THE SPANISH TRAGEDY

1930–1936

Dictatorship, Republic, Chaos

by

E. ALLISON PEERS
PROFESSOR OF SPANISH IN THE UNIVERSITY OF LIVERPOOL

GREENWOOD PRESS, PUBLISHERS
WESTPORT, CONNECTICUT

Library of Congress Cataloging in Publication Data

Peers, Edgar Allison.
    The Spanish tragedy, 1930-1936.

    Reprint of the 1936 ed. published by Methuen,
London.
    Bibliography: p.
    Includes index.
    1. Spain--Politics and government--1931-1939.
I. Title.
DP257.P36 1975   946.081   75-8724
ISBN 0-8371-8048-1

Originally published in 1936 by Methuen & Co., Ltd., London

Reprinted with the permission of Methuen & Co., Ltd.

Reprinted in 1975 by Greenwood Press,
a division of Williamhouse-Regency Inc.

Library of Congress Catalog Card Number 75-8724

ISBN 0-8371-8048-1

Printed in the United States of America

TO
J. L. G.

PREFACE

How can we explain all that is happening in Spain to-day?

Since the text of this book was completed, the two opposing forces in the Civil War have become locked in a still more desperate struggle, which is being pursued to the death in an atmosphere of dense political confusion and with a ruthlessness and ferocity which we had thought never to read of again, save in remote history and sensational fiction. It is useless to pronounce upon these events, as many are doing, by applying to them facile formulae transferred from the language of their own country and by censuring Spaniards for failing to act as they imagine they themselves would act in similar circumstances. Spain is not Britain, nor France, nor America, but herself—unique in many ways that in times of peace may well arouse our envy, but unique also in that the gods, while giving her so many gifts, denied her not only that of a good government, but others which just now she could have turned to excellent advantage. Let us cease taking sides in the conflict and try to understand.

Both geography and history protest against an attempt to judge Spain as though she were some other nation. Not only with a 'moat defensive', but with a strong mountain-wall she has been protected from her neighbours—and she has developed most of the characteristics of peninsularity. Spain is all but the most mountainous country in Europe, and shows incredible extremes of climate, together with variety, as well as abundance, of natural wealth, and violent regional dissimilarities in the temperament of her people. Though sparsely populated, in the main by agriculturists, she has two of her twenty-two millions crowded into her two greatest cities. The

Spaniards, who in the past have been so strangely romanticized abroad, are not one people but many: they share between them, not one mother-tongue, but four; and, quite apart from regional differences, almost any individual Spaniard will display so many apparently inconsistent traits of character that it will be the work of years to learn to know him. All these facts play their part in the present national tragedy.

The part played in it by history no doubt began when successive powers coveted and conquered the delectable Peninsula — Iberians, Celts, Phoenicians, Greeks, Carthaginians, Romans, Goths and Moors—the last remaining in the south-east for close upon eight centuries. Another problem was laid up for succeeding ages to solve when in the fifteenth century Castile and Aragon-Catalonia were united by the marriage of Ferdinand and Isabel, and still another when excessive centralization light-heartedly deprived Catalonians and Basques of their age-old privileges. The prize of the New World, which by a coincidence fell into the lap of Spain in the same year in which she freed herself from the Moors, was no unmixed blessing. Steadily bled, by the necessities of conquest and colonization, of her finest youth, ill-governed by weak or ambitious kings, impoverished by foreign wars and a benighted economic policy, condemned in the eighteenth century to ape the ways of France and reacting in the nineteenth by sinking back into her strange, reserved isolation, she found herself at the end of the War of 1898, shorn of her last colonies, far from the path of contemporary progress, despised by nations who centuries before had recognized her as a great Power.

It was then that the country, which for some time had been stirring uneasily, awoke to the greatness of her responsibilities and the extent of her decadence, and the spirit of reform, which had been alive throughout the nineteenth century, began quickly to make itself felt. This book is essentially a narrative of the most recent events in Spain, and to deal in the least adequately with her fundamental problems would be to write a second volume—quite unnecessarily, since other writers have treated them capably and at length. But briefly, before the reign of Alfonso XIII had begun, a divine discontent had effected vast improvements in social life, while at the same time it had started to make the cleavage between conservative and progressive Spaniards which in the last five years has so alarmingly widened. The rapid rise of Socialism from its modest beginnings in 1888, the development of Syndicalism, Communism and Anarchism (the latter now uniquely strong in Spain), the growing importunity of a few would-be autonomous regions, the clamourings of agricultural workers hungry for land, the increasing desire for religious tolerance, the splendid achievements and ideals of a few great educationists—all these things excited the opposition of those who preferred the former ways, and were content, when others decried the vices of the old order, to invoke and exaggerate its virtues. Once the progressives began to make themselves felt, the political pendulum, which for some time had been jogging to and fro harmlessly enough, quickly showed signs of becoming an alarming phenomenon. Could reform but have come gradually, we might have been spared the appalling catastrophe of to-day. But it had been delayed for so long that men demanded it quickly and there were always those who demanded more than the rest. So when in 1923 Primo de Rivera, in his impatience with the corruption and ineffectiveness of political and bureaucratic rule, agitated the pendulum more violently than had any before him, he was unconsciously preparing for the future not only recriminations but reprisals. Since then they have never ceased. The political prisoner of to-day is the Prime Minister of to-morrow. The hammer of the rebels quickly becomes the rebel leader. Years which are a mockery of peace end in open war. . . .

This book, though it appears in the midst of that war, was all but completed before the outbreak of hostilities.

When, about a year ago, it became increasingly clear that the Second Republic, founded with such high hopes by men of such high ideals, was, in the form that it then bore, doomed to disaster, I set to work to describe its career in a short and unpretentious chronicle. Chance has enabled me at the same time, without either undue hurry or delay, to write its epitaph. The last few weeks have been intensely painful for all who believe in Spain's future and can admire the men who, though sometimes blindly, have tried, nobly and single-heartedly, to lead her. Though elements of comedy—even of the broadest comedy—enliven some of the scenes of this drama, it is essentially, and in the Shakespearian sense, a tragedy, in which, as one looks back upon its course, all else seems weak beside the catastrophe.

For now nearly twenty years I have spent over one-quarter of my time in the Peninsula, and, though the personal pronoun intrudes but little in the narrative, much that is described in it has been not merely read but seen. A chronicle of events in Spain which I have written weekly since 1929 has been freely utilized, but my main sources, for book as for chronicle, have been the Spanish daily Press, together with the valuable articles of the correspondents of *The Times*, for which British students of Spanish affairs cannot be too grateful.

While complete impartiality is always difficult of achievement, I have tried to describe the events of these years with all possible objectivity; and party politicians, on whichever side, will look in vain for their pet exaggerations. I have neither declared, for example, with one recent writer, that 'the rigour with which war is waged against Roman Catholics surpasses anything imaginable', nor with another, more recent still, that 'the repression of the Fascist Spanish Government against the workers of Asturias is so frightful that it surpasses anything you may have heard up till now about any other country in the world'.

For the sake of readableness, I have used political terms familiar to English readers rather than strange-sounding ones, and have refrained from sprinkling the pages with such strings of letters as F.A.I., U.H.P., J.O.N.S., P.O.U.M., which are commonplaces of the Spanish Press. So far as I know, no substantial part of anything I have previously written is included in these pages, but short passages have occasionally been incorporated from numerous articles contributed to the *Nineteenth Century and After*, the *Contemporary Review*, the *Bulletin of Spanish Studies*, the *Commonweal*, the *Observer*, the *Liverpool Daily Post*, the *Church Times*, the *Nation*, and a few other periodicals, to whose editors I have often had cause to be grateful for much consideration.

E. A. P.

LIVERPOOL
September 15, 1936

CONTENTS

xiii

CONTENTS

CHAPTER I

THE COMING OF THE REPUBLIC

I

ON January 28, 1930, Don Miguel Primo de Rivera y Orbaneja, Marqués de Estella and Dictator of Spain, laid down the office to which, six years and four months earlier, he had appointed himself, and retired to Paris, where, after barely seven weeks, he died.

Primo de Rivera's experiment in dictatorship had started well, for it had represented a new and attractive-looking attempt to do away with Spain's unchanging phenomenon of continually changing governments, and to solve the problem of what to do with such problems as inefficient administration, which had previously refused to be solved. It ended badly—and a number of reasons are made to account for its bad end, but the real reasons were inherent in the character of the Dictator and of the Spanish people.

The Dictator was a benevolent Andalusian, with all the Andalusian's outstanding faults and virtues. He loved ostentation and parade; he talked too much, chiefly through the medium of fantastic official *communiqués*; he exaggerated freely; his generous promises were often in excess of what he was able to perform; and, when incensed, he acted like an imprudent and impulsive father, imposing the heaviest punishments, only to modify or remit them altogether as soon as his wrath had subsided. He liked to think that his rule was a mild and paternal one—not a 'dicta*dura*', to reproduce the play on words current at the time in Spain, but a 'dicta*blanda*'.(1)

Besides being an Andalusian, he was a soldier—and this at once by descent, by profession, and by temperament. Army officers, in effect, brought him into power, and army officers, in literal truth, brought about his fall. He trusted and believed in the officer class as he never trusted or believed in the *bourgeois* class, still less in the intellectuals. He had no conception of organizing a country otherwise than as a species of army. Unmindful of such phenomena as the rapid growth of Socialism and the increasing importunity of the regionalists, he attempted to drill the nation as though it were a single unit—much as he had once drilled his men. And so, despite his many excellent qualities—profound sincerity, intense patriotism, unfailing courtesy, steady perseverance, amazing industry, indomitable courage—he brought to nothing the pretentious edifice which he had reared with so much buoyant confidence, and ultimately caused the fall of the monarchical *régime*, to which he could probably have conceived no alternative but chaos.

In part, too, the termination of the Dictatorship was due to the character of the Spanish people. Up to a certain point the best in them can be brought out by effective leadership, for (to speak generally) they co-operate and organize but poorly, yet have a great love for the symbol, a rare idealism and a fine sense of loyalty. But the limits beyond which they refuse to follow blindly have in the last few decades become much narrower. Had Primo de Rivera lived in the seventeenth century he would no doubt have marshalled the nation with far greater success. Had Alfonso XIII been called to rule the people who groaned under his great-grandfather, Ferdinand VII, he would no doubt have gone down to his grave at a ripe old age beloved (or at least tolerated) by all. But Spain had changed tremendously in the century (1823–1923) between Ferdinand's victory over the Liberals and Primo de Rivera's victory over constitutionalism. It was the custom in Spain, during the Dictatorship, for Liberals to repeat appreciatively the blunt description of Alfonso XIII attributed to various notabilities—*Fernando VII y pico*: 'Ferdinand VII plus a bit more'. The description should have been accompanied by another of Spain itself: 'Ferdinand VII's Spain minus a great deal'. The Spaniards, taken all round, are not so democratically inclined as most other nations of Western Europe, nor are they as progressive a people as some of their intellectuals would like them, and us, to believe. If we reject, as we should, the 'Black Legend' which makes them a nation of ignorant, inquisitorial fanatics and picturesque brigands, we must not immediately give credence to a 'White Legend' which turns them into the most enlightened nation under the sun and invests them with an aureole of strictly undenominational sanctity. But we need not fall into that error in order to appreciate the fact that the Spaniards are a great deal more democratic and progressive than their immediate ancestors could have foreseen that they would be, or than Primo de Rivera and his royal master could have suspected. As a result, though at first resigning themselves to the Dictatorship, and even approving it, they gradually reacted against it with such determination that, had it not collapsed of its own weight when it did, only a few months more could have stood between it and a popular revolution.

The outstanding features of the rule of Primo de Rivera can be summarized quite briefly. It triumphed in a day—September 13, 1923—as a military movement, acquiesced in by the King, and probably, at that time, welcomed by the majority of the people.(2) Had it at once sought the approval of the Cortes, there is little doubt that it could have been constitutionally established, for, with the country weary to death of political instability and social unrest, the professional politicians were thoroughly discredited. But the Dictator believed that he could sweep away formalities like the Constitution with impunity; and besides, he announced, and continually repeated, that he had come to rule only for a period of ninety days, and aimed only at preparing the country for democratic government purged of impurities

3

the existence of which all admitted. He found it harder to lay aside his dictatorial powers than to assume them, but the change to a Civil Directory in 1925 and the creation in 1927 of a National Assembly—the hollow mockery of a parliament—were steps taken towards the goal which, as his health declined and his patience dwindled, he must have longed to attain more than any knew.

The achievements of the Dictatorship were numerous,(3) and, in their way, important, but, compared with its failures, superficial. Most of them came under the head of material reforms—a small item when weighed against the loss of independence and freedom. Nevertheless, they represented, and still represent, a certain positive gain and a foundation on which the Republic afterwards effectively built without saying too much about it. Just as the grand new University City of Madrid, beloved of King Alfonso,(4) will be a magnificent framework for a reformed and autonomous university when educational progress gets thus far, so the four thousand new schools erected by Primo de Rivera were by no means a negligible beginning for the much larger work of construction later inaugurated (partly at the expense of the religious Orders) by the Republic.(5) Roads were rebuilt and increased in number until it has become almost a commonplace with motorists that the main roads of Spain are among the best in Europe. The long-planned eastern and western trans-Pyrenean railway tunnels were completed; work on other much-needed lines was begun; railway services were augmented; trains were speeded up, and their hours were made to approximate more closely with those of the time-tables. Large irrigation schemes were set in motion and a generous programme was drawn up for similar innovations of the future. A brand-new and highly efficient telephone system was installed, by a new Spanish company of American origin. Hotels were augmented and vastly improved;

4

a State tourist service (*Patronato Nacional del Turismo*), still in existence, was created; and both the volume and the efficiency of the tourist business increased greatly. Two enormous exhibitions, at Barcelona and Seville, brought visitors from all over the world, and incidentally did much to strengthen the links between Spain and Spanish America.

Again, Primo de Rivera struck determinedly at corruption and disorder. In the Civil Service, where this was at its worst, he made a valiant though not wholly successful attempt to secure that those who drew salaries should also work for them. In the great cities, order was restored, and both gangsters and promoters of organized strikes and riots found it prudent to leave the country. Enemies of the dictatorship, at home and abroad (but chiefly abroad), declared *ad nauseam* that Spain was 'mute under a colossal military tyranny . . . a reign of terror'.(6) Everybody who travelled there between 1923 and 1929 knows well that the country showed every outward sign of prosperity and happiness.

But the prosperity was solely material and began to disappear as taxation increased; the peseta dropped and men realized that it would be decades before the great exhibitions were paid for. Except in one particular, too, the happiness was no more than a superficial contentment. That particular was the immense relief caused by Primo de Rivera's successful conclusion of the war in Morocco, which dated from 1909, and had come to be looked upon almost as an institution, taking a continual and often tragic toll of life and health from the people. The successes of the Riff leader, Abd-el-Krim, had culminated in a crushing disaster at Annual, in 1921, in which General Silvestre and an entire army had perished. When Primo de Rivera took the reins of government, he determined to give Spain a victorious peace, and, after a short period of apparent inactivity but of necessary retrenchment, he launched an attack, in close collaboration with the French, during the late summer of 1925, which led ultimately to a much-desired settlement in the following May.(7)

While all this must fairly be entered to Primo de Rivera's credit, there is a debit entry at once more extensive and more fundamental. Free speech and free expression of opinion were done away with; had it been possible to do away with free thought—'the disastrous mania of thinking', as it had been called in Ferdinand VII's time—the Dictatorship would doubtless have been functioning to this day. But it was not, and, even among those who in the main thought as the Dictator did, there was a gathering chorus of exasperation at his numerous repressive measures—newspapers censored and suspended; public meetings, and even banquets, policed with spies; leading men (and by no means always politicians) fined, imprisoned or exiled for the mildest indiscretions; clubs closed; associations abolished; universities suspended for indefinite periods; the Board for the Development of Studies (*Junta para Ampliación de Estudios*), Spain's most progressive educational institution, interfered with; religious tests imposed upon State officials, with dismissal for recalcitrants; and all this in addition to the sterner measures taken whenever there appeared the smallest sign of genuine revolt.

When the Dictatorship was three years old — the Dictatorship which was to have come to an end after three months!—Primo de Rivera went through the ridiculous pretence of making an appeal to the country. A four-days' plebiscite of both sexes—he was not likely to forget the women!—gathered together some 6,700,000 votes, recorded by whom, and how many by each voter, none knows.(8) In September 1927 came the creation of the equally farcical 'Supreme National Assembly'— a pseudo-parliament designed to 'represent all classes and interests' but consisting chiefly of members nominated by the Dictator. Its meetings in full session averaged about twenty-four hours a month, and it had neither legislative nor administrative authority, but was empowered merely to submit recommendations to the Government.(9) No more of the Dictator's critics were misled or pacified by the creation of such a body than by that of the 'Patriotic Union', a nation-wide organization of 'good citizens'—i.e., supporters of the Dictatorship—which was supposed to be the instrument for leading the country back to constitutional government, but which came into notice chiefly by its monster demonstrations, organized at enormous cost to bolster up the Dictator's policy and prestige. Meanwhile, he went on postponing the evil hour when he must inevitably relinquish authority. 'The Dictatorship, the people were told,' commented *The Times* in 1927, 'was to last for a week, then for ninety days, then for various undefined periods, but after four full years they see it continue as firmly established, and they believe as immovably established, as ever.'(10) At the end of five and a half years, Primo de Rivera announced the date of his retirement as still two years distant.(11) Perhaps, if it had been possible, he would have continued indefinitely in the path which he was wont somewhat airily to describe as 'illegal but patriotic':(12) none can say.

Of all the Dictator's puerilities and tyrannies, the most flagrant was probably his treatment of Catalonia. This region of Spain, which has its own language, its literature, its history, and its national character, had long been demanding some degree of the autonomy to which it believed itself to be entitled, and the small concessions which the Monarchy had made to it had satisfied none. But even these were taken away by Primo de Rivera. 'There was no regionalism in the army!' was his argument. 'Why should there be any in Spain? Let us all live like happy and contented Spaniards under Papa Primo!' So the Mancomunitat (a central organization co-ordinating the work of the local councils) was abolished; the Catalan flag was furled by order; the use of the

Catalan language at public meetings was prohibited; even the name-plates of Barcelona streets were cut in two by authority, only the Castilian name of each street being allowed to appear.

The situations to which such repression led are almost incredible. To take only one example, the council of the Bar Association in Barcelona was dissolved for attempting to issue the list of its members in Catalan and a fresh council was appointed in its place. Several of the newly appointed members refused to serve, whereupon the Government announced that, if they persisted in their refusal, they would be deprived of their citizenship, of the right to exercise their profession, and of their private property.

The marvel was that, under treatment which would have been so intolerably offensive had it not been so ridiculously childish, the whole of Catalonia did not turn separatist for ever. Instead, with commendable good sense, its leaders concentrated upon an intensive cultural propaganda, within the country, with an eye to the future of the region, and to political propaganda at a safe distance outside it. Only one serious attempt at revolution was made—the adventure of Prats-de-Molló, in November 1926, in which the exiled leader of the separatist organization, *Estat Català*, Colonel Macià, made a desperate but hopeless attempt to invade Catalonia with a voluntary army of exiles and foreign recruits, and to set up a 'provisional government of Catalonia' for the restoration of the 'national sovereignty'.(13) The leaders, who suffered the indignity of arrest on French soil, were tried and expelled from France, whereupon they went to Belgium.

Other attempts, however, to overthrow the Dictatorship by force of arms were made elsewhere in Spain. In the preceding midsummer a military rebellion at Valencia, under Generals Weyler and Aguilera, had been nipped in the bud, and exemplary punishment had been meted out to its leaders.(14) Valencia was also the scene of a second abortive outbreak three years later under a former Conservative leader, D. José Sánchez Guerra, who returned from a voluntary exile in Paris to lead it; and this was accompanied by a revolt of the artillery garrisons at Ciudad Real. These rebellions, like others of less consequence, were defeated without difficulty. Primo de Rivera, as a soldier, knew what to do with sudden military outbreaks; what he was entirely unable to cope with was growing civil discontent.

This began first to declare itself on a large scale early in 1929. In the first place, there was trouble with the Civil Service. Two distinguished writers, Don Enrique de Mesa and Don Ceferino Palencia, were dismissed from their posts in the Ministry of Education and clapped summarily into prison—no one seemed quite to know why. But a *communiqué* from the Dictator threatened meaningly to impose the severest penalties on public servants who criticized the *régime*, and the following notice to employees appeared on the walls of every Government office:

'Whether you like it or not, the Government is your master. You may have your own opinion about it, if you think yourself capable of holding one. But you are strictly to abstain from criticizing its actions.'(15)

Then came rumours of growing dissensions between the Dictator and the King. Primo de Rivera had determined to dissolve the artillery corps, which had been prominent in the rebellion; the King had refused to sign the decree, till the Dictator had threatened, if he delayed any longer, to resign. Riots among the cadets followed the promulgation of the decree, and even more serious riots broke out in the universities as the result of the concession of university privileges to the Jesuit college of Deusto and the Augustinian college of El Escorial. There was first of all a storm of verbal protest, and the Escorial College gave the Dictator rather more

9

than a hint as to the course he should pursue by declining to accept the privileges. But, as he made no move, words gave place to actions, and violent agitations began all over the country. Led by Madrid University (which is known as the 'Central University' of Spain), students in each of the university cities struck work, organized demonstrations, stoned buildings, fought the police. . . . The thing could obviously not continue, but once again the Dictator knew no remedy but repression. He closed the University of Madrid for no less than eighteen months and a number of other universities for lesser periods.

The intellectuals of Spain, already estranged from the *régime*, protested anew. Professors resigned their posts. Sr. Menéndez Pidal, President of the Spanish Academy, wrote a well-nigh unanswerable open letter to the Dictator, containing the sternest public censure that the latter had yet encountered. Every university senate in Spain, declared Spain's foremost scholar, had condemned this action against which the students were quite properly protesting. 'The harm you have done is irreparable. Besides the mischief wrought to intellectual life, it will ruin the careers of thousands. What seeds but those of rancour are being sown in the minds of youths who, students to-day, will be the leaders of to-morrow?'

All this happened in the spring of 1929, a few days before Easter. Primo de Rivera was really annoyed! Then he made a tour of Catalonia and Aragon and at the sound of the usual plaudits his heart melted. A group of subservient professors uttered some 'noble words' in the National Assembly, and, soon after, the Minister of Education pronounced a few touching phrases of forgiveness. One of the grand Madrid demonstrations of the Patriotic Union put everybody in a good humour again. Soon it was being rumoured that the University would be closed for six months (including the Long Vacation of four months) instead of for eighteen. Then, that it would be opened again in a fortnight. . . .(16)

So, like a doddering old man, the decrepit administration stumbled downhill to meet its destruction. By the end of 1929, it was admitted on all sides that its days were numbered. *Don Dinero es el mejor informado*— 'Mr. Money always knows'—says the Spanish proverb, and it was significant that at the close of the year sterling stood at 36.50 as against 29 at the beginning: the peseta was, in fact, lower than it had been at any time since the beginning of the century. The university disturbances were growing worse and worse: soon, it seemed, there would be no universities open at all. The project for drawing up a new Constitution had failed; the Dictator found fewer and fewer people willing to collaborate with him. At the beginning of 1930, he yielded to the inevitable and suggested that the Dictatorship should come to an end, not in March 1931, as he had said ten months earlier, but on its seventh anniversary in September 1930. But this period of grace, as Primo de Rivera has himself left on record,(17) was considered too long, and by no less a person than the King. So the Dictator revised his announcement and undertook to quit office in five months' time, elections to be held at the end of June.

But the life of the Dictatorship was to be shorter even than that. In the last week of January, the Dictator's bright young Finance Minister, Sr. Calvo Sotelo, resigned, and there was no one to be found both able and willing for so short a time to succeed him. Primo de Rivera began to wonder if he could with any show of dignity escape from his self-created office immediately.

His next act, which aroused the entire country to indignation, was an inexplicable piece of lunacy, attributable only to incapacity or mental fatigue. His own description of it was 'a sensational and decisive proof' whether or no he should remain in power. 'As the Dictatorship came by military proclamation,' he announced, 'so the military or naval chiefs shall now decide if it is to stay.'(18) So he authorized the captains-general and the officers in high command in the Army and Navy to make a brief, discreet and private examination of the situation and to decide his future. Should they oppose his continuance in office, he would at once hand the King his resignation.(19) To the people, this was a frank abandonment of the country into hands even less fitted to guide it than his own. Whatever the reply had been, he could hardly have survived a week after it was given. But, as it fell out, the officers made the right and obvious decision. They could only support a Government which had the confidence of His Majesty. Primo de Rivera thereupon offered the King his resignation so that His Majesty might complete the answer to the original question. His Majesty replied by accepting the resignation, and Primo de Rivera went.(20)

'And now,' he wrote in the last of those garrulous official *communiqués* which he had made notorious, 'for a little rest, after two thousand three hundred and twenty-six days of continuous uneasiness, responsibility and labour.' But his rest, as it proved, was to be eternal. He died, with tragic suddenness, on March 16. His body was brought back to Spain and given a wonderful funeral. Tens of thousands stood in the steadily falling rain as the procession passed by, and behind the private and the official mourners came a huge unorganized concourse of the people. With its never-failing generosity, Spain forgot for a moment the sins which the Dictator had committed against liberty and remembered only his positive achievements, his good intentions and his sincerity. Women, in particular, hailed him as the man who had made peace in Morocco. And such may yet be the principal verdict upon him of posterity. For, with all his faults, he worked, according to his lights, for the welfare of Spain, and he should not be unworthy of a niche in Spain's noble history.

II

For a short time Spain now grew more placid. '¡Aquí no pasa nada!'—'Nothing happening here!'—men had said sarcastically to each other during the Dictatorship when seething discontent was being checked by ruthless repression. But now that the check had been removed, and nobody would have been surprised to see a violent reaction, it really seemed that nothing *was* happening and the country was preparing for a peaceful and gradual return, according to Primo de Rivera's recipe, to constitutional rule. A temporary Government, under the presidency of a former War Minister, General Dámaso Berenguer, had issued a decree of amnesty, and set out to pave the way to a more liberal rule—which was warmly welcomed, most of all in Catalonia. The Press censorship was raised. Reforms in education began to be spoken of. There was talk of elections. . . .

But soon indications began to appear that all was not well. The sterling exchange during the autumn dropped steadily till it stood at 51, and thereafter rose but slowly. General strikes, though unaccompanied by violence and lasting each only a day or two, occurred with disagreeable frequency all over the country. June saw them in Seville, Málaga, Granada and Bilbao; September, in Galicia and Asturias; November, in Madrid and Barcelona. Mass meetings of Republicans seemed to be making numerous converts to a creed which had in appearance flourished little during the Dictatorship. Not only so, but it was rumoured that leading Republicans had formed a Revolutionary Committee, which had met leaders of the movement for Catalonian autonomy at San Sebastián and drawn up a pact binding the Catalonians to work for the Republic, and the Republican leaders, in return for their help, to bring an Autonomy Bill before the Constituent Cortes as soon as they should be in power.(21) When the universities re-opened, in October 1930, a recrudescence of student riots increased the general feeling of uneasiness. In the next month it was no student, but a professor of philosophy, Don José Ortega y Gasset, who declared in Madrid's most respected and respectable periodical that General Berenguer's errors were irremediable. 'Spaniards,' he cried, 'your State is no more. Reconstruct it! *Delenda est Monarchia.*'(22)

An attempt to put this counsel into practice was made in December by the garrison of the little Pyrenean town of Jaca.(23) The mutiny was to have been merely the vanguard of a much more extensive attack on the *régime* which the Revolutionary Committee had planned for December 15. Hearing that the Jaca leaders had determined to strike first, the Committee sent one of its members, Sr. Casares Quiroga, to dissuade them. He reached his destination late on the night of December 11–12, in order to interview the revolutionary leaders early the next morning. But the mutineers were earlier still: the signal for action had been the first note of the *réveillé* and the Committee's delegate was wakened by the noise of arms.

The soul of the mutiny was a young Andalusian, Captain Fermín Galán, who had already spent three of his thirty years in prison for military rebellion against the Dictatorship, and was a man of highly advanced ideas as well as of remarkable persistence, initiative and courage. His second-in-command, Captain Ángel García Hernández, was a man of a very different type—among other things a practising Catholic—but of equal determination and valour. Galán and his men began by disarming any who resisted them, arresting the Military Governor, cutting telephone and telegraph wires, intercepting railway traffic, hoisting the red, yellow, and purple flag of revolution over the Town Hall and issuing a ruthless proclamation threatening to shoot without trial any who opposed the 'newly born Republic', not only by force of arms but by 'speech or writing'.

Early in the afternoon, the mutineers, eight hundred strong, began to march southwards towards Saragossa with the intention of occupying Huesca and thus establishing themselves in an important strategic position while their numbers grew and revolution broke out elsewhere. But, after a brush that night, near Ayerbe, with loyal forces hastily raised from the Huesca garrison, they met with stronger opposition in a few hours' time ten miles farther on and were at once overpowered. Several hundreds of the rebels were taken prisoners; six of the ringleaders were court-martialled; and, in order to turn the incident into a salutary example, Galán and García Hernández were shot.

This last event made a deep and tragic impression on public opinion, the more so since at the time it was widely believed that some of the ministers had counselled leniency and that the King had intervened in favour of the execution of the sentences.(24) This would seem unlikely to have been the case, considering the sacrifices made by Don Alfonso four months later to avoid bloodshed, but it undoubtedly exacerbated feeling against the Monarchy, and, so soon as the Republic was declared, the portraits of Galán and García Hernández were displayed everywhere in homage to the 'martyrs of the Revolution'.

Meanwhile, it seemed as though the failure of the Jaca *coup* had temporarily restored order, for, apart from a few isolated strikes, nothing came of the revolution planned for December 15. But the Revolutionary Committee issued a long, oratorical and somewhat violent manifesto, at the end of which the twelve signatories declared that, with full consciousness of their 'mission and responsibility', they 'assumed the functions of public authority as the Provisional Government' of Spain's Republic.(25) Several of the signatories were, naturally enough, at once arrested; others succeeded in eluding the police and escaping from the country. But the appearance of the manifesto marked a decisive stage in the history of the Republican campaign even more clearly than did the Jaca rebellion.

One more demonstration occurred in this troubled

week, which, though chiefly spectacular, added greatly
to the impression created by the revolutionaries. One
of the points in Madrid which was to have been occupied
by them, had the rising of December 15 materialized,
was the aerodrome in the suburb of Cuatro Vientos, and
the leaders who had been detailed to carry out this enterprise, Commandant Franco and General Queipo de
Llano, saw no reason why they should not make an
effective display. Accordingly, believing, as it seems, that
in Madrid, at least, the original plans would be carried
out, they made themselves masters of the aerodrome,
and flew over the city, dropping pamphlets headed:
'Spaniards! The Republic has been proclaimed!' and
containing threats that troops obeying orders to quell the
movement would be bombed from the air, whether they
went out into the streets or whether they remained in
barracks.

Detachments of infantry and artillery were immediately
moved to Cuatro Vientos and within a few hours the
leaders had either escaped or surrendered. This, presumably to the Government's great relief, brought an end
to the December demonstrations. Everything possible
was done to calm the country. Martial law was declared,
and the censorship re-imposed, for a period of six weeks.
But this had not the slightest effect upon the irrepressible
general strikes, especially in the north of Spain—at
Coruña, Santander, Bilbao, Tolosa, Pamplona, Logroño
and elsewhere. The universities were closed again lest
they too should increase the disorder. The most hopeful
sign of the times was that the Government began to
think seriously—and talk loudly—about the forthcoming
General Election.

But perhaps nothing took place during these months of
more striking import than the grouping together of the
intellectuals of Spain in favour of the formation of a
Republic. The Ateneo of Madrid, Spain's famous
literary club, and the home of Liberal opinion, had been
re-opened after the fall of Primo de Rivera, closed at the

first outbreak of trouble, and re-opened by its own officers without the authorization of the Government. As a result it now found itself closed more or less continuously. In the preceding June, during one of its short periods of activity, it had elected as president a middle-aged Civil Servant named Don Manuel Azaña, a man of some literary pretensions, who had translated Borrow's *Bible in Spain* and written several novels and dramas. Sr. Azaña was known to be an out-and-out Republican, and his election at this time was highly significant. Then, again, three prominent personalities had actually formed a 'League for the Service of the Republic'—for all the world as if the Republic had already arrived! One of them, Dr. Gregorio Marañón, was a fashionable Madrid specialist, with a *clientèle* that included the aristocracy and even royalty. The second, Don Ramón Pérez de Ayala, was one of Spain's leading novelists, a man not yet fifty, who had made his name early and might still have his best work before him. The third, Don José Ortega y Gasset, the professor of philosophy just referred to, was (and is still) immensely respected in the world of ideas and progress. A manifesto signed by all three maintained that the Monarchy was now in the 'last stage of decomposition' and must give place to a 'genuinely national' form of government—a Republic which would combine 'dynamic force with discipline' and would 'invite all Spaniards to join in the supreme enterprise of resuscitating the history of Spain'. 'We call upon all professors and teachers,' continued the signatories, 'upon writers and artists, doctors, engineers, architects and every kind of technical expert, upon advocates, notaries and other members of the legal profession. In particular we need the collaboration of the young. . . . The Republic will be the symbol of the fact that Spaniards have at last resolved to act with vigour and to take into their own hands their own destiny.'(26) The manifesto created a profound effect on the class to which it was addressed, and it is hard to estimate the embarrassment which the publicity given to it must have caused the Government.

By February 1931 the situation was so chaotic that the Government found itself unable to remain in office till the General Election, which had been fixed for March, and on the 14th of February resigned precipitately. It is probable that King Alfonso now found himself more completely isolated than at any previous crisis of his reign. His original Dictator was removed, the Dictator's hardly less dictatorial successor was discredited, and the old party system of collective responsibility had fallen to pieces. So the King emerged, as he had never done before, as the one person who must find a way out of a situation which he might after all have prevented, or must suffer the consequences.

The Press censorship had been re-imposed immediately upon the Government's resignation, but rumours regarding the future of the Monarchy were flying everywhere. Some said that Don Alfonso would abdicate unconditionally; others, that he would resign his powers in favour of his brother-in-law, Don Carlos; others, again, that he would be asked to leave the country until after the elections, and that guarantees to rule constitutionally would then be required of him. None of these dramatic events took place, however. After consulting, in the conventional way, with leading statesmen, the King took what must have been the most unpalatable course of asking his enemy, Don José Sánchez Guerra, to form a Left Government, insisting, however, that a trusty friend of his, the Conde de Romanones, and another of his own nominees, should figure in it as ministers without portfolio. To this Sr. Sánchez Guerra would not agree, but he did make an attempt to form a Government acceptable to the people, and in order to do so he paid a visit to Madrid's so-called Model Prison, where he actually solicited the collaboration of members of the Revolutionary Committee. Had they accepted, the situation of the King would have become still more embarrassing, but the only reply of the revolutionary leader, Sr. Alcalá Zamora, was to issue a new statement reiterating his former defiance:

'The Republican-Socialist coalition [it said] remains inseparably united. . . . Refusing to have any part in the Government . . . it will continue its labours from without, and will await the Republic's inevitable triumph. . . . We are certain that the elections will bring in the Republic legally and we are resolved that no intrigue or influence of traditional powers shall rob us of this victory.'(27)

So Sr. Sánchez Guerra returned from the prison to the Palace, to decline the King's offer. In the end it was the astute Conde de Romanones who saved the situation, not by forming a Government himself but by fashioning a new one of the Berenguer type—under an admiral, Don Juan B. Aznar, instead of a general. He himself, its real strength, was content to take the Foreign Office. None viewed this Government with the slightest confidence save a few ultra-Conservative newspapers (28) and foreign periodicals which took their opinions from such sources. These last believed—to quote one of them— that 'King Alfonso's great diplomacy' had at one and the same time discredited the Republican opposition and averted a new military dictatorship. 'The Monarchy is more firmly established than during any period in the past seven years', added this newspaper, and the King 'has added greatly to his prestige and perhaps to his personal popularity'. (29)

Any one in Spain who held such idealistic opinions was destined very shortly to be disillusioned. But it is true that the new Government got to work with great celerity and made several most important decisions. First of all, elections would be held throughout the country, on Sunday, April 12; these, however, would not be parliamentary but municipal. Next would come parliamentary elections, and the Cortes then elected would be expressly empowered to draw up a new constitution. At the same time, the whole work of the dictatorial *régime* would be revised, and a determined attempt would be made to deal with a few century-old problems, such as that of Catalonia. So often had such attempts been promised before that the undertaking inspired little confidence. But at least it showed that the Government was alive to the gravity of the situation.

But the new team was no sooner in harness than it began to exacerbate public opinion with a series of solemnly staged trials for rebellion.

First, on March 13, came the court-martial held at Jaca on over sixty prisoners taken in the December rebellion. The whole country was deeply moved to learn that the Attorney-General was asking for five capital sentences, in addition to the two already executed. The defending advocates issued a public plea which might almost have been called a solemn warning.

'Always so terrible [they said] because so completely irreparable, capital punishment inflicted three months after an attempted revolt could have no exemplary value; it could only be interpreted as an act of vengeance, and this is absolutely incompatible with public feeling at the present time. . . .

'In issuing this protest and plea, we ask for the collaboration of all Spaniards. It is addressed to all Spaniards . . . even to those whose opinions differ most widely from our own. We desire also to appeal to the Church, that greatest of institutions founded upon the principle of compassion. Only recently, at the time of the execution of Galán and García Hernández, the Church was silent. Let it now recall the Decalogue, which makes no distinction between Republicans and Monarchists. In the past, the Church has besought pardon for common delinquents: political offenders are surely more worthy of its endeavours. . . .

'Violence sets the worst possible of examples.

It hardens opinion. It sows the germs of vengeance. . . .'(30)

After a three-day trial, and deliberations extending over thirty-two hours, the Court passed sixteen sentences of from six months' to twenty years' imprisonment, one of imprisonment for life, and one of death. Petitions for reprieve of the death-sentence poured in from all over the country. The national Socialist organization known as the General Union of Workers declared that 'the unrest prevalent in the country would be greatly aggravated by the shedding of a single drop of blood'. The Government evidently agreed with this view, for within twenty-four hours the King had granted a reprieve.

Exactly a week after the Jaca court-martial, there began, in Madrid, the trial of six members of the Revolutionary Committee who had signed the seditious manifesto of the preceding December and, instead of escaping from the country, like their fellow-signatories, had been incarcerated in the Model Prison, which, especially during the February crisis, had become a centre of the most fervid Republican enthusiasm. The names of all six were to figure prominently in the later political history of Spain. The acknowledged leader was Don Niceto Alcalá Zamora, a lawyer of Andalusian birth and a former Minister of the Crown. Don Miguel Maura was the son of one of the most distinguished Prime Ministers in Spain's history and brother of the Duque de Maura, Minister of Labour in the Aznar Cabinet. Don Fernando de los Ríos had for years been a professor at the University of Granada and was a nephew of the famous Liberal educator, Francisco Giner de los Ríos. Don Álvaro de Albornoz was a lawyer in late middle age who was afterwards given one of the most highly paid posts in the Republic. Don Francisco Largo Caballero, a leading Socialist, was Secretary-General of the General Union of Workers. Don Santiago Casares Quiroga was the luckless envoy to Jaca, who on the outbreak of the mutiny had been discovered and arrested on something rather more than suspicion.

The Press Censor, though allowing the trial to be reported in fair detail, forbade description of the manifesto which was its cause. Nevertheless, it was generally known that the signatories had allotted themselves posts in the provisional Republican Government which they hoped to establish, Sr. Alcalá Zamora being given the presidency. The knowledge served to raise expectation to fever-heat. 'The trial', says a contemporary periodical, 'was a great Republican demonstration, more effective even than those which have been held in the bull-rings of Madrid and Valencia.' (31) The accused were popular heroes, and authority was powerless to prevent homage being paid them. Vast crowds cheered their approach. As they entered the court, lawyers and public rose as a tribute of respect. After the hearing, they were fêted by the College of Advocates. Even their wives and daughters received gifts of flowers. The significance of it all was unmistakable.

It would not have been hard to predict the lines of defence taken up by the prisoners and their advocates. Logically, there was simply no reply to them. 'You can only convict my friends and clients', said Sr. Ossorio y Gallardo, 'by proving the legality of the Dictatorship.' And that was just the impossibility. Sr. Alcalá Zamora, in a long speech delivered with great sincerity, went farther. He caused a tremendous impression by making the simplest possible statement of the reasons which had led him, an ex-minister, to Republican sympathies, and one could not but be struck with the elaborateness of the Committee's plans and the confidence with which they had laid them when he showed how such detailed preparations were essential, when the Republic should come, to the avoidance of bloodshed and the safety of the Royal Family.

The remainder of the accused departed little from the fundamental argument just enunciated—the breaking of the Constitution by the King, the illegality of the Dictatorship, the state of oppression in which Spaniards had lived for the past seven years, and the complete moral and legal incompetence of the Tribunal which was trying them. All denied strenuously the nonsensical accusation that they were in any way inspired by Communism. 'An abyss yawns between the Communist creed and mine,' declared Sr. Largo Caballero. 'The workers, realizing that Spain was rushing headlong towards the most terrible state of anarchy, ordered me to sign the manifesto in their name, and we were firmly convinced that by my doing so we were escaping from Communism and leading Socialists away from its tortuous path.'(32)

On March 23, sentences were pronounced—six months and a day's imprisonment for each offender—the whole of which term, at the end of the following day, was remitted. It was the clearest admission of the complete impossibility of stemming a tide of which the steady rise was visible to all. The enthusiasm of the thousands who stood for hours outside the prison to greet the liberated heroes was indescribable. Surrounded, each one, by so dense a crowd that to reach their cars and waiting relatives was impossible, they could only fight their way to taxis, and, with the greatest difficulty, drive off to the accompaniment of deafening 'Vivas'. But they made no speeches, or even declarations of policy, save for one short sentence:

'¡Y ahora a luchar!' ('And now for the fight!')(33)

As all knew, the fight was to come very soon, though few, perhaps, guessed how quickly it was to be ended.

III

Palm Sunday in 1931 fell only five days after the release of the revolutionary leaders and exactly a fortnight before the municipal elections. So the ceremonies and processions of Holy Week, which foreigners come hundreds and even thousands of miles to see, kept strange company with crowded and turbulent election meetings and demonstrations in favour of immediate amnesties for all political prisoners. Not that the country was by any means in a state of tumult. During the last week in March there had been some grave riots in Madrid, where students in the Faculty of Medicine had defied the Civil Guard, one member of which had been killed, while several medical students and guardsmen sustained serious injuries. In Barcelona University, too, bodies of students had taken possession of the main building and defended it against the Civil Guard, and in Valencia students had been fired on by the Guard in the course of a Republican demonstration. But the beginning of the short Easter vacation prevented matters from becoming more serious, since for a few fateful days the ringleaders were safely dispersed to their homes.

During the days preceding the elections, something like a hush fell upon the country, and the prevalent impression was one of intense seriousness of purpose. There was much activity, but hardly any excitement. Men debated whether the elections (which, though municipal, were of course entirely political in character) would be dominated by the party bosses, as had so often been the case in the past, or whether they would be a genuine expression of opinion. The general belief was that being the first for eight years, with so many young electors who had never before voted now on the register, they could not fail to be entirely sincere. There might be gerrymandering here and there—perhaps, in the country districts, on a large scale—but throughout Spain as a whole, and certainly in the largest towns, which contributed about one-fifth of the electorate, the results would be a key to the people's mind.

At the same time, it may be stated, without risk of contradiction, that few, if any, expected these elections to bring in a Republic immediately. Most Republicans believed, to quote the very words used by Sr. Alcalá

Zamora, that 'they might be the first step towards the Republic', (34) but that was a different matter. Well-known public men, who were in the innermost counsels of the Revolutionary Committee, have testified that its very leaders had no expectation of a change of *régime* before the summer. They thought that opinion in April would show a distinct inclination towards republicanism and that the movement of minds thus initiated and demonstrated so clearly would cause a landslide in the parliamentary elections in June. Should the Government postpone these elections for fear of the consequences, the moment might well be ripe for a revolution. Therefore their plans were cut and dried, down to the smallest detail. But the rapidity and the ease with which the historic Monarchy collapsed was probably as great a surprise to the majority of those who had worked to procure its fall as to the merest spectator.

April 12

The Sunday of the municipal elections was a warm, sunlit day, and, though on its eve there had been a few sporadic disturbances, it passed almost as quietly as a day of national humiliation. I remember that I spent the morning in the peace of a monastery garden some miles from Barcelona, and, on returning to the city at the busiest hour of the day, was more struck with the tranquillity of the main thoroughfares than with the contrast between the cloistered garden and the world outside. It was freely said by those whose memories went back many years that no quieter election-day had ever been known. In Madrid there was more activity than in Barcelona, but even here, where most was at stake, no one would have suspected that such transcendental events were in preparation.

Monday in Spain is, till evening, in compliment to the principle of *descanso dominical* ('Sunday rest'), a day without newspapers, except for the official news-sheet, which supplies the barest outline of news. For some time, therefore, the results of the elections were not at all generally known. At first it seemed as though they were favouring the Monarchists. At two o'clock in the afternoon, the figures received down to that hour, and published by the Home Secretary, showed that 22,150 seats had gone to Monarchists and only 5,875 to Republicans. The country districts had, with few exceptions, supported the Monarchy; in Madrid, the numbers of seats gained by each group were exactly equal; and only in the principal provincial capitals, and in the northern and eastern districts of Vizcaya, Logroño, Huesca, Lérida, Barcelona and Tarragona were there Republican majorities.

But these figures, as many realized at the time, were no guide as to what was likely to happen. In the first place, everybody knew them to be incomplete. In the second place, Spain was not likely to wait for the rural constituencies to turn Republican before she threw off the Monarchy. And, most important of all, the figures given by the Home Secretary took no account of the immense size of the Republican majorities in the great cities. In the Madrid district, for example, where Sr. Alcalá Zamora, as befitted the leader of the Revolutionary Committee, headed the poll with 12,048 votes, each of the two Socialists who came next to him received over 11,000, and the three Monarchists only some 4,000 each, while of the seven remaining candidates the most popular scored 577 votes, and the least popular 8. In another district, though two of the five councillors elected were Monarchists, they each scored less than half the votes of each of the Republicans. In Barcelona, the Republicans averaged about 90,000 votes to 33,000 of the Monarchists.(35)

Such a decisive expression of opinion in Spain's two great cities alone would account for the defeatist attitude at once taken up by the Government. Madrid learned of this very early on the Monday evening. The Prime Minister, besieged by reporters (a tribe far more importunate and ubiquitous than in our own country), had made a possibly unpremeditated and certainly indiscreet reply to one of their questions.

'Is a crisis imminent?' they had asked him.

'What greater crisis do you want,' he had replied, 'than the spectacle of a country which we believed to be Monarchist turning Republican in twenty-four hours?'(36)

Frankness could go no farther. Even the War Minister's dispatch to the captains-general—'the Monarchists have been routed and the elections lost in the chief provincial capitals'(37)—was outdone by it. By nightfall, the answer to the reporters' question, with all that it implied, was being discussed by every Madrileño. On the Tuesday morning, the papers appeared with 'Republic' written on every page of them. The prominently featured messages from the revolutionary leaders, at home or in exile, came almost as an anti-climax after the Prime Minister's admission. It was presumed that the Government would duly resign and the Republicans would claim power, but that question no longer interested the crowds who gathered at street corners or walked along the avenues, deep in discussion, stopping every now and then to drive home their arguments with excited gestures. The question that absorbed them went beyond the Government and the Revolutionary Committee to the man in whose hands, as never before, lay the destiny of Spain. Yonder, in the great Royal Palace, with its courtyard thronged by anxious crowds and its glorious view over the splendid Guadarrama mountains, Don Alfonso XIII, by the grace of God King of the Spains, must even now be debating the most momentous question that he had had to solve in his lifetime of kingship.

'Monarchy or Republic? Chaos or union? War or peace?'

And those were the alternatives which in the streets as well as in the Palace were being debated on that fateful Tuesday morning.

IV

A large part of what actually happened was made known through the medium of the Press almost at once: the Republicans had everything to gain, and nothing to lose, by a policy of complete frankness. Details were added, and others corrected, in a number of books which appeared subsequently,(38) so that the fullest account of events can be read in Spanish sources. Here it will suffice to narrate the story in its main outlines, for which purpose a brief retrospect will not be superfluous.

From an early stage in the history of the Dictatorship—perhaps even before he accepted it—King Alfonso cannot have failed to realize the personal responsibility for the change of *régime* which fell upon his shoulders. Undoubtedly, as even his warmest apologists allowed,(39) he had acted unconstitutionally when in November 1923 he declined to summon the Cortes on his ministers' demand, thereby confirming his acceptance of the illegal Dictatorship. His was not the easy, expansive temperament of an Andalusian; he could not, like Primo de Rivera, refer lightly to his 'illegal but patriotic' actions: on the contrary, he never forgot that some day he would have to render his account to history, if not to his own subjects.

One may imagine his feelings, then, after Primo de Rivera's fall, when he foresaw the improbability of a return to constitutional government without disaster. It is unlikely that he shared in the shallow hopes of muddling through indulged by the more myopic of the Monarchists; on the contrary, it is known that, during the crisis of February 1931, Queen Victoria, on a visit to London, where her mother had met with an accident, was gravely concerned for his future and his safety. But her return, on February 17, gave the supporters of the throne an opportunity to demonstrate their loyalty. As the proud royal train, with its ducal driver, passed through the provincial capitals, music, flowers, and frenzied applause greeted her everywhere. In Madrid, tens of thousands thronged the streets and surrounded the Palace till the King and Queen appeared at the balconies. It was 'one of the most striking manifestations of enthusiasm that the Royal Family had ever received'. (40)

A month later, with the elections near at hand and the Aznar Government apparently in command of the situation, King Alfonso thought it practicable to pay a visit to London also. Though no facile optimist, but, as a highly critical historian has allowed, a politician of the first order, (41) he had that naturally buoyant personality which so often goes with great physical energy, and he no doubt hoped that, however greatly weakened his position might be by the parliamentary elections, he would be able to strengthen it once they were over. That the municipal elections could bring about his fall was an idea probably as far from his own mind as it was from that of nearly everybody. When, through the night of that fateful Sunday and in the early hours of the day following, the first results came through to him by telephone, he can hardly have found it possible to believe that his people were throwing him over. Neither the defeatist Aznar nor the hopeful but clear-sighted Romanones could persuade him that, for the moment at least, all was lost. His first idea was a month's truce with parliamentary elections to follow, (42) but it was not long before his ministers convinced him, as he may well have been inwardly convinced all the time, that such a course would not conceivably be agreed to by the other party.

On the Monday evening a three-hour meeting of the Cabinet was entirely dominated by the outstanding personality in the Government—the Conde de Romanones. To make any show of force, maintained the veteran statesman, was out of the question; it was not an illegal act of the people that was the problem, but their democratically and constitutionally expressed opinion. His

29

logic and sincerity carried conviction, and only two advocates of force—Bugallal and La Cierva—stood out against him. With these exceptions, the Cabinet agreed, in the first place, to resign, and then to see the King two by two, so that he might ask their advice, should he so desire, on the course to be followed in such critical circumstances.

But by Tuesday morning the situation was graver still. Practically the whole of the large towns were now known to have turned Republican, most of them by decisive majorities, and in one small town—Eibar, in the northern province of Guipúzcoa—the Republic had been officially proclaimed. Before many hours had passed, other and larger towns—San Sebastián, Saragossa, Córdoba—had followed Eibar's example. It was clear that the King must be persuaded to leave the country, at least for the present. So the Conde de Romanones telephoned to one of Don Alfonso's personal friends, the Vizconde de Casa-Aguilar, begging him to represent to His Majesty the possibility that the Army and Civil Guard might join the Republicans and to advise him to summon the Cabinet and make an act of renunciation in all due form so that the transference of powers might be effected legally.(43) The Vizconde agreed to convey a written message to this effect to the King, who at once sent for the Conde de Romanones and instructed him to communicate at once with Sr. Alcalá Zamora with a view to making the best terms possible.

It was midday when Romanones left, and the succeeding hours were spent by the King in interviewing his ministers, as the Cabinet had suggested on the preceding evening. Meanwhile, unwilling to meet Sr. Alcalá Zamora at his own residence, the Count interviewed him at the house of Don Gregorio Marañón, the aristocratic doctor who had so recently come out as a Republican. It was a strange meeting. Alcalá Zamora had once been Romanones' political follower and private secretary; both had been Ministers of the same monarch on whose staff the doctor had also served; they had disagreed and fallen out; now they came together again, from opposite sides, to decide the future of Spain.

Romanones began by asking for the truce which Don Alfonso had originally proposed and which he apparently still hoped might find favour.

Alcalá Zamora refused to hear of it. Not for that had members of the Revolutionary Committee risked their personal safety.

Then the King would abdicate, provided a regency were established under the Infante Don Carlos.

Still, it seemed, there was no basis for argument.

'What, then, does the Revolutionary Committee require of His Majesty?' asked Romanones.

'The King must hand over his authority to us and leave Spain immediately.'

'And when?' asked Romanones.

'Before daylight goes [*Antes de que se acabe la luz del día*],' answered the President-designate, 'the power must be in our hands. That is final.'(44)

So, by two o'clock, it was amicably arranged that, without formal abdication, the King should leave Madrid that same night. Five minutes later, the Count was on his way back to the Palace.

The battle was lost. The King received several more of his advisers, but, as soon as he knew that the alternatives were bloodshed or resignation, he made his choice with perfect serenity.

Already, news had been received that the Republic had been proclaimed in Spain's 'second capital', Barcelona. At half-past three the Republican tricolour of red, yellow, and purple was hoisted over the Madrid Post Office in the Plaza de Cibeles, and, like magic, the tricolour began to appear on taxis and trams, in the windows of shops and private houses and over public buildings, till, by evening, it was fluttering over the Royal Palace itself. People formed themselves into groups, and, with banners improvised from crude posters representing

31

Lady España fondling a lion or Galán and García Hernández, the 'martyrs of liberty', paraded the streets shouting wild *vivas* for the Republic. Red-capped youths commandeered taxis and jumped upon omnibuses and tramcars for gratuitous rides without number.

As time went on, the excitement increased, and, lest it should become ungovernable, a group of ministers decided to declare martial law. The proclamation was duly made, but disregarded. For a few hours there were two governments in Spain. At four o'clock Sr. Alcalá Zamora issued a statement that the Republic would be established before nightfall. At five o'clock it was informally proclaimed from the Ayuntamiento, or City Hall, of Madrid. A few minutes later the outgoing Cabinet met the outgoing King. The two die-hard ministers still counselled resistance, but Don Alfonso cut them short.

'I do not wish a single drop of blood to be shed for me,' he said. (45)

Then, after reading a message to the nation drawn up by the Duque de Maura and revised by himself, he briefly took leave of his ministers. Twice during the Cabinet meeting insistent messages had been received from the Provisional Government of the Republic, which had met at the house of the Duque de Maura's brother, Don Miguel. Sunset was approaching, they said, and power must be handed over immediately. So, with the meeting at an end, preparations began to be made for the King's departure.

v

Meanwhile, what of the Revolutionary Committee, now the Provisional Government of the Second Spanish Republic?

On the Monday afternoon, while those of its members who had been in exile were returning post-haste to Spain, the remainder met at the house of Sr. Alcalá Zamora and drew up the following manifesto, to be issued over their joint signatures:

'The representatives of the Republican and Socialist forces, united for joint action, feel the imperative necessity of addressing Spain in order to impress upon her the historic transcendence of the events of Sunday last, the twelfth of April. Never, in all our past history, has there been an achievement comparable with that of last Sunday, for never has Spain given proof of such strong civic sentiment and enthusiastic conviction, nor has she ever so determinedly revealed the firmness and dignity which she is capable of displaying in defence of her political ideals.

'There are civic events in the modern history of Europe comparable with that which took place in Spain on the twelfth of April but there is not one that can surpass it. The results of the elections in the Spanish capitals and chief urban centres are in effect a plebiscite against the Monarchy and in favour of the Republic, while at the same time the extent they have reached amounts to a verdict of "Guilty" against the present holder of the supreme power. This adverse judgment has been reached by the collaboration of all social classes and all professions in the country, while in the streets the youth groups of Spain, unable to record their votes, have given a thrilling demonstration of the fervour with which they support us.

'Now that this hour has come, we invoke those supreme civic virtues which in every cultured nation are respected by the foremost institutions of the State, the official organs of the Government and the armed forces. It is imperative that all should submit to the national will, which it is useless to endeavour to misrepresent by silence or by an appeal to the votes cast by rural feudalism. On the twelfth of April was legally recorded the voice of living Spain, and, if what she desires is now as clear as day, what she rejects is no less evident.

'If, to the great misfortune of our Spain, those who through the power of force hold official positions, or who serve in subordinate positions, should not make adequate response to the great and noble expression of civic sentiment which she has given, then, in the presence of the country and of international opinion, we decline responsibility for what must inevitably happen, since, in the name of this young and eager Spain, which has at last arrived at its majority, and which in these present circumstances we represent, we declare publicly that we shall act promptly and energetically, in order to give immediate effect to her wishes by establishing the Republic.' (46)

This note, if a little high-flown and confused in its terminology, was firm in tone, explicit in intention and as unprovocative in expression as could reasonably have been expected. At approximately the same time the Socialist General Union of Workers issued a slightly more bellicose statement, promising to see to it that nothing should interfere with the implementing of the national will. On the Tuesday afternoon, as though in response to these demands, that distinguished soldier General Sanjurjo, Director-General of the Civil Guard, who had originally declared himself a neutral, placed himself and his forces at the disposal of the new Government, which, that evening, from the house of Sr. Maura, sent and repeated to the King and his Cabinet the ultimatum already mentioned.

Then came the move which to the ministers themselves must have been the most dramatic in those two crowded days. 'I shall serve the Government which issues its commands to me from the Home Office,' Sanjurjo had said on the Tuesday morning to a messenger from the Provisional Government who had visited him to inquire his intentions. Sanjurjo, as it proved, had already come over, but it was sunset, the hour which the President-designate had named to Romanones as the latest time for the King's surrender. The King, in effect, was king no longer, and it was time for ministers of the new *régime* to take possession. To the Home Office, in the Puerta del Sol, the centre of Madrid's political life and popular activity, they must go.

So, in Sr. Alcalá Zamora's words, 'before daylight had quite gone, we went in two cars to the Home Office, where an advance guard consisting of the two newly-appointed sub-secretaries of the Prime Minister and the Home Secretary had already made a discreet arrival. . . . We were fortunate enough not to be noticed by the people until we were some three hundred yards from our goal. Thence onwards, our cars could only crawl along: the delirious enthusiasm of the masses was something indescribable. To go even so short a distance took us nearly half an hour, and it was a miracle that we got through at all without causing any accidents. In the end, by some inconceivable means, the crowds squeezed us a passage . . . and we knocked insistently on the shut and closely guarded doors of the Home Office. To all of us the few moments' delay seemed endless. . . . But if there had been any hesitation within, it was soon overcome: the door opened, the officers and the men of the Civil Guard stood to attention, and saluted the representatives of the new *régime* as they entered. We were at last the Government; we had won.' (47)

With the Republican tricolour waving for the first time from a Government building, the sub-secretary and other officials of the old *régime* silently gave place to those of the new, the first Republican Civil Governor received his orders, and Don Miguel Maura, Home Secretary in the Provisional Government, stepped out on to the well-known balcony and in historic fashion addressed the seething and cheering crowd in the Puerta del Sol below.

At eleven o'clock that night the new City Council of Madrid formally took office, and at two o'clock on the next (Wednesday) morning (by no means as unearthly an hour in Spain as in other countries) the Government entered into full possession. Its first decree, issued an hour or so later, but dated Tuesday, was one conceding 'the fullest amnesty' to political offenders and signed 'Niceto Alcalá Zamora y Torres, President of the Government of the Republic'. But previously to this, the seven other members of the Provisional Government who were in Madrid had signed and circulated a document announcing the advent of the new *régime* and appointing its first Prime Minister. It ran thus:

'The Provisional Government of the Republic has assumed power without prolonged negotiations and without any kind of formal opposition or resistance. It is the people who have raised it to the position which it now holds, and it is the people who, throughout Spain, render it homage and invest it with authority. In virtue hereof, the President of the Provisional Government of the Republic henceforth assumes the headship of the State with the express assent of the triumphant political forces and the will of the people, acquainted as they were with the composition of the Provisional Government before recording their votes at the late election.

'Interpreting the unmistakable desire of the nation, the Committee formed by the political forces which have collaborated for the installation of the new *régime* designates Don Niceto Alcalá Zamora y Torres for the office of President of the Provisional Government of the Republic.'

Having twice addressed the country by radio, established the members of his Government in their respective offices and declared the following day (which, in fact, had already begun) a national holiday, the new President went, it may be presumed, to bed. In a few hours, the last of the exiled ministers had returned to Spain and the full list of the Government was published. In view of the later history of some of its members it may be interesting to give their names.

Prime Minister	.	Don Niceto Alcalá Zamora
Foreign Affairs	.	Don Alejandro Lerroux
Justice	.	Don Fernando de los Ríos
Home Affairs		Don Miguel Maura
Finance	.	Don Indalecio Prieto
Public Works	.	Don Álvaro de Albornoz
Education .	.	Don Marcelino Domingo
Army	.	Don Manuel Azaña
Navy	.	Don Santiago Casares Quiroga
Economy	.	Don Luis Nicolau d'Olwer
Labour	.	Don Francisco Largo Caballero

The national holiday, in Madrid, as elsewhere in the country, passed with an almost complete absence of disorder. Though the noise of shouting and singing was tremendous, only the very slightest damage was done to property. At one time people feared for the Royal Palace, but the renaming of it the 'National Palace' and the affixing of notices which read, 'People, respect this building: it is yours', preserved it from harm. The injury done to property in Madrid, though regrettable enough, was not serious in extent. The rather vulnerable statue of the goddess Cibeles, opposite the General Post Office, suffered amputation of its arms and sceptre; the figure of Philip III, in the Plaza Mayor, was knocked off its pedestal; and, finally, the statue of Isabel II, in the square which at that time bore her name, was first decapitated and then adorned with a red flag and an inscription: 'Long live the martyrs of Jaca!' (48)

VI

In Barcelona, which alone of the cities of Spain may with truth be called Madrid's rival, the change of *régime* was being celebrated with not a whit less fervour. This one would certainly have expected, not only because

Catalonia and its capital lost more than the rest of Spain during the Dictatorship but because they had more to gain from the establishment of a Republic. It so happens, too, that in the light of later events the details of the proclamation of the Republic in Barcelona became of unusual importance, and they must therefore be described with some fullness.

The suppressed excitement in Barcelona, when the enormous Republican majorities were made public, was more intense even than that in Madrid. Everybody knew what was likely to happen, but no one knew whether in fact it would happen, nor how nor when nor where. Rumours became whispers, whispers became *vivas*, and at last word went round that in the Square of St. James, either from the City Hall or from the sixteenth-century palace formerly known as the Palace of the Generalitat, the seat of Catalonia's ancient parliament, a proclamation of transcendental importance would be made at about two o'clock in the afternoon. But what would the proclamation be? In this part of Spain alone could there be any doubt. In the uncertainty of the moment people asked if Catalonia was to break loose from the rest of Spain and become an independent Republic. Or if, as elsewhere in Spain, the Provisional Government was to rule. Or if there was any possibility of the proclamation of the United States of Iberia, in which case Castile and Catalonia would certainly share the pre-eminence.

It was not learned till afterwards that, at about eleven o'clock in the morning, the news of the proclamation of the Republic in some of the smaller towns in Spain had reached one of the Republican councillors returned with a huge majority on the Sunday—a lawyer named Lluis Companys. Walking through the streets, he fell into conversation with some colleagues, during which it was suggested that a move for the proclamation of a Republic might be made independently of Madrid. The move being agreed upon, it took but a short time for Sr. Companys to assemble the majority of the newly-elected Republican councillors, and it was only one o'clock when he marched with them into the City Hall and claimed possession of it in the name of the Republic.

'Here,' he said to the acting Mayor, 'are the genuine representatives of the people. We have come to take over the government of the city.'

'I shall offer no resistance,' answered the Mayor, and pointed to his wand of office.

Sr. Companys took the hint—and the wand. Then, with his companions, he proceeded to hoist the Republican flag over the City Hall. The crowds already gathered in the square below knew that in some form or other Catalonia was about to declare for the Republic, and there began a singing of the *Marseillaise* and a shouting of *Vivas* and *Mueras* (or, more correctly, to use the Catalan words, of *Visques* and *Moris*), which, as I can personally testify, were heard continuously, except during some four hours before dawn on Wednesday, for no less than forty hours on end.

Denser and denser grew the crowds until all traffic ceased; denser and denser, until, even in that vast square, one could hardly move. As nearly as possible to two o'clock there was a stir of excitement in the crowd as Sr. Companys appeared on the balcony of the City Hall and announced that the Republic was to be proclaimed in Barcelona. Then the tall spare figure of Colonel Macià, the leader of the victorious Esquerra, or Catalan Left party, was seen behind him. The crowd burst into excited cheers, which suddenly died as Sr. Macià came forward to make the shortest of speeches.

'People of Catalonia:

'In the name of the people of Catalonia I proclaim the Catalonian State, which, with all cordiality, we shall endeavour to incorporate in the Federation of Iberian Republics.

'From now onward is formed the Government of

the Catalonian Republic which will meet in the Palace of the Generalitat.

'Those who form the Government of Catalonia will now and henceforward be ready to defend the liberties of the Catalonian people and to die for them. Let us hope that you, Catalonian people, will be prepared, like all of us, to die for Catalonia and the Republic.' (49)

As he ceased, the cheers redoubled. Some one with a cornet began the *Marseillaise*. The whole crowd took it up. One felt it must have been heard for miles.

Meanwhile, accompanied by his fellow-councillors, Colonel Macià crossed to the Palace opposite for his formal election to the presidency of the new Government, before which ceremony he addressed the people again, this time from the Palace balcony.

'In the name of the people of Catalonia I proclaim the Catalonian State, under the *régime* of a Catalonian Republic, which freely and with all cordiality desires and requests the collaboration of the other and sister peoples of Spain in the creation of a Confederation of Iberian Peoples, and offers to free them from the Bourbon Monarchy.

'Here and now we raise our voice to all the free states of the world, in the name of liberty, justice and the peace of nations.' (50)

It was not till the small hours of Wednesday morning, when the news from Madrid just narrated had become public, that the victory of this bloodless revolution in Barcelona was made certain by the submission of the Army. But the people took it for granted—so much so that it hardly occurred to them to answer the questions which they had been asking before the time of the proclamation.

These, none the less, were of some importance. What exactly had Sr. Macià proclaimed? Well, clearly, a Catalonian republic, for not only did the Catalonian flag fly from the Palace high above the Republican tricolour, but the words 'República Catalana' headed the official proclamation, copies of which were posted all over the city. But only a Catalonian republic in the federal sense of those words. Though nothing whatever was said of Sr. Alcalá Zamora and his Provisional Government in Madrid, it was clear from the second proclamation that collaboration with the 'sister peoples' of Spain was to be an integral part of the new order, and enough was known of the Pact of San Sebastián, which had been signed in the preceding August, to guarantee the faithful collaboration of Barcelona with Madrid in the building up of the Spain of the future. It was also observed that among the ministers of the Provisional Government was a well-known and trusted Catalonian, Sr. Nicolau d'Olwer, a fact which gave assurance both, on the one hand, that Catalonia had not been forgotten and, on the other, that she would do her part in the future.

So but little heed was paid to the terms of the proclamation, and it was only the Provisional Government that scanned it with some anxiety. There was, of course, to be no nonsense about a Federal Republic—that was an idea which would require decades, if not centuries, of development, before it could become practical politics. But that the Catalonians should have started their new *régime* in the wrong direction was an error that affected Madrid closely, for the Pact of San Sebastián committed them to the sponsoring of a Catalan Autonomy Statute in the Constituent Cortes, and for the peace of the Republic it was essential that the governments of Madrid and Barcelona should see eye to eye both now and subsequently. So, when the Republic was but a week old, three ministers flew from Madrid to Barcelona, interviewed the Catalonian Government and persuaded them to change the phrase 'Catalonian State' (*Estat Català*), which had a somewhat sinister association with pure separatism, to the historic one of 'Generalitat of

Catalonia', and at the same time to resign themselves to becoming an autonomous region in a unitary state if such should be the decision of the Cortes. Always reasonable as they are when reasonably treated, the Catalonians made no difficulty about agreement and for the time being the matter was amicably settled.

Republic Day—the national holiday—in Barcelona was a *fiesta* not soon to be forgotten. There was delirious excitement, but complete good humour with absolutely no disorder, the only known casualties being framed portraits of the King which some one conceived the idea of dropping from upper stories of apartment-houses on to pavements. It can best be described as an Armistice Day followed by a Boat Race Night; add to that short phrase a dash of local colour and you have the situation exactly.

Imagine, if you know Barcelona, the scene as one looks up the plane-lined Ramblas to the Plaça de Catalunya. As far as the eye can reach, a sea of humanity. A sea with yellow and red sails upon it for the Catalonian Republic—with red, yellow and purple sails for the Republic of Spain. Down from the houses fly pennons, flags and streamers—red, yellow and purple these, too, against the azure sky. Taxis are completely swathed in the colours of Catalonia or of Spain. Along the tree-lined central avenue, the youth of the Republic, some of them red-capped, others with Republican favours, marching who knows where. Along the outer roadways, no tram-cars for once: on the preceding evening they had all been commandeered by the people, who rode on them without ever paying for a ticket even with so much as a by-your-leave, and not only rode on them but filled them to overflowing—squeezed tightly, on top and bottom alike, crowding the platforms, hanging on the back and swarming up steps and staircase. Black with such shouting loads of humanity, the cars plunged at breakneck speed down the Ramblas—making one shudder both at the thought of their overturning and at the symbolic picture which they offered of a people plunging into the immensity of the unknown.

But no Catalonian could think of such a thing on this night when he celebrates his country's liberation. *Visca la República!* . . . Only in the rare welcome moments when no one is either playing or singing the *Marseillaise* can the words be distinguished, but they come full-throated from this city of a million gone mad. Marching who knows where—up the Ramblas to the Plaça de Catalunya, down the Ramblas again, along the Quay, through the Gardens, up the higher boulevards, out to Pedralbes, and at last, when all is dark, up to the fortress-hill of Montjuic, where there will be dancing and fire-works and the night will wear itself out in rejoicing.

At last the harbour darkens, the sun sets; but still the cries grow louder and the crowds denser. Aeroplanes circle overhead, the twin flags of liberty fluttering from their wings. Slowly they turn and make for Montjuic. The people, from all parts and quarters of the city, do the same. Little by little, Old Barcelona empties. As the tramp of many feet recedes, the shouting becomes fainter.

The Republic is on the march again. *Visca la República!*

VII

As the members of the Provisional Government sat in their cars outside the Puerta del Sol listening to the plaudits of the people, there must have been, at least to the more imaginative of them, one faintly jarring note in the music. However loudly they might proclaim the Republic, the King was still in the Royal Palace, and, however vehemently the crowd might hurl its *mueras* at the 'Bourbon tyrant', there was always a danger that the bellicosity of the die-hards, or the magnetic person-ality of Don Alfonso himself, would change those *mueras* into *vivas*—so undependable, even at its best, is the People!

Sunset had passed, night had fallen, and still there

was no news of the King's departure. But the ministers need have had no fear. Brave enough to risk death, as he had often done, when his personal safety was at stake, he was brave enough even to risk being thought a coward for the sake of the safety of his people. From the beginning he had seen that if terms with the enemy were impossible it was best for all that he should slip away from Spain, hoping, no doubt, that the Second Republic would go the way of the First and that he would be called back again in the near future. So, after his last meeting with the Cabinet, he negatived alike the entreaties of the die-hard ministers, the protestations of his personal attendants and the offers of a valiant general to muster what he could of the Army. His mind was made up: he would leave Spain that night.

His immediate goal was France—but the question was how best to get there. The direct route, by way of Irún, was out of the question. Gibraltar, though in itself a convenient exit, was inconveniently distant. At their meeting with Dr. Marañón, Romanones and Alcalá Zamora had favoured Portugal; and, till a late hour on the Tuesday evening, the crowds in the great cities, who thronged the newspaper offices and other places displaying periodical news-bulletins, believed that Portugal had been decided upon.

In the end, however, the King adopted the less easily calculable plan of driving on Tuesday night to Cartagena, and in the small hours of Wednesday morning boarding the cruiser *Príncipe Alfonso*, which would take him to Marseilles. At a quarter to nine, with a small retinue, he left the Palace by a private exit, and travelled through the night, arriving at Cartagena at four o'clock the next morning and at Marseilles twenty-six hours later. As soon as he had disembarked, the Commandant hoisted a Republican flag which had been specially made during the journey, as though to show that his passenger had not been the King of Spain, but Don Alfonso of Bourbon-Habsburg.

The Queen had all her children with her, except the Infante Don Juan, who was studying at the Naval Academy of San Fernando and rejoined his family a few days later in Paris. It was thought that they might safely make the direct journey to France by the morning express, but at the last moment they decided to join the train at El Escorial rather than in the capital. The story of their preparations and journey may not unkindly be said to belong to the anecdotal history of the reign of Alfonso XIII rather than to the history of the Republic. It will suffice to record that, after a night of anxiety not lessened by the shouts of the surging mob as they filled the courtyard and assaulted the very doors and windows of the Palace, they entrained safely in the royal Pullman which was awaiting them at El Escorial and reached the French frontier without suffering any kind of molestation.

Two days later, somewhat to the general surprise, the Provisional Government authorized the publication of the manifesto which the ex-King had read at the last meeting of his Cabinet. Two short and harmless messages, to the Army and the Navy respectively, written by Don Alfonso on board the cruiser and entrusted to Admiral Rivera, who had accompanied him to Marseilles, were not allowed to appear and became known only much later. But so sure did the new Government feel of its hold on the country—'so free was it,' to use its own words, 'from all fear of Monarchist reactions' —that, although some might think it had been rash in allowing the King to leave Spain without formally abdicating the throne, it saw no objection to allowing the publication of the longer document, prefacing it with only a few words to justify its action. The manifesto read as follows:

'The elections which took place on Sunday show me clearly that I no longer have the love of my people. My conscience tells me that this indifference will not be final, for I have always done my utmost to serve

Spain, and even on the most critical occasions I have made the public interest my sole endeavour.

'A king can make mistakes, and no doubt I have sometimes erred, but I well know that our country has always shown herself generous towards those whose faults are devoid of malice.

'I am the king of all Spaniards and I am also myself a Spaniard.

'I could find ample means to maintain my royal prerogative by making effective use of force against those who contest it. But I desire most resolutely to abstain from any course which might plunge my compatriots into a fratricidal civil war.

'I renounce none of my rights, for they are not so much my own as a trust committed to me by History, for which one day I shall have to render her a strict account.

'I await the tidings of the authentic and adequate expression of the nation's collective conscience, and, while the nation is speaking, I deliberately suspend the exercise of royal power and leave Spain, thus showing that I recognize her as the sole mistress of her destinies.

'By doing this I believe I am fulfilling the duty dictated to me by love of my country. I pray to God that other Spaniards may feel it as deeply and may fulfil it as I do.'

'ALFONSO R.H.'(51)

It was a magnificent farewell, and a far more restrained one than might have been expected from the last of the Bourbons, in whom initiative and personal courage had always been more prominent than insight, sensitiveness or prudence. None would have been surprised if, with a lingering trust in the Divine Right of Kings and the inherent monarchism of the symbol-loving Spanish people, he had pointed to the non-political nature of the elections or to the published figures, which of course gave a large Monarchist majority, and, calling upon his ministers to support him and his army to fight for him, had challenged the revolutionaries to do their worst. The eventual result of such a proceeding, it can hardly be doubted, would have been civil war first, followed (whichever side won) by the worst kind of political chaos. Nor can one refrain from admiring the tone of the manifesto, which reflects credit alike upon its gifted composer and its royal signatory. Though it is probable that, optimistic to the last, Don Alfonso hoped that the June elections would bring him back again, the magnanimity of his attitude is in no way based upon any such expectation. When for the last time he spoke to his people, it was as a King indeed, but no less as a Spaniard and a fellow human being. Of him it may be said, as it was said of an earlier sovereign who found that kings may err, and must suffer for their errors, but learned his lesson more tragically,

> He nothing common did or mean
> Upon that memorable scene . . .
> Nor call'd the gods, with vulgar spite,
> To vindicate his helpless right.

And for an epitaph on his entire reign we may go to Shakespeare and say, still more briefly:

> Nothing in his life
> Became him like the leaving it.

CHAPTER II

THE REPUBLICAN CONSTITUTION

I

THE King was now satisfactorily disposed of, and the new Government's next thought was for the consolidation of the Republic. For until the elections, fixed for June, had been held and a Republican Constitution firmly established, there was always a possibility of counter-action by the supporters of Don Alfonso.

Expedients of many kinds were invoked to bring the new *régime* popularity. One of such expedients was the handing out of presents. On the second day of the Republic's existence, life pensions, dating from the previous December, were awarded to the dependants of the 'martyred' heroes of Jaca.(1) The royal parks of Madrid and the royal palace of Pedralbes at Barcelona were made over to the inhabitants of those cities. Seville, where extremism was so rife that Communistic literature was being sold from the very steps of the cathedral, was granted 500,000 pesetas towards the immediate relief of unemployment, and smaller grants were made in other parts of the country. Before April was out, Sr. Alcalá Zamora had paid an official visit to Barcelona, and both in Catalonia and in other parts of the country it became known that the aspirations of the people towards autonomy would receive the most sympathetic consideration.

The intellectuals, who had lent the young Republic such valuable and timely support, were conciliated principally by assurances of the aid that would in due course be given to learning; intellectuals are patient and, as a rule, harmless people, and will wait longer for the fulfilment of promises than the proletariat. But as an earnest of what was coming—and it proved to be well worth waiting for—the principal ambassadorships were bestowed upon men of letters. Don Salvador de Madariaga, who had for some time been in effect the future Republic's principal ambassador-at-large, went from the King Alfonso XIII Professorship at Oxford, which he had so strangely consented to hold, to the Embassy at Washington. Don Salvador Albert, the poet, went to Belgium; Don Américo Castro, the Cervantes critic, to Berlin; and the novelist Don Ramón Pérez de Ayala, who for some months, as we have seen, had been working to bring in the Republic, to London. The Paris ambassadorship was offered, first, to the eminent specialist, Dr. Marañón; and then to the Socialist professor Don Julián Besteiro. Both of these having refused the post, it was given to an historical novelist who has aspired to be a second Pérez Galdós, Don Alfonso Danvila.

Another expedient for the popularization of the Republic over Spain as a whole was the organizing of demonstrations. The success of the national holiday of April 15 had been greater than its promoters had dared to hope, and on the following Sunday a monster demonstration organized in Madrid to honour the memory of the Socialist hero Pablo Iglesias passed off in perfect order. Labour Day (May 1), at which some serious ebullition of extremist feeling was always a possibility, loomed perilously near, but it was proclaimed an official holiday, work being specifically forbidden, and, except for some minor incidents in Barcelona and Bilbao, there were no disturbances. Truly this, as a British journalist observed, was an 'immaculate republic'!

It is worth while pausing for a moment to admire what was perhaps the greatest achievement of the makers of the Second Republic—the bringing of it into being with such tranquillity. Primo de Rivera had prided himself on the ease with which he struck his *coup d'état*, but what had his task been beside that of the new Provisional Government? 'Here was a Monarchy which had been in existence for fifteen centuries annihilated in the space of forty-eight hours by the sheer irresistible force of the popular will—and not a drop of blood spilt in the process.'(2) The oldest monarchy in Europe, wrote Sr. Alcalá Zamora in an article the boastfulness of which would have been pardonable had it not been premature, had gone down before the indomitable will of the people. And what was the state of Spain, he continued, at the time of this bloodless revolution:

> 'The forces of law and order remain within barracks, or, if ordered out, fraternize with the people. . . . There is no need to guard any bank, church or convent, for they are threatened neither by greed nor by sectarian passion. Shops are left open without the slightest anxiety or danger. . . . Even jewellers take no particular precautions. Women, and indeed children, go freely about the streets. . . . On the fifth day of republican rule, a civic procession of over one hundred thousand people made its way through Madrid without the least disorder. . . .(3)

These, as it proved, were unlucky words, very soon to recoil cruelly upon the writer. But the paragraphs which follow, describing the thoroughness and minuteness of the preparation made by the Revolutionary Committee, are even more deserving of quotation. Being a coalition of widely differing ideas, it had worked together until there was not the slightest fear that it would fall apart when it began to govern. Every step to be taken had been discussed beforehand; all the portfolios had been assigned exactly as they were announced in April; every important position in the State had been filled in advance, even to the civil governorships of the provinces. All the early reforms which it was proposed to establish had been worked out down to their smallest details. For two months after the Provisional Government had been formed in the summer of 1930, it had met, not occasionally, nor even frequently, but daily, 'lest for a single moment, when the victory had been won, the machine of government should become paralysed'.(4)

It was all remarkable—one hardly knows whether to marvel more at the industry and thoroughness which characterized the work of these highly practical idealists or at the completeness of the success which rewarded it. But worse times were at hand, and it must unhappily be chronicled that a third measure which had to be adopted for the consolidation of the Republic was repression. The new *régime* was not a month old before drastic action had to be taken in an attempt to quell serious disorder, and this action, in its comparative ineffectiveness, showed that the passions of the mob were more profound and violent than the amiable and well-intentioned Prime Minister had suspected.

The troubles of May 1931 began with a journalistic scoop achieved by the famous Monarchist newspaper *A.B.C.* The editor of *A.B.C.*, Sr. Luca de Tena, had, like his father, its founder, long been the personal friend of Don Alfonso XIII, and, three weeks after the proclamation of the Republic, he had paid a visit to the King, who was now in London, to secure a personal interview, which became the sensation of the moment. There was nothing in the content of the interview, as we look back on it to-day, which was in the least degree inflammatory; indeed the remarkable feature of it is that the exiled King could express himself with such moderation. 'I will not put the slightest difficulty in the way of the Republican Government', he was reported as saying.

> 'Monarchists who wish to follow my advice will not only refrain from placing obstacles in the Government's path but will support it in all patriotic enterprises. . . . High above the formal ideas of republic or monarchy stands Spain. . . . I may have made mistakes but I have thought only of the good of Spain. . . . I declined the offers made me to remain and rule

by force and . . . for Spain I made the greatest sacrifice
of my life when I found she no longer desired me.(5)

It was not the sentiments expressed in the interview
that alarmed Republican opinion so much as the facts
that the editor of a leading newspaper had travelled to
London to get it; that, having got it, he had written it
up so attractively and featured it with such prominence;
and that he had added to it an expression of loyalty
to the 'Parliamentary and Constitutional Monarchy'.(6)
Nor was it so much the content of Cardinal Segura's
famous pastoral that incensed this opinion as the words
in which the Cardinal had clothed it and the feeling that
he could not be relied upon to remain neutral.

The striking and dynamic personality of Dr. Pedro
Segura, Cardinal-Archbishop of Toledo and Primate of
all Spain, could hardly be kept for long in the background at a time of national turmoil. A Bishop at
thirty-five, Primate and Cardinal eleven years later, he
was still on the right side of fifty. A scholar, he had won
no less than three doctorates at college. A social re-
former, he had become known throughout Spain for his
humanitarian work in its most poverty-stricken region,
Las Hurdes. A devoted pastor, he lived the simplest
of lives in his Toledan palace, and, during diocesan
missions, had been known to work as hard and as long
as the humblest parish priest.

Since the fourteenth of April, report had been busy
as to the attitude of the Cardinal-Archbishop to the new
régime, and on the very day after the publication of the
A.B.C. interview, the Press reproduced the long text
of a pastoral which set the entire country talking. By
no means the whole of it could be interpreted as provocative, but the language and the sentiments of several
paragraphs, on which the Press naturally laid emphasis,
were, to say the least of it, unfortunate. It was hardly
prudent, for instance, at such a time, to begin by expressing 'grateful remembrance of His Majesty King

Alfonso XIII, who during his reign successfully preserved the ancient traditions of faith and piety of his ancestors', to devote the three following paragraphs to a eulogy of 'his fallen Majesty' and to hint that 'the enemies of the kingdom of Jesus Christ' are advancing. The climax of his argument was nothing less than a call to battle.

'In these moments of terrible uncertainty, every Catholic must measure the magnitude of his responsibilities and valiantly perform his duty. If we all keep our eyes fixed on higher interests, and sacrifice what is secondary to what is important; if we unite our forces and prepare to fight with perfect cohesion and discipline, without vain parade, but with faith in our ideals, with abnegation and the spirit of sacrifice, we shall be able to look at the future with tranquillity, confident of victory.

'If we remain "quiet and idle"; if we allow ourselves to give way to "apathy and timidity";(7) if we leave the road open to those who are attempting to destroy religion or expect the benevolence of our enemies to secure the triumph of our ideals, we shall have no right to lament when bitter reality shows us that we had victory in our hands, yet knew not how to fight like intrepid warriors, prepared to succumb gloriously.'(8)

From one point of view these were splendid words; none will deny that they were brave words; yet most people to-day would agree that they were also provocative words. It was not surprising that an anti-clerical Minister of Justice should condemn them as 'bellicose,' or that the Government should decide that this kind of thing 'could not be permitted to continue' and request the Holy See to remove the Cardinal from his arch-bishopric.(9) Nor could it be wondered at that *A.B.C.*, when it described the pastoral as 'irreproachably loyal to the Government'(10) and saw in it 'not a paragraph, assertion or counsel that was open to question', should be attacked by extremists.

This, and more, was what happened. On Sunday, May 10, exactly four weeks after those momentous municipal elections which put an end to the Monarchy, Spain's immaculate republic soiled its record.

The trouble began in Madrid, where, in the Calle de Alcalá, a new Monarchist Club had been founded, and on this Sunday morning was holding a private meeting to elect its Committee. Some reports had it that passers-by heard the Royal March being played inside the house on a gramophone; others alleged that members of the Club were indulging in provocative demonstrations from the balcony. Whatever the cause, a crowd col-lected, and when two men paying off their taxi before entering the Club heard the commotion, cried 'Long live the Monarchy!' and struck their driver, who had shouted for the Republic, its smouldering passion was kindled. A free fight began—and unfortunately it be-gan in the pre-luncheon hour when the Alcalá is always packed to capacity.

Somehow a rumour started that the taxi-driver had died from the effect of the blows he had received. The rumour spread like wildfire.

'Down with the Monarchists!' yelled the crowds. 'Down with the house! Down with the balcony!'

By this time the Civil Guard had arrived in force, but its attempt to disperse the crowds was completely ineffective. The excellent idea was circulating that it would be an amusing game to set fire to the waiting cars of the members of the Club before their own eyes. No sooner said than done: in a few minutes two of the cars were blazing merrily.

From the standpoint of the authorities, the problems of how to clear the streets and of how to get the Monarch-ists safely out of the house were now equally pressing. Three large police motor-vans were brought, and, to the accompaniment of jeers, curses and blows, the members of the Club were packed inside. But none of them could go, for scores of men flung themselves on the ground to impede their passage. At last the Home Secretary, Don Miguel Maura, mounted one of the vans and tried to harangue the crowd. Worse and worse! 'What! Maura?' yelled the mob. 'Down with him! Down with the son of his father! Down with the Monarchist's son!'

By this time it was four o'clock. The driver of one of the motor-vans, by means of a pretty reverse feint, had managed to clear a way through the human barrier which impeded his progress, but the crowds grew larger and larger, till the whole of the Alcalá and the streets beyond it were one mass of humanity.

Then suddenly some one started a new cry:

'*A.B.C.*! To the offices of *A.B.C.*! Down with *A.B.C.*!'

Instantly the situation changed. In a few moments, thousands were charging down the Alcalá, across the Cibeles square, up the Paseo de Recoletos and by all other possible routes until they joined forces in the Calle de Serrano, where the offices of the Monarchist daily were situated. On their way they recognized Don Leopoldo Matos, a former minister of King Alfonso, paying an afternoon call. Immediately they set upon him, pummelled him, beat him, tore off his coat, trampled on his hat, and might well have lynched him had he not, for his own safety, been taken into custody.

At last, after a number of such incidents, the crowd arrived at its goal. A few sentries who had been detailed to guard the offices were soon disposed of, and in a few moments, to the cheering of thousands, several hundred people were engaged in stoning the windows and flinging petrol on the walls with the intention of setting them on fire. The Civil Guard, in desperation, retreated into the building and thence fired several shots into the air. This sufficed to disperse the crowd, which, unlike similar crowds of later days, was unarmed, and soon groups of frenzied Republicans, with tales of machine-guns being trained on them from the *A.B.C.* offices, were busy working off their hostility on buildings in other parts of the city. The Government, as though completely unprepared for events which had been freely forecast, appeared to be powerless, and all the Home Secretary could do that night was to attempt to appease the mob by announcing that *A.B.C.* had been suspended, its offices searched and its editor put into prison.

But the blood of the mob was up and on the next day incendiarism, directed this time against the Church, began in earnest. In broad daylight—to be exact, at half-past ten in the morning—a body of men set fire to the Jesuit Church of the Calle de la Flor, in the very centre of the capital. Not till it was completely alight did firemen arrive, and then the crowds, who had been watching the scene as placidly as though it were a municipal firework-display, set upon them and prevented them forcibly from extinguishing the flames till the church was burned to the ground. Even mounted police and cavalry could do little against this determination of the people.

Next, crowds with red flags formed up and marched to the magnificent new convent[1] and church built by the Carmelite Fathers in the Plaza de España, to the residence of the Jesuits in Alberto Aguilera, to the Mercedarian convent in Bravo Murillo, to the College of Maravillas in the suburb of Cuatro Caminos, to the College of the Sacred Heart in Chamartín, and to a number of other buildings, all of which they set on fire and more or less completely destroyed. Many convents were disbanded as a precaution, and monks, friars and nuns escaped in lay attire. Some of them wandered through Madrid that night, with nowhere to go, and were taken in by private families.

Still the Government failed to take effective action.

[1] The word 'convent' is used in Spain to denote either a monastery or a friary or a religious house for women and in that general sense it is used in this book.

The Cabinet sat continuously for thirteen hours, but about the results of their long deliberations the less said the better. In an official statement they laid the principal blame, not, as might have been expected, upon the mobs, but upon the most unpopular people in Spain, whom any stick was good enough to beat—the Monarchists. These 'reactionaries', ran the statement, had 'deliberately chosen to excite disturbances' and to 'defy the people'. Even the circumstantial accounts of the disturbances given by the staunchest of Republican papers belied this imputation.(11) But its effect was, of course, merely to stimulate the crowds to further effort, and the suspension of the Catholic daily *El Debate*, as well as of the Monarchist *A.B.C.*, could hardly have been more timely if its object had been to applaud the incendiaries' achievements. For the rest, martial law was proclaimed, the Exchange was closed and an appeal was made to the country by radio.

But, though the Madrid mobs had by now had their fill of violence, the fires so light-heartedly set ablaze at once spread over the country. North of Madrid there were no disturbances, nor in Catalonia, which was occupied, as we shall see, with other matters. But in Andalusia—*tierra de María Santísima*; *tierra bendita de Dios*—a terrible toll was taken by ungoverned passion. In almost all the large cities of the South martial law was proclaimed. In Valencia, Alicante, Murcia, Granada, Seville, Córdoba, Cádiz and Málaga, convents and churches went a-blazing. The city hit worst of all was Málaga, where on May 11 and 12 fires continued uninterruptedly. Not only were the Episcopal Palace, the Jesuits' residence and convents of Augustinians, Carmelites and Marists set on fire, but various churches, containing valuable works of art, were destroyed, together with numerous shops and public buildings. (12)

For forty-eight hours something like panic reigned in Spain and men talked wildly of Russia and Mexico.

There was much removal of Church treasures to places of safety. In the midst of it all, the Cardinal-Primate, not without suggestions from the secular authorities, slipped quietly over the frontier and made his way to Rome. But at the end of five days the country was completely quiet again. The wave of feeling which had surged up, without, as it seemed, any adequate cause, had subsided with equal suddenness. *A.B.C.* and the *Debate* remained suspended; a few public functionaries resigned their posts; and newspaper reporters began hunting for news again.

So ended the first calendar month of the second Spanish Republic.

II

The attacks on churches and convents demonstrated clearly to the Government the necessity for more effective control of mob-passion, and there is no doubt that they profited from the lesson. The strengthening of the Civil Guard, a brave and loyal body of men to whom all pay tribute, dates from this period, as does the establishment of the more drastically intentioned Shock Troops, or Guardias de Asalto. But for the moment the chief effect which the outbreaks seemed to have was the straining of relations between Church and State which even now were none too easy. Already, before it had been a week in office, the Government had announced the secularization of cemeteries, the cancellation of compulsory church parades in the Army and a more ample toleration for non-Catholic worship. At the end of May a decree was passed giving all denominations equal rights as to worship, forbidding any functionary to inquire into an individual's religious beliefs, and removing the obligations on individuals to take part in religious practices or ceremonies. Unhappily, there were those who interpreted this to mean that Catholics might be persecuted with impunity, and numbers of practising Catholics, in no way connected with politics, lost their employment for reasons (to quote a phrase which was made to cover a multitude of sins about that time) of 'incompatibility with the *régime*'.

Meanwhile, to the virtual expulsion from Spain of the Cardinal-Primate had to be added the actual expulsion of the Bishop of Vitoria, who was alleged to have used diocesan visitations for purposes of political propaganda. It seemed as if a complete impasse had been reached between Madrid and Rome when the Holy See refused its *placet* to the newly appointed Ambassador to the Vatican and made a condition of his being accepted the safeguarding of the lives and property of the faithful. The Government issued no reply to this announcement, for it had no reply to make. At that time it was incapable of safeguarding the lives or property of any group of citizens whatsoever.

Perhaps the tension caused by this situation of mutual inactivity was somewhat relieved by an undignified incident which occurred in the middle of June. The Cardinal-Primate made a secret return to Spain— *incognito*. Evidently, though he had not been formally expelled, he was aware that the frontier officers would not re-admit him, so this Prince of the Church re-entered Spain by one of the little-used Pyrenean passes, and it was not till he had reached Guadalajara that he was stopped, detained for the night and on the next day ejected by way of Irún. Whether because the blow was too much for his pride or because the Holy See thought it best to yield to the demands of the Spanish Government, he never repeated the attempt. Shortly afterwards, his see was declared vacant, and he was succeeded in it by Mgr. Goma, of Tarazona, an elderly man who proved to have considerable administrative ability, though at the time of his appointment he was noted chiefly for his prowess in theology.

By the time of the Guadalajara incident, the Government was occupied with matters which it judged to be more important than the pursuit of recalcitrant cardinals.

The general elections of the first Cortes of the Republic
—the Constituent Cortes, as they were called—were
approaching and with them new pitfalls both for the
Government and for the *régime*. Revolutionary strikes,
which began soon after the proclamation of the Republic,
were growing uncomfortably common. Martial law and
riots resulting in six deaths had accompanied a three-
day strike at San Sebastián, and sympathetic strikes had
developed along the coast. The Syndicalists of the
northern provinces threatened a general strike unless
two ministers were sacrificed. A serious strike was
attempted in the Asturian mines, and, though it was
confined to about twenty per cent of the miners, the
collisions that occurred between strikers and men at
work made it necessary to take military action

Another cause of anxiety was the peseta. For nearly
a month after the incendiary riots of May, and despite
the care taken by the Government to prevent the exportation of capital, it dropped continuously. In the
middle of May, sterling stood, approximately as in the
preceding December, at 48; by the end of the month,
it had reached 62 and the Finance Minister, Sr. Prieto,
was threatening resignation. Gradually, however, the
peseta began to recover and the middle of June found
the rate at 48 again.

Meanwhile the stage was being set for the meeting
of the new parliament. Some weeks previously, the
minimum age for the franchise had been fixed at 23
years; eligibility for membership of the Cortes had been
extended to women and priests; and the electoral divisions
of the country had been revised so that each province
could elect one deputy for every 50,000 of its inhabitants.
Now the unicameral parliament, though not yet elected,
was solemnly invested, by proclamation, with full
constituent and administrative powers, the first of these
to be exercised being the ratification of the authority
assumed by the Provisional Government. Signed by
the whole body of ministers, the proclamation was as

imposing as no doubt it was intended to be; and, in order that disturbances should be reduced to a minimum, widespread *fiestas* were organized as a preliminary to the elections—the *fiestas* in Madrid lasting for no less than a fortnight.

The elections, like the fateful municipal elections of April, passed off quietly, and the results were all that the Provisional Government could have hoped. In Madrid, the Government's candidates averaged 120,000 votes as against 30,000 polled by the candidates next in order. Only a single new deputy in the whole of Spain described himself as a Monarchist, and those Conservatives who might have been presumed to be of Monarchist sympathies numbered no more than 19. Even the right-wing Republican Party, under Sr. Alcalá Zamora, which had presented over one hundred candidates, had only 28 in the new House. The left-wing Republican Alliance, on the other hand, numbered 145; the Socialists, 114; and the Radical Socialists, 56. It was clear that Spain was still under the influence of the Republican reaction of April, and it seemed as if there would be no difficulty in maintaining an unbroken progressive coalition for an indefinite period.

Before the new parliament met, the Provisional Government published the first draft of the Constitution, which throughout the session would form the principal subject of discussion. In the main it bore a close resemblance to the document which was eventually approved by the Constituent Cortes. One notable divergence was in the creation of a Senate of 240 members: 60 to be elected by employers, 60 by workers, 60 by the liberal professions and 60 by universities, cultural institutions and religious bodies. Half of each group would be re-elected at a time, the Senate as a whole to be indissoluble. As the bi-cameral principle, however, was decisively rejected a few months later, the ideas of the first Republicans on this subject are of only historical interest.

No sooner were the general elections safely over than

social disturbances broke out anew. This time they took the form, which later became only too familiar, of relays of revolutionary strikes, organized by the Sindicato Unico, as the Syndicalist Confederation is called, all over the country.

One of the targets of the strikers was the telephone system, which had been made efficient under the Dictatorship. For weeks a telephone strike rendered the service ineffective throughout Spain, while, in Madrid, groups of Syndicalists attacked the Central Telephone Building in the Gran Vía and had to be charged by mounted police. In Valencia, hotel and restaurant employees came out, and even the cafés were half empty. But the worst disturbances took place at Seville—the metropolis, as it were, of the vast regions of Andalusia and Extremadura, where there was so much unrest among the peasants. In Seville, for ten days, mob rule threatened to triumph. A general strike was declared on July 20; in the accompanying riots a man was killed, and at his funeral further shooting caused three deaths and numerous injuries. The authorities acted more determinedly than had yet been done anywhere in Spain. The Syndicalist and Communist centres in Seville were closed; prominent Syndicalists were arrested; and, when the shooting still went on, artillery destroyed one of the Syndicalist centres which had been found to be a nest of gunmen. When martial law was declared and armed aircraft began regularly to patrol the city, the situation became easier and by the end of the month all was quiet. The casualty list of 30 killed and 200 wounded seemed at the time enormous. Alas, that it was again and again to be so greatly exceeded in the years that followed!

III

Day after day, from July till December, through the torrid heat of a Madrid summer, the newly elected Cortes debated the Republican Constitution. No one who followed the course of the debates could have questioned the intense earnestness of all parties in their search for a stable foundation on which the Republic might rest. Nor could any doubt the determination and the industry which kept the Cortes unremittingly at work during what is normally a season of prolonged vacation. When, before the end of the year, the Constitution was duly promulgated, the Government must have felt intense satisfaction.

Any reader of the Constitution of 1931 must feel that he has been carried far away from the Spain of history and legend(13)—especially from the Black Legend of a country opposed to every kind of innovation and to all forms of progress. 'Spain', declares the first article, 'is a democratic republic of workers of all classes, organized in a *régime* of liberty and justice.' Its authority, continues the text, 'emanates from the people'; all its citizens 'are equal in the sight of the law'; it has 'no official religion'.(14) Spain no longer glories in splendid isolation: 'the Spanish State will respect the universal rules of international law'.(15) Nor does the new Republic dream of empire or conquest: 'Spain renounces war as an instrument of national policy'.(16) These introductory articles, like the first scenes of a drama, give the atmosphere of the whole and prepare us for what is to follow.

The first section of the Constitution, which relates to the organization of the country, will be referred to again in connexion with regional autonomy. Here it will suffice to say that, while for Spain as a whole the existing provincial and municipal organization is retained in the new Constitution, it is specifically laid down that, under certain conditions, groups of provinces may apply for a Statute of Autonomy,(17) with the proviso that 'in no case is a federation of autonomous regions permissible'.(18) In the following articles a broad delimitation is made between the powers of the Central Government and those of the autonomous region, and

general principles are detailed to be observed in case
of dispute.

Following a brief section on Spanish nationality
comes the longest and in many ways the most important section of the entire document—on 'political and
individual guarantees'. Of this the dominant notes are
equality and freedom. No titles of nobility are henceforth recognized. No special privileges are to be
accorded to citizens on account of sex, wealth, social
class, political opinions or religious beliefs.(19) All are
free to choose their professions, and to 'express in any
form their ideas and opinions, without previously being
subjected to censorship'.(20) Both sexes are given the
franchise, on equal terms; the age for enfranchisement is
fixed at twenty-three.(21) These and other provisions
clearly do their utmost to create a free Spain. At any
time of national emergency, however, many of them may
be 'totally or partially suspended, by decree of the
Government, over either the whole or a part of the
country', subject to subsequent confirmation by the
Cortes. The suspension can last only for a maximum
period of thirty days without renewal.(22)

This vital section of the new Constitution also contains some of the most hotly debated of its clauses—
those relating to religion and the religious Orders. The
payment of the clergy by the State is to come to an end
after two years from the promulgation of the Constitution. No favour or financial aid is to be given to any
religious institution by State, provinces or municipalities.
All religious confessions are henceforth to be considered
as societies, subjected to a special law.(23) The freedom
of conscience already guaranteed to the individual by
decree is reassured to him; he may profess and practise
any form of religion provided it does not transgress
public morals. All denominations may worship as they
please in private, but for any public manifestation of their
religion they must obtain the sanction of the Government.(24)

Of the religious Orders, those which require a vow to be taken, 'besides the three canonical vows, of obedience to an authority other than the legitimate authority of the State', 'are dissolved' (*quedan disueltas*) and 'their property is to be nationalized and used for educative and charitable purposes'. All other Orders will come under the scope of a special law which will dissolve such of them as (presumably in the opinion of the Government of the day) 'constitute a peril to the safety of the State' and oblige the remainder to register with the Ministry of Justice. No Order shall be permitted to hold more property, directly or indirectly, than it needs for its own subsistence. No Order shall engage in industry, commerce or education. All Orders shall be obliged to submit their annual accounts to the State and (a final threat held over the heads of the contumacious) 'it shall be permissible for the property of the religious Orders to be nationalized'. (25)

Lest it should be thought that the Orders are unduly penalized, further articles proceed to declare that 'all the wealth of the country, whosesoever it be, is subordinated to the interests of the national economy' and that 'all the historical and artistic wealth of the country, whosesoever it be, constitutes the nation's cultural treasure and is under the safe custody of the State, which may prohibit its exportation and alienation and decree the legal expropriations which it deems opportune for its defence'. In no circumstances may the confiscation of property be ordered as a penalty, but any property may be 'forcibly expropriated', conditionally upon the approval of the Cortes, 'on payment of an adequate indemnity'. (26) Adequacy, as we shall shortly see, is a term susceptible of varied interpretations.

Another group of articles regulates marriage, divorce, and the education of children. Marriage, in the new Spain, is to be founded on sex equality, and any union may be dissolved 'as a result of mutual disagreement or on the petition of either party, just cause being shown'. (27) Parents are obliged to educate their children, legitimate

5

or illegitimate(28); primary education (as previously) is to be compulsory and free(29); and all education will be secular and (magnificent phrase!) 'inspired by ideals of human solidarity'.(30)

Such, in necessarily concise form, are the articles in the new Constitution which have the greatest interest for others than Spaniards. The remainder are chiefly concerned with parliamentary administration and may be dismissed more briefly.

The legislative authority, which resides in the people, is to be exercised in a unicameral parliament, whose members are to be elected, by universal suffrage and secret ballot, for a maximum period of four years.(31) The President of the Republic, head of the State, 'personifies the nation'.(32) He is to be chosen in a curious way—by an electoral college consisting of all the members of the Cortes and an equal number of electors, or *compromisarios*, themselves chosen *ad hoc* by means of elections similar to those held for the return of parliamentary deputies.(33) The President's mandate is for six years and cannot be renewed till at least six more have elapsed.(34) Instead of taking an oath on the Gospels, as did the Kings of Spain, he will 'promise fidelity to the Republic and the Constitution' before a 'solemn assembly' of the Cortes.(35) His powers, defined in some detail, include the nomination of the Prime Minister—a point of some interest, as will later be seen—and the submission to the Cortes of any decree of the Government which may seem to him contrary to existing laws.(36) His authority over the Cortes is considerable: he may convoke a special session 'whenever he thinks fit', suspend ordinary sessions for brief periods and dissolve the Cortes altogether on two occasions during his six years of office, provided that, on each dissolution, he orders new elections to be held within sixty days, and that, on the second dissolution, the new Cortes may censure his action, an absolute majority for the vote of censure to involve automatically his deposition.(37)

This last provision renders the position of a President faced with numerous political crises extraordinarily insecure, and, as his deposition may also be effected at any time by the votes of three-fifths of the deputies, subject to the approval of the electoral college,(38) it would seem that the new Constitution had no great hopes that six-year mandates would often be completed.

Another interesting limitation of the President's powers has reference to the promulgation of laws passed by the Cortes. All such laws must be promulgated within fifteen days of their being passed, or, if a two-thirds majority of the Cortes has declared a law to be of urgency, it must be promulgated 'immediately'. Laws not declared urgent may be sent back to the Cortes by the President, together with a 'reasoned statement', and a two-thirds majority then becomes necessary for their promulgation.(39)

A final article in the long section on the presidency declares the President to be 'criminally responsible' for any infraction of his constitutional obligations and provides that he shall be tried before the Tribunal of Constitutional Guarantees (of which more will be said hereafter) on the vote of three-fifths of the deputies of the Cortes.(40) Given the markedly political character of the Tribunal, this provision seems likely to lead to some delicate situations. Distinctly it will be no bed of roses that awaits the first President of the Spanish Republic.

IV

Though several parts of the new Constitution have of necessity been omitted from the foregoing survey, the articles described indicate at least the main lines followed by the five-months' almost continuous discussion. There were naturally other debates during this period than those on the Constitution, for pressing problems had to be solved without delay and malcontents had to be satisfied all over the country. No sooner were the warlike scenes in Seville brought to an end than Catalonia held a peaceful referendum for the ratification of her Statute of Autonomy, which thereupon, for the sake of the continuance of this peace, had to be considered, at length and in detail, by a special Committee of the Cortes, and in the following spring, as we shall see later, was debated *pari passu* with the equally important laws on agriculture. The urgency of these last was continually impressed upon the Government. Distress was not uncommon, and discontent was particularly rife, in the central and southern areas of Toledo, Ciudad Real, Extremadura and Andalusia. An agrarian reform bill, making it illegal for a proprietor to hold more than 300 hectares, was introduced immediately in the new Cortes, in the hope that within a year some 70,000 families would be settled on their own land. But it was easier to pass such a law than to carry it into effect, and recourse was necessary to various temporary expedients during the period now under discussion.

The debates on the Constitution took place to the accompaniment of strikes and disturbances throughout the country, though none of the strikes, except a complete stoppage for two days in Barcelona during the month of September, caused serious inconvenience, and the disturbances were only sporadic. It was clear that serious unrest would be a constant menace till the aspirations of the extremists were satisfied, if that were possible, and this gave the greater impetus to the Constitution-makers. The Government, diverse as were the political affiliations of its members, did its utmost to sink differences for the common good, and it must be added that the Press showed admirable restraint in its treatment of the most difficult situations.

Two crises of some importance—the first for its ultimate effects and the second for its immediate effects— characterized the debates on the Constitution. The earlier of the two concerned women's suffrage. There are many women in Spain (6,500,000 of the 12,500,000 voters on the 1933 register were women), and it was with something of a shock that foreign observers saw a country which had only just rid itself of a seventeenth-century monarch prepare to adopt such an entirely twentieth-century reform. Many of the most advanced feminists in Spain, both in and out of the Cortes, felt that women, whose education had been so greatly neglected in the past, were as yet hardly ready for the franchise. To put it in another way, the anti-clericals feared that, once enfranchised, the large majority of women would (as the saying went) all vote 'to a single priest'; and, while in some of them Liberalism was stronger than anti-clericalism, a large section feared to let Liberalism take its course. Some argued that, with few exceptions, only women of progressive opinions would exercise the vote, since only these would recognize its value; and that, as education grew more potent and the number of such women increased, they would become a great force for good. In support of this argument, they pointed to the large majority obtained by the Left parties at the June elections—the first held under the Republic and the first at which women had voted. But their opponents replied that these last elections were abnormal: the country was still under the influence of pristine Republican enthusiasm and many supporters of the Right had thought it useless to vote at all. One of the leading women deputies, Doña Victoria Kent, who had just been appointed Director of Prisons, was among the strongest opponents of women's suffrage. 'If all Spanish women were university women or manual workers,' she declared in the Cortes, 'I would give them the vote at once; but as things are, to give them the vote is to take votes from the Republic, and I must in conscience oppose the article.' (41) In the end, the suffragists won, but only by 39 votes. The division was a remarkable one: the majority, chiefly composed of Socialists, was reinforced by almost the whole of the minute Catholic party—a fact which speaks for itself and on which the elections of 1933 proved to be an eloquent commentary.

The second and much more violent crisis arose from the debates on the religious question. Again and again during the history of the Second Republic the essentially religious character of the Spaniard becomes evident. Attempt after attempt is made by the enemies of religion to attack it or expel it from the minds of the people, and again and again the people themselves instinctively defend it and secure its victory. It is surely a fact of the greatest significance that at a moment of supreme enthusiasm for the Republic and at a time when its very nature was under discussion, persons of no less importance than the Prime Minister and the Home Secretary should resign from the Government in defence of the Church to which they professed fidelity. It was not the first time during the debates that a secession from the Cabinet had been threatened: the Finance Minister had handed in his resignation at the end of September and the Prime Minister had done the same a week later, but in both cases pressure from the remainder of the Cabinet had kept them in their offices. Now, however, conscience dictated a course which no merely political pressure could alter, and from defeat itself the Church snatched a victory.

The anti-clerical articles described above were introduced on October 8, 1931, not by their chief supporter, Sr. Azaña, whose heavy guns were kept till the last, but by a somewhat more doctrinaire opponent of the Church, Don Fernando de los Ríos, Minister of Justice. Don Fernando had no great difficulty in making out the usual case for disestablishment: at one and the same time it increases the spiritual strength of the Church and the financial resources of the State—an attractive argument. And although, in such discussions, disendowment is always a more delicate proposition, he made skilful work of the contention that the already poorly paid clergy might reasonably be supported by their parishes instead of by the State, which expends upon the Church an average sum of over 44,000,000 pesetas.

After a preliminary discussion on these lines, the article was sent back to a Standing Committee of the Cortes for certain revisions, and it was not until October 13, after the separation of Church and State had been agreed to, that the article on the religious Orders, which caused the split in the Cabinet, again came up for discussion. The outstanding speech in this debate, and one of the outstanding speeches in the entire history of the Second Republic, was delivered by that doughty enemy of the Orders, Sr. Azaña.

Some of the most amazing statements that have ever been made in the Cortes can be read in the Spanish equivalent of *Hansard* for October 13. First, Sr. Azaña made a pure debating point, which could hardly have influenced a single deputy: this was not a religious problem, he said, that was being discussed, but a wholly political one, since a religious problem is concerned only with the conscience of an individual and this question related to the constitution of a secular State. Then he went on, with perfect seriousness, to declare that Spain was no longer a Catholic nation! He admitted that there were still millions of practising Catholics in the country but considered that 'since the last century Catholicism has ceased to be the expression and the guide of Spanish thought'.

'Spain in the sixteenth century was a Catholic country despite the fact that numerous and most distinguished Spaniards were dissenters, a few of whom are the glory and splendour of Spanish literature. To-day Spain has ceased to be Catholic, despite the fact that there are many millions of Spaniards who are practising Catholics.'(42)

After emitting this puny paradox, Sr. Azaña entered the realms of finance and then went on to what he described as the 'dramatic' part of the Government's

71

proposals—the treatment of the religious Orders. Here he was frank enough to show the weakness of his case side by side with its strength. It is necessary, he said, to respect the principle of freedom of conscience—Christian as well as non-Christian—but it is no less so to protect the Republic. The two necessities being (as he considered) incompatible, he proposed to put the State first. Forcibly, but cynically, he likened the so-called 'reform' of the religious Orders to a surgical operation performed without an anaesthetic. The operation might occasionally prove fatal—'for which of them I cannot say, but no doubt for some of them'. (43)

For one of them he proposed that it should prove fatal without delay. This 'Order which has not been named', as he put it, and which he proposed to kill outright, takes a vow of obedience to an authority other than the State. Everybody knew what he meant, and the announcement 'I mean the Jesuits' caused no sensation. Of the Society of Jesus he would make an example. The Jesuits must go.

As to the remainder of the proposals, Sr. Azaña admitted that they were illiberal and regretted that he was 'going to shock Liberal opinion'. But there must be no half-measures. Earlier in the debate Sr. de los Ríos had spoken with some sympathy of the numerous Orders that engage in works of mercy, as well he might, for they have deserved well of all Spaniards. But would Sr. Azaña allow any exception to be made in their favour? Not for a moment. They proselytize, he cried, as well as nurse and heal. And proselytizing we cannot for a moment tolerate.

So the Orders are not to be allowed to engage in 'business', whether it be the sale of embroidery and sweetmeats by nuns who devote their lives to doing good or the publication of learned journals and works of erudition by monks who include some of Spain's leading scholars. And, most serious matter of all, 'not for a moment, at no time and under no conditions whatever' must the Orders be allowed to teach.

'I greatly regret it, but this is necessary for the genuine defence of the Republic. . . . The continual influence of the religious Orders on the consciences of the young is precisely the secret of the situation through which Spain is now passing and which as Republicans—and not only as Republicans but as Spaniards—we are in duty bound, at all costs, to prevent. Do not tell me that this is contrary to freedom: it is a question of public health. Would you, who oppose this measure in the name of Liberalism, permit a university professor to lecture on Aristotle's astronomy and to say that the stars are fastened to spheres which make up the heavens? Would you permit sixteenth-century medicine to be taught from a Chair in a Spanish university? You would not; in spite of the professor's right to teach and in spite of his freedom of conscience, such a thing would certainly never be permitted. And I tell you that, in the sphere of the political and moral sciences, the Catholic religious Orders are compelled, by virtue of their dogma, to teach everything that is contrary to the principles which are the foundation of the modern State.'(44)

So Sr. Azaña went on. It was an all-night sitting, and, when the division was taken, at seven o'clock on the morning of the fourteenth, the article was approved by 178 votes to 59. Perhaps the most significant and striking fact which emerged from the announcement of the result was that, despite the importance of the question, almost half the members were absent or did not vote. Strange as it may seem, three members of the Government, Sres. Domingo, Albornoz and Lerroux, were absent, and as Sr. Alcalá Zamora and Sr. Maura voted with the opposition it can hardly be said that the Government gave enthusiastic support to its own proposals.

At six o'clock that evening, notwithstanding the absence, as a sign of protest, of the Basque Catholics, there was a far fuller House than eleven hours earlier. The Prime Minister and the Home Secretary had had the courage of their convictions and had resigned. The situation was not an easy one. With unrest abroad in the country, a false step might be fatal to the Republic, yet there was no head of the State to appoint a new Prime Minister and no legal machinery for selecting one. Don Alejandro Lerroux, the senior member of the Government, which as a matter of course had announced its collective resignation, interpreted the feeling of the House in addressing its President, Professor Julián Besteiro, and asking him to act as though he were President of the Republic. As he signified his acceptance, the whole assembly, glad of an opportunity to relieve its pent-up emotions, rose like one man and cheered him to the echo.

'I shall not leave this House,' cried Sr. Besteiro, 'until the crisis is over.'

'Long live the Republic!' cried Don Alejandro. 'Long live Spain!'

'Long live the Republic and the Spanish nation!' responded Sr. Besteiro.

Once more the House rose to its feet and shouted *Vivas*.

In less than three hours, the crisis was over. As the Ministers trooped in and took their seats on the *banco azul* it was at once observed that Sr. Azaña was at their head. Without great reluctance, it may safely be presumed, he had taken over the responsibilities to which the leading part he had played in bringing about the crisis had entitled him. A slight shuffling of personnel sufficed for the formation of a fresh Government, and in a brief speech the new Prime Minister announced that all was ready for pushing on with the Constitution. Encouraged by vociferous applause, he indulged in a more than usually emotional peroration:

'Never, gentlemen, while in my hands, shall authority be weakened! Never, while in my hands, shall the

74

Government of my country be the object of contempt, scorn and reviling! Never in this ministry shall there be hesitancy in the service of the commonwealth! The Republic belongs to us all. Woe to the man who dares to lift his hand against it!' (45)

The House stormed its applause.

'That's the way to talk to the country!' shouted a deputy.

The sitting had lasted but half an hour when the House rose.

On the next evening the debate on the Constitution continued as if nothing had happened.

v

Nearly eight weeks elapsed before the Constitution was ready for promulgation but nothing that took place during the discussions was comparable in interest with what has just been related. Quite a number of the remaining articles were non-contentious, and, though many others, such as those on divorce facilities and the use of regional languages in schools, were valiantly challenged, point by point, by the little handful of Conservatives, some of the Opposition groups, like the Basque Catholic party, thought they could better serve a temporarily lost cause by returning to their constituencies. Attendances dwindled, often to half the total number of deputies, a fact to which the Press of all parties continually drew attention. Now and then articles were passed by the smallest majorities: only 14 votes, for example, secured the principle of the election of the President by the electoral college instead of by popular suffrage. But for the most part even the rousing speeches of the new Prime Minister failed to awaken interest, and it was outside the House, rather than within it, that public attention was centred.

A number of mild sensations enlivened the days of late autumn. One of them was provided by Sr. Azaña, whose 'Law for the Defence of the Republic', passed with little opposition by the Cortes only a week after his accession to power, and incorporated, for the term of these Cortes, in the Constitution, was destined to become the best-hated measure of the day. Only the gravest fears for Spain's safety could have justified 'the paradox of having a Constitution which guarantees the rights of the individual together with a law which places them at the mercy of a single minister'.(46) The law gave the Home Secretary power to suspend public meetings, suppress associations, close clubs and take possession of illicit arms, while eleven 'acts of aggression against the Republic', including not only strikes, rioting and violence but such vague offences as incitements, the spreading of subversive rumours, defence of the Monarchy, profiteering and official negligence, were declared to be punishable with fines or exile. Necessary such a measure might be, but the abuses to which it could hardly fail to lead were obvious, and few Ministers would find much satisfaction in applying it.(47) In all quarters it was bitterly attacked—and not only by prospective strikers and rioters. As time went on, its similarity to measures enacted under the Dictatorship became more evident.

A second sensation was the work of Don Ramón Pérez de Ayala, then Ambassador at the Court of St. James's and one of the leading intellectuals who had come out early in support of the Republic. Twenty years earlier, as a young man, Sr. Pérez de Ayala had written a satirical novel called *A.M.D.G.* which attacked the Jesuits to whom he owed his early education. Spain is not the only country in which excellent and efficient schools have been held up by former pupils to attack or ridicule, and the youthful novel, though not forgotten, had long been surpassed in merit by the author's more mature productions. It was therefore a painful surprise to many that the Republic's Ambassador in London should have chosen this moment, when passions were at their highest, to stage a dramatic version of his novel in the Spanish capital. It was certainly not in England that the Ambassador had learned to attack a defeated enemy. The staging of the play was, not unnaturally, a signal for demonstrations, and if, as a result, the incendiarism of the preceding May had broken out again, one may wonder to whom would have been attributed the responsibility. At the first performance, reported the *Sol*, the noise was so great that not a word of the first act was audible.(48) Uproar was succeeded by violence, which continued after the play was over, and broke out sporadically at future performances.

But the prime sensation of the late autumn in Madrid was the spectacular trial—*in absentia*—of Don Alfonso XIII in the Constituent Cortes and his condemnation to perpetual banishment. Only a few days after the advent of the Republic it had been announced that a number of investigations would be held to report upon the Dictatorship, the trial and execution of Galán and García Hernández, and other questions of a similar nature. It was fortunate for the public that, at a period when interest in the Cortes was flagging, the Committee investigating the alleged guilt of Don Alfonso should issue a report of a sensational character. It was really more exciting even than the famous 'Hang the Kaiser' agitation in England. The almost unanimous report of the Committee found the criminal guilty of high treason against the Spanish people and deserving of death. Only because of its objection on principle to capital punishment could it recommend the Cortes to sentence the ex-King to life imprisonment should he re-enter Spain, and to death only if he should 'continue in his acts of rebellion'.

With the prospect of enjoying this fantastic bill of fare, flavoured most opportunely by the alleged discovery of a Monarchist plot of which no one seemed to know any details, the Cortes sat down on the night of November 19 to a rare feast of oratory and remained sitting until sentence was passed, by acclamation, at 4 a.m. on the following morning. The proceedings were described by

A. B. C. as a 'rancorous and needless act of persecution'—
for expressing which sentiments it was suspended for
three days and fined one thousand pesetas. But the
comments made on the charges by the Madrid correspondent of *The Times* support this view, and one may be sure
that, in years to come, the Spanish people, always so
generous when not moved by passion, will unite in its
sincere regret for the entire proceedings.

The four counts of the indictment against Don
Alfonso were as follows: (1) Neglect of his duties as a
Constitutional sovereign; (2) acceptance of the *coup d'état*
of 1923; (3) *lèse-majesté* towards the people; and (4) com-
plicity in administrative immorality. On these the *Times*
correspondent comments as follows:

> 'From his accession in 1902 up to 1923 it would seem
> that King Alfonso cannot be accused under the first
> count, because all decrees during this period were
> countersigned by responsible Ministers. As for the
> second count, the document produced by Count
> Romanones shows that, in September 1923, abdication
> —which would have been desertion of the nation,
> as the King was under a solemn oath to serve as a
> soldier—was the only alternative to acceptance of the
> Military Directorate, which, moreover—and this is so
> notorious that it is not disputed—held at that moment
> the sympathies of the mass of the nation. As regards
> the crime of *lèse-majesté* towards the people, no one
> seems to understand what it means, or to have
> attempted to urge it in Cortes. Nor was any attempt
> made to produce evidence of complicity in administra-
> tive immorality.'(49)

The only feature of the debate worthy of record was
the defence of the ex-King by the one confessed upholder
of the Bourbon Monarchy in the Constituent Cortes—
that veteran parliamentarian, the Conde de Romanones.
After challenging ex-ministers of the Monarchy who
were present to say that they had ever signed a decree

at the King's wish and against their own will, he proceeded to read the document referred to above, which, if it be accepted as genuine, shows that in 1923, as in 1931, the ex-King had to choose between a *coup d'état* and civil war, and that on each occasion, rightly or wrongly, he chose the course which avoided shedding the blood of his people.

The document, the authenticity of which was afterwards confirmed by the Marqués de Alhucemas, who was Prime Minister at the time, is a telegram from Primo de Rivera, then Captain-General of Barcelona, to the Captain-General of Madrid.(50) It reads as follows:

'I beg Your Excellency to point out respectfully to his Majesty the King the urgency of deciding the issue raised, on which I am continually receiving fresh and valuable support. We have reason on our side, and therefore force, though so far we have used force with moderation. If any endeavour is made to trick us into a compromise which our conscience would consider dishonourable, we shall make demands for greater penalties and impose them with severity. Neither I, nor the garrisons with me, nor the garrisons of Aragon from which I have just received a communication to this effect, will consent to anything but what we have demanded. If in an attempt to defend themselves the politicians form a united front, we will do the same, with the help of the people, whose reserves of energy are great. To-day we are resolved on moderation, but in the other extreme we should not shrink from bloodshed.'

It is difficult to see how after such evidence the trial under the second head could have continued. But passion was still blinding judgment, and the Count, though given the respectful hearing due to his status and seniority, was never seriously answered. The whole trial was no doubt staged in order to add stability to the Republic and inflame the people still further against the fallen

79

Monarchy. And in this respect it was undoubtedly successful.

A few days later, attention was diverted from the fallen idol to the figure about to be erected in his place—to the election of the first President of the Republic.

For some weeks rumour had been playing around the names of prominent personalities who were thought to be likely candidates. Ideally, the most suitable would have been the venerable Don Manuel Bartolomé Cossío, well known as an authority on Spanish art, as a pioneer in Spain of modern educational theory, and as a fearless and original thinker. But, though in full possession of his mental faculties, Sr. Cossío was seventy-three years of age and had for some time been bedridden with a painful malady, from which, three years later, he died. Another striking figure, whom many would have liked to see in the Presidency, if only because he stood outside the circle of professional politicians, was Professor Rafael Altamira. This writer and critic, author of the well-known *History of Spain and Spanish Civilization*, is one of a small band of internationally minded and internationally reputed Spanish scholars. As a warm supporter and friend of the progressive Institución Libre de Enseñanza, he would have made a strong appeal to the Left, while the Right could not have disputed his intellectual distinction. He was no more than sixty-five years of age, and his election to the highest office in the land would have been a fitting climax to the appointment of so many scholars to posts of lesser distinction.

But it seemed that a politician was most generally favoured for the office of President, and here the choice was narrowed to two possible candidates. One of these, a wily parliamentarian of nearly seventy, with long experience and a record of hard work, was the Radical leader Don Alejandro Lerroux, whom we have already met in the two Republican Governments as Foreign Secretary. Sr. Lerroux was excessively unpopular in Catalonia, and his election as President would have

exacerbated opinion in that important part of the Peninsula. In other respects he was fully qualified for the
office, and the prestige which he had acquired as a
representative of Spain in the League of Nations would
have made his appointment a welcome one abroad.

The Government, however, had another and a subtler
proposition, which combined the advantages of political
expediency and popular appeal. Why not appoint the
recently resigned Prime Minister, Don Niceto Alcalá
Zamora? This, to the world at large, would seem an
entirely natural and fitting selection, for Sr. Alcalá Zamora
had been head of the Revolutionary Committee and
Provisional Government, had represented the Government in the negotiations leading to the transference of
power, and had, until a few weeks previously, been the
Republic's first Prime Minister. But there were arguments in his favour more potent even than these. Since
his resignation from the Cabinet, he had been known to
be considering a step which might greatly prejudice
progressive interests—the leading of a campaign in favour
of the revision of the Constitution so that the obnoxious
anti-clerical articles might be altered. True, the Constitution provides for its own revision only under conditions
so stringent that there would be no risk whatever of their
fulfilment until after fresh elections. But one of the
contingencies which the Government was particularly
anxious to avoid was any rallying of the forces of
organized religion, and an ex-Prime Minister who could
present himself as a martyr for conscience' sake would be
an exceedingly useful leader for such a rally and an
exceedingly inconvenient opponent for a Government
none too sure of its stability. Furthermore, Don Niceto
had once been a Monarchist and a Minister of the Crown:
what if, as leader of a strong and united Catholic party,
he decided, sooner or later, to lead it back to Don
Alfonso? Altogether, the situation gave cause for grave
misgivings.

Surely no better plan, then, could be conceived than

6   81

to set Don Niceto safely out of harm's way in the National Palace. As a constitutional President, he would be removed to a suitable distance from party politics. He could do little harm, and, as we have seen, the Constitution envisaged a number of circumstances in which a strong Government or an astute Prime Minister might bring about an unwanted President's deposition. The idea seemed altogether an excellent one: the best thing would be to accustom the victim and the public at large to it as soon as possible, and, if practicable, to obtain a unanimous vote of the Cortes, which, on this initial occasion only, would sit alone, without its equal number of *compromisarios*, to elect the first head of the Republic.

Accordingly, one day early in November, a deputation of ministers waited upon Don Niceto at his residence, acquainted him formally of the honour which Providence and Sr. Azaña had in store for him, and respectfully intimated that, if he thought well of it, he might cease talking about a revisionist campaign and refrain from taking any further share in party politics until the day of his election. He certainly thought well of it. Spain might have discarded the Monarchy but she had not shed her ideas of the dignity which should hedge the Monarch's successor. There was to be a salary attached to the office of President of the Republic—nothing less than one million pesetas a year[1] was being talked about, with another million and a quarter for expenses. He was a married man, with three sons and three daughters, and now he would be the highest-paid President in the world.

The deputation returned whence it had come, quite satisfied with the assurances Don Niceto had given it. Now it had only to obtain the consent of the political parties and that should not be difficult.

In many ways Don Niceto was by no means a bad choice, though not even his closest friends would have

---

[1] Nominally £40,000; at the rate then current, about £25,000.

described him as an imposing figurehead. Fifty-four
years of age, a Cordoban by birth, with a marked Andalusian accent and all the oratorical mannerisms of the
lawyer-politician, he appeared to the public as a benevolent little *bourgeois*, of medium height, with rather a good
head but an unfortunately weak mouth, which called
attention to itself whenever he smiled—and that was
often, especially on occasions of ceremony. To the
public, who were impressed rather with the alleged size
of his feet, he became known early in his presidential
career as *Botas* ('Old Boots') and the name never left him.
Still, he enjoyed great prestige as a politician. In his
younger days, as we have said, he had been a protégé
and associate in politics of the Conde de Romanones, and
after he had parted company with him, and later with
the Monarchy, his entrance into the Republican party
brought him at once to its head, since there were not
many men of position in it who had been Ministers of
the Crown.

By the beginning of December, the Constitution was
completed, and, after a verbal revision, it was ratified on
December 9. For a Spanish parliament, which, as a wit
once remarked, is generally 'conspicuous by its absences',
the House was well filled: there were only ninety-eight
absentees, the majority of whom were deliberate absten-
tionists, Basque Catholics or extreme Conservatives of
the type which at that time called itself by the harmless
name 'Agrarian'. On the following day, by 362 votes
out of a possible 466, Don Niceto Alcalá Zamora was
elected President of the Republic. A few other individuals received odd votes, totalling thirteen; there were
thirty-five blank papers and fifty-six abstentions through
absence. Don Niceto might therefore be fairly considered
to have the confidence of the Cortes, and presumably
of the nation, and both Cortes and nation celebrated
accordingly.

On December 11, in the Spanish phrase, the President
'took possession' of his office. Arrayed for the most part

in evening dress, the deputies, together with representatives of the Diplomatic Corps, stood in their places while
the ministers trooped on the platform to form a background for their successful nominee, as he 'took the
promise' of fidelity to the Constitution and received the
supreme distinction—a strange one to be conferred by an
anti-clerical and Republican Government—of the Grand
Collar of Isabel the Catholic. The form of promise used
was based upon the oath formerly taken by Spanish
sovereigns, all references to God and the Holy Gospels
having been deleted from it. The ceremony was a brief one.

'I solemnly promise, by my honour,' repeated Sr. Alcalá
Zamora, 'before the Constituent Cortes, as the organ of
national sovereignty, that I will serve the Republic
faithfully, keep and ensure the observance of the Constitution, observe the laws and devote my activities as
head of the State to the service of justice and of Spain.'

'In the name of the Constituent Cortes, which elected
you and which now invest you with office,' replied Sr.
Besteiro, 'I say this to you: "If you act thus, let the nation
reward you for it; and if not, let it call you to account."'

As the promise was given, salvos of artillery outside
the Chamber were heard, and these were redoubled as
the deputies emerged from it. Huge and orderly crowds
lined the route from the Chamber to the ex-Royal Palace,
where the President was to make his home—though
afterwards, on second thoughts, he decided it would
be more prudent to use it only as an office. When
the procession of notabilities entered the Palace, the
Presidential flag—a red flag bearing the national arms
—was hoisted; the Republican tricolour was already
flying. Aeroplanes circled round the Palace; bands played
national airs; and copies of the newly promulgated
Constitution, gaily bound in paper of yellow, red and
purple, were distributed to the crowds. Finally, following a well-established Royal precedent, the genial form
of the new President, smiling expansively, appeared
with his Ministers on one of the Palace balconies.

Two days later, President Alcalá Zamora held his first diplomatic reception. The deputy doyen of the Corps, to. whom it fell to deliver a formal address of congratulation and goodwill, was the Papal Nuncio. There was irony in the coincidence. The Cardinal-Primate of Spain having been expelled and deposed, the Spanish Ambassador at the Vatican having been refused a *placet*, the Church being disestablished and disendowed, the religious Orders crippled and the Society of Jesus under sentence of expulsion from the country, one would suppose that the Nuncio's address was one of more than ordinary formality.

CHAPTER III

TWO YEARS OF THE LEFT

(December 1931 *to November* 1933*)*

I

THE President being safely deposited in what henceforth was generally known as the 'National Palace', the Government, before deciding upon the dates for a short and emphatically well-earned Christmas recess, underwent an important reconstruction.

During the months devoted to the framing of the Constitution, the Republican coalition had found quite considerable difficulty in remaining united, and, now that they felt freer to act on their own initiative, the Radicals, under Sr. Lerroux, resolved to separate from a Government which they considered excessively Socialistic and to go into Opposition. As a result, Sr. Azaña's reconstituted team—the fourth Republican Government in eight months—found itself predominantly Socialist, with two portfolios in the hands of Radical-Socialists, and finance in the very able grasp of an Independent, Sr. Carner, a Catalonian largely responsible for the draft of the Statute of Autonomy, which was on the point of coming up to the Cortes for ratification. Sr. Lerroux's Foreign Office portfolio, it may be noted, went to Don Luis de Zulueta, the non-placeted Ambassador to the Vatican.

Christmas and the New Year passed quietly in Spain. The chief subject of conversation was, as in the olden days, the great National Lottery, the first prize in which, as it chanced, went, perhaps rather appropriately, to the State. On Christmas Eve, two Spanish aviators, Haya and Rodríguez, flew from Seville, across the Sahara, to Bata, in Spanish Guinea, a journey of about 3,000 miles, in twenty-seven hours. Such eminently uncontroversial subjects as these filled the papers, and for a short time political crises were forgotten.

But not, unfortunately, for long. On the last day of the year 1931 occurred the first of those terrible village tragedies which later became so frequent and seemed impossible either to predict or to prevent. To the holiday-maker, one of the greatest charms of Spain is the picturesqueness and variety of its tiny villages. Every tourist knows the little groups of brown houses, scattered here and there on the long white road which leads across the vast Castilian tableland to the horizon: the fresh green villages, shaded by trees, that make the northern provinces such an oasis in the desert of Spain's long, hot summer; the sleepy little palm-fringed hamlets of Andalusia, with their acacia-lined streets and the orange-groves but a little way outside them. It would seem impossible that riot, violence, and murder could spring up, like evil spirits, in the midst of such peaceful surroundings.

Yet, whether because the rapid (perhaps over-rapid) improvements in communications have facilitated the spread of subversive doctrines among uneducated villagers, or for whatever other reason, village riots in Spain came gradually to be a normal feature of the news. The first group of reports of such riots burst upon Spain with terrible suddenness, from almost opposite ends of the country, in the first days of the year 1932.

Hardly any Madrileño who opened his morning paper on the second of January had heard of Castilblanco, that delightfully named little Extremaduran village near the Guadiana, in the province of Badajoz. The nine hundred inhabitants of the village, as an official report afterwards showed, were in no kind of distress: food was plentiful and nearly all the villagers had their own land. Drunkenness was unknown; a violent death of any kind had hardly been heard of. Until the advent of the Republic, no interest had been taken in the world outside:

there were only two radio sets—the parish priest's and the doctor's—and no one, even during the Dictatorship, had discussed politics. (1)

Yet only political motives could have been responsible for the tragedy which occurred there on New Year's Eve. Permission had been refused by the authorities for a political meeting to be held in the village. The promoters determined to hold it. The Civil Guard, which came to the defence of the authorities, was set upon by a mob, and four guards were murdered. As it happened, a general strike in the city of Badajoz had extended to this and other villages; the strikers threatened to shoot the telegraph operator if she communicated the news of the massacre; and so for about eight hours nothing was heard of what had happened. When reporters arrived, they were aghast at the revelation of brute passion. The murdered guards had been battered with their own rifles beyond recognition. Their heads had been beaten in, their eyes gouged out and their bodies knifed, stoned and mutilated. (2) On one of the bodies were counted thirty-seven knife-thrusts. To crown all, the very women of the village, so eye-witnesses declared, had danced round the disfigured corpses.(3)

This was only the first, though the worst, of a number of similar outrages which in those dark January days were reported from this southern province. Almost at the same time news of a similar kind arrived from the north: the little town of Arnedo, near Calahorra, had gone on strike; the Civil Guard had broken up a meeting in the *plaza*; both sides had fired; and six people, including four women, had been killed in the *mêlée*.

All this, pending the reassembly of the Cortes, gave the Government food for serious thought. Extremists, both in the Cortes and in the country, declared that the Guard had on each occasion behaved brutally and should be restrained by authority. It seemed impossible, however, to establish what had really happened. Centuries ago, in one of his plays, Lope de Vega describes the

peaceful little village of Fuenteovejuna, where, so runs
the story, a tyrant was killed for his misdeeds; when the
villagers were questioned, and even tortured, till they
should reveal the names of the murderers, they cried
with one accord: 'Fuenteovejuna'. The same thing seemed
likely to happen in Castilblanco. Forty arrests had been
made but there was little possibility of inflicting effective
punishment.

In the Cortes, the Prime Minister protested vehemently against the attempts which were being made to
'use the bodies of the victims as arms of aggression
against the Republic'. But that was precisely what did
happen and what continued to happen. Of the parties
belonging to the extreme Left, the Socialists were loyal
to a Government in which they themselves were strongly
represented: only later, when they had been defeated,
did they join the revolutionaries. But their rivals, the
Syndicalists, did their utmost to stir up strife, and with
them, knit in a strange alliance destined to persist to an
extent beyond belief, were Anarchists and Communists.
Such grievances as the alleged brutality at Castilblanco
were quite sufficient pretext for a crop of revolutionary
strikes accompanied by violence, and these, which
broke out all over the country, now aimed avowedly,
however remotely, at substituting for the newly constituted *régime*, which they stigmatized as 'bourgeois',
another of more advanced tendencies. 'We have got
our Republic,' was their nation-wide slogan; 'now let us
have our Revolution!'

Since Anarchists, Communists and Syndicalists have
quite distinct and even incompatible ideals, it may seem
surprising that they should have united in this way, for,
had they succeeded, there and then, in destroying the
Second Republic, they would indubitably have fallen
out over the next step to be taken and the result would
have been immediate chaos. But the fact remains that,
very early in the history of the Republic, the small but
determined Anarchist Federation joined forces with the

much larger Syndicalist organization, known as the National Confederation of Labour,[1] and this Anarcho-Syndicalist combination was responsible for most of the early disorders. From time to time, Anarcho-Syndicalism also united with Communism, which, in these early years, was itself a somewhat vague and mobile influence. 'The Communists in Spain', as *The Times* remarked about this period, 'seem to be indistinguishable from Anarchists; their aim is the overthrow of any Government just because it is a Government, and their methods are disruption and havoc.' (4)

As every traveller who has talked with Spanish workmen knows, they tend to follow individuals rather than principles; Nin and Maurín in Catalonia and the quasi-Messianic Dr. Vallina in the south draw their adherents by tens of thousands, but these adherents have frequently only the haziest idea as to what their leaders represent. It is therefore impossible to make a clear demarcation between the three disturbing elements and the principles for which they stand, though in the future these may well become clarified.

In January 1932, these disruptive forces were for the first time unleashed simultaneously. For days, the city of Bilbao, in the north of Spain, was the centre of riots attended by constant shooting and arson. Another focus of unrest was Valencia, in the east, where mobs made unsuccessful attacks on churches and the Civil Guard became a target for their fury. The most serious disturbances, however, took place at the end of the month, in Catalonia.

So great had been the enthusiasm shown for autonomy in that region that up till now it had been one of the quietest parts of the country. The Generalitat, too, was

---

[1] Though these rather confusing terms have in the interests of simplification been avoided as much as possible, it may be convenient to state here that the Socialist 'General Union of Workers' (Unión General de Trabajadores) is known in Spain as the U.G.T., the Syndicalist 'National Confederation of Labour' (Confederación Nacional del Trabajo) as the C.N.T., and the 'Iberian Federation of Anarchists' as the F.A.I. (Federación Anarquista Ibérica).

on by no means bad terms with the Syndicalists, and
Catalonians take much more kindly to the methods and
ideals of Syndicalism than to those of Communism.
But the Communists, who for the past nine months
had been returning to Spain from their long exile in
great numbers, and who were in general opposed to any
form of regionalist government, had been working
steadily to undermine the Statute of Autonomy before it
should ever come into being, and this revolt may probably be correctly described as the first determined and
organized attempt to establish a Communist State in
Spain. It lasted for about a week, but although, on its
outbreak, sympathetic revolts began in Bilbao, in the
Catalonian outpost-city of Lérida, at Seville and in
various other parts of Andalusia, the idea of the rebels
seems to have been to establish their rule, first of all, in
northern Catalonia, and their action was too strictly
localized to prove of real danger. Its centre was the
Llobregat valley, between the manufacturing towns of
Manresa and Berga. The rails of the narrow-gauge
railway joining these towns were torn up; general strikes
were called throughout the locality; and at Sallent a
powder magazine was seized, while a 'Revolutionary
Committee' hoisted on the Town Hall the red flag which
in Spain does convenient duty for Socialists, Syndicalists
and Communists and issued a Communist proclamation.

The revolt had one excellent result, which perhaps,
from the point of view of the existing *régime*, almost
justified it. It was the first serious test of the Government's efficiency and that efficiency stood the test in a
way that evoked universal praise. Sr. Azaña's firm and
prompt action, which in the years following saved the
country from civil war again and again, quelled the
rebellion immediately. Infantry, cavalry and artillery
were hurried from other parts of Catalonia and the
military Governor at Barcelona was ordered to act without fear of consequences. By the time Sr. Azaña had
occasion to address the House, practically everything

was over, and he was able to assume an air of easy satisfaction which he may well have been far from feeling but which gained him a vote of confidence with only four dissentients.

While the Prime Minister was striking determinedly at the extremists of the Left, he was also preparing to give effect to his earlier attacks on the Right by putting into operation the twenty-sixth article of the Constitution and expelling the Jesuits. By a decree of January 23, 1932, the Society of Jesus was 'dissolved on Spanish territory', on and after February 3, and its property passed to the State. The President of the Republic, whose conscience had forbidden him to remain in the Government when the article was passed, had apparently no scruples about signing the decree without comment, and within a fortnight of its promulgation the Jesuits were leaving the country.

As the Society of Jesus had not been specifically mentioned in the article, it was clearly necessary for the decree to justify the application. This it did by referring briefly to 'the bull of Paul III, which serves as the canonical foundation for the institution of the Society', and to 'its own Constitutions, which dedicate it pre-eminently to the service of the Apostolic See'. The Spanish Press, however, had a few days previously published a statement drawn up by five leading lawyers, and endorsed by a large number of others, which showed, in the opinion of many, that, whatever the intentions of those who promoted it might have been, the article was not in fact applicable to the Society.

The Jesuits, declared the document, like all the other religious Orders, take 'the three vows of poverty, chastity and obedience to their superiors', and, in addition, the professed, who number less than ten per cent of the total membership, take the additional vow, approved by Paul III, which binds them 'to accomplish that which the Pontiff of to-day or his successors may command, in

whatever concerns the welfare of souls, and the propaga-
tion of the faith, and any missions to which they may
be pleased to send us'.

This undertaking, the document proceeds, can in no
way prevent lawful obedience being paid to the State.
It points out that all religious, and all priests of the
Catholic Church, are bound to the Holy See in exactly
the same way as that in which the Jesuits specifically
bind themselves by this additional vow as an act (in
the words of the vow) of humiliation. The very Article
26 of the Constitution, it continues, tacitly recognizes
the permissibleness of the vow of obedience 'to the
spiritual power of the Roman Pontiff, whom all Catholics
must obey', and only when it is explicitly referred, by
those who take it, to the welfare of souls or the propaga-
tion of the faith, does the new Constitution consider it
illegal. Concluding with a plea for religious liberty,
addressed to the head of a Government which has
professed to stand for religious liberty, the signatories
declare that the dissolution of the Jesuits in Spain will
be a measure of pure injustice.

Even before the publication of this statement, there
was little pretence that the expulsion of the Jesuits was
more than a measure of expediency. Nor, except with
anti-clericals, was it particularly popular.[1] We have
already seen that barely more than half the deputies were
present when Article 26 of the Constitution was passed,
that two members of the Government voted against it,
and that three were absent. What of the rest? 'I have
voted for a bad measure,' wrote Sr. Nicolau d'Olwer,
the then Minister of Economy, 'yet not to have voted
for it would have been to have opened the way for a

[1] 'The Second Republic', wrote Don Salvador de Madariaga, whom no one
would describe as a clerical, 'has ruined a magnificent opportunity of directing
the problem of secondary education towards a satisfactory solution. Obsessed
by its anti-clericalism, it has light-heartedly closed down the only type of school
that, for all its imperfections, bore some slight resemblance to a secondary school
—the Jesuit college. And having done this it has created more and more . . .
spiritless caricatures of universities. . . . In matters of secondary education, the
Republic has failed dismally.' (*Anarquía o Jerarquía*, p. 248).

worse and more illiberal article still.' He referred, of course, to the original draft of the Constitution, which would have dissolved all the Orders. The Jesuits, in other words, not for the first time in their history, were being thrown to the mob in the hope that the mob would be satisfied.

The Press were, for the most part, as critical of the decree as they dared to be, though the recent suspension of the Catholic newspaper, *El Debate*, for its criticisms of the Government, made caution essential. No paper calling itself Liberal could tolerate such a measure. The leading article of the Left Republican *Publicitat*, normally a staunch supporter of the Government, ran:

> 'The decree now published can surprise no one, though it is arousing protests which we ourselves recognize as logical. . . . As Liberals, we are opposed to all that impedes the exercise of individual rights, and for that reason we entirely deprecate the illiberal nature of Article 26 and the decree which is the result of it.' (5)

The excellence of Jesuit education is proverbial the world over, and in a country like Spain, where for centuries education has been neglected, it has been a god-send. At the time of its dissolution, the Society had some seventy residences and thirty colleges in Spain. Of the best-known of the colleges, that of Sarrià, near Barcelona, had a School of Ecclesiastical Studies, an Institute of Chemistry, and laboratories for Biology and Experimental Psychology. The theological studies of the college at Comillas and the astronomical studies of that at Granada were equally noteworthy. The poorest classes were poorer for the loss of the Jesuits. The church of the Sacred Heart, at Barcelona, maintained five working-men's clubs, and, in 1931, educated over 1,200 children. The Jesuit Workmen's Club at Burgos, with 1,500 members, included housing and pension schemes, a sick benefit club, a savings bank and day and night classes.

So one might go on throughout the country. A progressive nation, with well-organized schemes of education and social progress, might possibly cut off such institutions without much loss, but for a *régime* which began by acknowledging the country's backwardness and its intention of remedying it to proceed to close so many of Spain's best schools and to expel so many of her most gifted teachers was to put intolerance and prejudice above a desire for educational and social progress.

The first week in February saw the departure of large numbers of Jesuits and the abandonment of their residences, schools and other establishments. Dignified as always, having quietly made their collective protest, they left the country without parade or demonstration and the only disturbance occasioned by their departure occurred in the Cortes, where a retrospective debate on the decree which expelled them was guillotined amid scenes of great disorder. In the Basque country, whence their founder came, they were given an impressive, but again a quiet, farewell. At the Basilica in the hamlet of Loyola, St. Ignatius' birthplace, the total numbers present at the Masses on the day of the Fathers' departure was computed to be twenty thousand.

Having struck so effectively at the Right, Sr. Azaña next turned Left again, and aroused the indignation of many of his own adherents by deporting a hundred of the Communist rebels, without trial, to Spanish Guinea. The majority of these were from the humbler classes, and the action was freely described as a class measure. But the Government was both united on the question and inexorable, and, although as a result more than twenty general strikes were called, extending all over Spain, to Guinea the rebels went, and in Guinea, for many months, they remained.

And now followed a period of comparative calm for a country grown weary with excitement. Strikes—general and partial—continued in monstrous succession all over Spain, but most of them lasted only for a day or two and they rapidly became part of the Spaniard's normal existence. Many of these strikes entailed no inconvenience greater than the non-appearance of breakfast-rolls and the closing of theatres and cafés. They were little more, indeed, than Bank Holidays, with the additional thrill of coming unexpectedly. In Madrid, a large proportion of the inhabitants would spend the day in the Sierra, and the main streets of the city would be occupied chiefly by children playing football. Occasionally, general strikes were accompanied by rioting, but even this often loomed larger in next morning's paper than in the experiences of those who read it. Half a dozen people out of half a million would be injured—and the half-dozen would get the publicity. On the whole—and I can speak here from personal experience—conditions in Spain from March to August might fairly have been termed tranquil.

The Cortes were busy, but with the exception of the Agrarian Law and the Catalan Statute of Autonomy, which were debated through the summer, there was little legislation of outstanding interest. February saw the definition and approval of the new divorce laws. These widened still further the rift between Church and State, for, while the Church still declared marriage to be indissoluble, the State now proposed to concede divorce after five years' agreed separation, for a period, however short, of desertion, for a sentence of imprisonment of more than six years' duration, and for half a score of other reasons. Yet these proposals, of such transcendental importance in family life, aroused but the slightest interest even among deputies: attendances in the Cortes began to fall as low as eighty; divisions had to be postponed; and a Committee was even set up to discuss if it was practicable to levy fines for absence.

The first Holy Week to fall under the Republican *régime*, and the traditional outdoor processions, had been dreaded by lovers of peace, lest the passions of anti-clericalism should again be loosed and cause more irreparable damage. But there was no justification for alarm. Most of the processions, from motives of prudence, were cancelled; Seville, the home of the greatest of them, was sad—but tranquil. The *Debate* was allowed to reappear, after sixty-six days' suspension. All seemed well. Even Labour Day passed with nothing worse than a few skirmishes, and, of course, with an almost complete stoppage of work throughout the country.

After Easter, men made merry over the first anniversary of the Republic. It might be thought that there was little cause for rejoicing, but there was at least this—that the Republic had survived for twelve months and might be considered as definitely established. 'Much, very much,' wrote Dr. Marañón on the anniversary day, 'remains to be done. But the period of danger is over. The Republic can never again be a subject of mere village gossip. It is a consummated fact . . . a part of the structure of history.' (6)

This may be a suitable place to record a few general impressions of life in large Spanish cities during the first year of the Republic as compared with that of the last years of the Monarchy. It cannot be said that the comparison is altogether a flattering one to the new *régime*. There was a noticeable increase of ebullience, especially in streets and public places, among the young of both sexes. This was, perhaps, to be expected at a time of political and social upheaval, and the new order should not be censured for it. Nevertheless, in the later and darker days of the Republic, it degenerated into the most shameless and disgraceful licence. Since so many of the richest families had left the country, there was presumably less wealth, but there was certainly much more display of wealth, and especially of motor-cars *de luxe*. Again, there may or may not have been in fact more immorality, but there was certainly a great deal more

display of immorality, principally in the shape of porno-
graphic literature, which was prominently featured in
kiosks and bookshops, and, with Marxist literature, was
sold outside the very entrances of the churches.

But the principal superficial characteristic of social
life in the early days of the Republic was the vast increase
in mendicity. 'The streets of Madrid and many other
towns', wrote the Madrid correspondent of *The Times*
a few days before the Republic's first birthday, 'have
become so infested with beggars that it is almost impossible to walk even a hundred yards without being
accosted not only by the old-fashioned and tolerated
blind, halt or maimed professionals, but by bands of
two, three or four men carrying a blanket or a large
handkerchief to catch pennies and imploring charity
"for the poor unemployed".'(7) From my own observa-
tion, Barcelona was a striking exception to this rule,
and such show-towns as Toledo and Granada were at
least no worse than before. But most of the capital
cities and large towns of the provinces, and, most
markedly of all, Madrid, were riddled with mendicity.
The Calle de Alcalá had become a continuous exhibition
of physical deformities; old men and young women with
children stepped across the walker's path and waylaid
travellers by tram-car or omnibus; while unsightly groups
would cluster on the steps of Metro stations, leer un-
pleasingly beside the booking-offices and spring out
upon one at the turn of each corner leading to or from
a platform.

Precisely to what this increase in begging was due is
uncertain. Trade depression, though considerable, was
insufficient to explain it, for Spain, with about half the
population of Great Britain, had at that time less than a
quarter of its unemployment. Nor were the homeless
and helpless unprovided for; the religious Orders, it is
true, had been deprived of much opportunity for doing
good, but, on the other hand, many municipalities,
including that of Madrid, were setting on foot schemes

of help on a scale previously unknown. One could only surmise that mendicity, with its accompanying mendacity, had grown because of the greater independence and indiscipline which came in with the Republic, combining with a well-marked tendency on the part of country folk to gravitate to the towns.

Only some rather serious outbreaks of rioting in the universities and a week's successfully organized transport strike disturbed the harmony of the early summer. And the Cortes worked their way steadily through the Agrarian Bill and the Catalan Statute, with every prospect of having to sit continuously for a second summer. The Catalonian question is so complicated that it may best be treated separately, but something must be said here about the Agrarian Law, the first part of which was passed by the Cortes in July 1932, and the second part in September.

For decades past, discontent and distress among agricultural labourers in the south of Spain have been serious problems, but under the Monarchy, though land reform had often been talked about, nothing fundamental had been done. The agrarian difficulties in the north and the south were quite unlike each other. In the north, the problem was that of the over-division of holdings, often themselves quite insignificant in size. In the south, enormous estates, known as *latifundios*, consisting sometimes of hundreds of thousands of acres—principally in Extremadura and Andalusia—were held by absentee landlords and tilled by peasants for wages so small that in 1931 they were calculated to average no more than 900 pesetas (nominally £36) yearly. Bad seasons, which are frequent, would produce widespread misery barely alleviated by uncertain private doles. The increasing influence of political organizations upon the peasantry and the rapid growth of Socialist and Syndicalist organization led to peasant strikes and demonstrations which Governments too often solved by authorizing the Civil Guard to practise ruthless repression and closing their eyes to the consequences. Long before the Republic came into power it was agreed among progressives that expropriation and redistribution of the land was the only remedy. It was just a question of whether the Republic would come in time (and, having come, would act in time) for the step to be taken constitutionally, or whether it would be effected forcibly by a gigantic peasant revolution.(8)

The Agrarian Law of 1932 was a courageous and an able attempt to meet the downright claims of the Syndicalist leaders, to offer some kind of compensation to landowners who would naturally resent confiscatory legislation, and at the same time to strengthen the Republic. Thus, on the one hand, all land of more than a certain area (the limit varying with the district) was made liable to expropriation, but on the other hand indemnification was to be allowed only on the value of the land as assessed for taxation, which would often be far below its real value, and payment was to be made in Government bonds, the disposal of which would be restricted.

The application of the Law was to the provinces of south and central Spain—Andalusia, Extremadura, Ciudad Real, Toledo, Albacete and Salamanca—and to all other lands of feudal origin which had descended to their owners by direct succession. Royal estates, and the lands of conspirators against the Republic, as provided in the Constitution, were to be confiscated without indemnification, while grandees were normally to be indemnified only for recent improvements. The land expropriated was to become national property and to be cultivated by peasant tenants, either by families or in communal groups.

For the administration of the new Law the Cortes created a central Institute of Agrarian Reform, which was to receive a substantial credit from the State. The general board of the Institute was to be composed of twenty-one members: landowners, tenant farmers, agricultural workers and financial and agrarian experts. The Institute would act largely through regional committees and would set to work as soon as might be on the huge task of taking the necessary censuses and proceeding with the redistribution. The pessimistic doubted if this task could be accomplished, and the land system completely revolutionized, in the lifetime of any one in the country; conservative and optimistic estimates put the period necessary at from twenty to thirty years.

Such were the main lines of the 1932 Agrarian Law. Opposed in the Cortes at every stage only by the small minority representing the landowner class, it was welcomed in the country by the man in the street and as a rule by the man in the field, though, as the sowing season drew near, frequent reports from the south were received of groups of peasants taking land by force. But it was chiefly the extremists—the grandees and the Syndicalists—who looked upon the new law with disfavour. Both classes, however, saw, or thought they saw, their opportunity coming in the future, and both were prepared to wait.

II

From what has been written on the Pact of San Sebastián and the proclamation of the Republic in Barcelona, some idea will be gathered of the importance of the Catalonian problem in the recent history of Spain.(9) The depth of feeling which characterizes Catalonia's attitude to the question of regional autonomy could only be adequately explained by a digression so long that it would throw this narrative completely out of proportion. Only a brief backward glance at her story can here be attempted.

During the Middle Ages, for some three and a half centuries, the north-eastern part of Spain made history. While Castile attempted to drive the Moors southwards to Africa, Catalonia, once freed from Moorish incursions, looked eastward to conquest and commerce across the Mediterranean. The Balearics, Corsica, Sicily, Sardinia fell into Catalonian hands as Valencia, Játiva and Murcia had done on the mainland. There followed the expedition to Constantinople, the extension of the Catalonian empire into Asia and the establishment, in 1311, of a Catalonian Duchy of Athens, which lasted for almost eighty years.

But the union of the Spanish kingdoms gradually led to Catalonia's submersion in a centralized State. The Catalan language, which had produced at least as many masterpieces as Castilian, now ceased to be the mouthpiece of literature. Politically, things went from bad to worse. The immemorial privileges of the Catalonians began to vanish. They had to keep up part of an army in which they had but small commands. In taxes they paid heavily for the virtue of industry and for the natural fertility of their country. Even their treasured shrine of Montserrat fell into the hands of Castilian monks, who told Catalan penitents to speak in a 'Christian language'. Little by little a temperamentally loyal people was being turned into a nation of rebels.

Twice the national spirit blazed forth—in 1640, the Catalonians rose against Philip IV in a revolt commemorated by their patriotic hymn *Els Segadors*, and in 1714 their refusal to accept the first of the Spanish Bourbons, Philip V, led to the terrible siege of Barcelona and their return to subjection. The beginnings of the partial liberation effected by the fall of the last of the Bourbons may be traced to the literary renaissance which began in 1833. The rich, virile and graceful Catalan language had for centuries been proscribed and neglected, but never forgotten, and now, under the impulse of a few patriotic men of letters, the glories of medieval Catalan literature were splendidly revived, to become in these latest years increasingly fruitful.

The cultural renaissance brought with it political

progress. In 1893 the Catalanist Union produced the famous 'Bases of Manresa', on which have been founded most of Catalonia's modern claims. During the present century practically all the Catalan deputies to the Spanish Cortes have been Catalanists. In 1913, the creation of the Mancomunitat, already referred to, marked a further advance. Upon its foundation were reared propagandist schemes without which it would have lacked reality: the 'Municipal Weeks' of 1918 and the resulting negotiations with Madrid; the virile *Acció Catalana* and its organ *La Publicitat*. Though but slowly, and sometimes almost imperceptibly, progress continued, till in 1923 Primo de Rivera began a new era of repression.

One of the great virtues of the Catalonian people, however—a virtue perhaps unlooked-for in a people so full of energy, initiative and imagination—is their patience. No nation could have borne the persecutions of the Dictatorship, often most aggravating when most puerile and trivial, with greater dignity, or have more calmly endured the delays and disillusionments which, perhaps inevitably, came to them in the early years of the Republic. Any one unfamiliar with Catalonian history might be forgiven for underrating the profoundness of their attachment to their country and for misreading the demonstrations of April 14 and 15 as superficial ebullitions of comparatively little meaning. But such is not the case. The Catalonians, during the last century, have so often met with disillusionment from their friends, as well as with persecution from their enemies, that they have become resigned to the slowest progress, and though their hopes, justifiably high in 1931, have in the intervening years been more than once disappointed, they have always been willing to accept what they have contrived to gain as an earnest of more to come.

It is a popular but mistaken belief that the Catalonian people are anxious for complete separation from the rest of Spain. The separatist party is, as a matter of fact, a very small one, and the principal cleavage between Catalonians on matters of political principle is on the question of federalism. When the Catalan Statute of Autonomy was published in the form drafted for submission to the people, and, if duly approved by them, to the Cortes of the Spanish Republic, there was no suggestion in it of complete separation, and the wishes of the Provisional Government, which had already been made known at Barcelona, were meticulously observed. Thus the word 'Generalitat' was found where one might have expected the word 'State', and the federalism expressly repudiated in the Spanish Constitution was excluded also from the draft Statute. From first to last, the Statute was characterized by statesmanlike moderation, and this was generally recognized by people outside Catalonia who were familiar with the country's history. Submitted, as was provided by the agreement with the Republic, to all the Catalonian municipal councils and approved by them, it was then sent to the people for a referendum, which took place on August 2, 1931. The general belief was that, if the people should give it their clear approval, it would go through the Cortes without serious modification.

There was no doubt about the approval of the people. The referendum was duly held on a hot August Sunday which will live in the memory of those who spent it in Catalonia, and the result must have been one of the most decisive electoral affirmations in history. The majority was in the proportion of nearly 200 voters to 1. There voted for the Statute 592,961 electors; against it, 3,276. Of the dissentients, 2,188, or almost exactly two-thirds, voted in Barcelona, a city whose inhabitants are notoriously of diverse shades of opinion. In the rest of Catalonia the proportions were astonishing: 421,231 against 1,088—or 99.997 per cent for approval. If votes ever show anything, these votes showed beyond a doubt that Catalonia was as nearly as possible unanimous in support, not merely of a vague ideal of autonomy, but of a clearly defined document of which the terms were known to all.

But those who were optimistic enough to believe that this decisive expression of opinion would be generally respected throughout Spain were destined to be quickly disillusioned. Upon the proclamation of the Republic, as also earlier, upon the dissolution of the Dictatorship, there had been a striking *rapprochement* between Barcelona and Madrid and a determined attempt by each party to see the question from the other's standpoint. But once the Catalan Statute was on the way to the Cortes a most violent reaction against it began. For about a year there raged a fierce agitation against the 'separatists'. Certain newspapers fulminated against the Statute daily; clubs and societies sent incoherent telegrams of protest; enormous public meetings were addressed by well-known traditionalists; and countless delegations of patriotic provincials (one recalls the 'Patriotic Union' of Primo de Rivera) celebrated demonstrations, chiefly in the Spanish capital.

The agitation was supported by many who had made no protest against the autonomy clauses of the new Constitution and who apparently did not see that their action was completely illogical, since the Constitution definitely approved the principle of regional autonomy. But the majority of the protesters were Conservatives who were stoutly opposed to the greater part of the Provisional Government's programme, and were, to say the least of it, lukewarm towards the Republic itself. The fact is that anti-Catalanism was an extremely convenient form of opposition to the *régime* and about as safe a form as it was possible to find. Though in the main things were going smoothly during 1931–2, feelings ran high whenever conversation was invaded by such subjects as the restoration of the Monarchy, the re-establishment of the Church, the return of their lands to grandees, or the reinstatement of Civil Servants who had been dismissed from their posts for 'incompatibility'.

It was not practicable to attack the Government publicly
for its ecclesiastical or agrarian policy, but it was perfectly
practicable to attack a policy to which the Government
was, by the Pact of San Sebastián, actually committed,
but which had originated elsewhere. Further, there was a
magnificent slogan which sounded splendidly patriotic:
'Vote for a united Spain!' 'The dismemberment of our
country' was a phrase worked by opponents of the
Statute to its uttermost limit—at a safe distance, of course,
from Barcelona. It was an unexceptionable proceeding,
politically, to defend a united Spain, and if (it was argued)
the Government could be weakened by the defeat of its
regionalist policy, other defeats might soon follow.

There was naturally little risk of the defeat of a
coalition Government, with so huge a majority behind
it, on a bill to the support of which it was more or less
definitely committed. But in the passage of the Statute
through the Cortes, from May 6 to September 9, 1932,
it was sadly mutilated in clauses which its progenitors
considered to be little less than fundamental. Once
again, the Catalonians showed admirable restraint. Their
deputies made every kind of protest against successive
mutilations and the people trusted them to do what they
could and left the rest to the future. 'I warmly appreciate
the admirable example you have set of discipline,' said
Sr. Macià to his people on the night of September 9,
'and I have every confidence in the good-will with which
you will receive this Statute . . . *though it is not the
Statute for which we voted.*' It is well that, in any estimate of
the position and conduct of Catalonia under Republican
rule, this simple truth should be remembered.

A detailed comparison of the draft Statute with its final
form would occupy too much space for a short survey.
A few examples, however, may be given.

One of the most delicate points of the whole discussion was the use of the Catalan language, for, while
politically it may be a matter of little moment, its
sentimental importance is very great and it was in his

attempts to repress the language that Primo de Rivera earned for himself, among Catalonians, the greatest obloquy. The draft Statute had provided that 'the Catalan language shall be the official language in Catalonia, but in relations with the Government of the Republic the official language shall be Castilian'. In its final form, the Statute made an unsatisfactory, if not a meaningless, compromise: 'the Catalan language, *like the Castilian language*, is the official language in Catalonia'. After making Castilian alone the official language for communications between Catalonia and any other part of Spain, it went on to detail numerous cases in which both languages must be used, or in which either might be chosen by the other party than the representative of Catalonia.(10) These were only pin-pricks, but, pressed home as they were in debate, they had their full effect on a sensitive people.

A more vital point was education. Catalonia had long been denied the right of organizing any part of the education of her people. Catalonian professors and school-teachers had found themselves unable to obtain posts in certain other parts of Spain, while on the other hand Catalonian schools and colleges were filled with teachers whose mother tongue was different from that of their pupils, and what should have been the specifically Catalonian university of Barcelona was, like all other Spanish universities, administered from Madrid. The wish of Catalonians was that (to quote the Draft Statute) 'education in all its grades and orders, and the services of public instruction, fine arts, museums, archives, libraries and the conservation of monuments' should be in the hands of the Generalitat, due precaution being taken, in the interests both of Catalonia and of the Republic, as to the equalization of standards.(11) All they were given was permission to 'create and maintain such centres of instruction as the Generalitat may think fit, independently of the cultural and educational institutes of the State', together with control of the services of fine arts, museums, and libraries and the conservation of monuments and archives with the exception of the Archives of the Crown of Aragon.(12) A peculiar situation was created with regard to the University of Barcelona. On the proposition of the Generalitat, the Central Government was to be empowered to grant the University autonomy, with a Patronato, or Board of Control, which would secure equality in every respect as between the Castilian and Catalonian languages and culture.

This was no doubt the honest attempt of a House hampered by criticisms which, though not emanating from any great number of persons, had all to be taken into consideration, to resolve age-old problems in a way that would be acceptable to all. But it fell so far below the desires of the Catalonians that there seemed to be grave danger of complete disaffection. 'To-day,' declared Sr. Companys, the chief spokesman of the Esquerra in the Cortes, 'all Catalonia is Republican, more solidly so than any other part of the country.' She had believed, he continued, that her all but unanimous wishes would be respected, but she was rapidly becoming disillusioned. If the present unsatisfactory article were passed, it would be applied with the utmost loyalty. But the Catalonian deputies could not possibly vote for it, so they would refrain from voting altogether.

The Prime Minister attempted in vain to induce the Esquerra to modify this extreme position. He had long been known as an ardent supporter of Catalonia, and, earlier in the debates, had completely won regionalist sympathies by a speech lasting for three hours—one of the most powerful and effective he had ever made. After tracing the history of the Catalan problem since, by methods of repression, the first of the Bourbons believed he had solved it for ever, Sr. Azaña had shown that, unless it were now handled with decision, it would become insoluble. The Constitution of the Republic, he asserted, plainly authorizes the Statute: the Cortes had no alternative but to pass it. Having on that occasion clearly demonstrated his entire community of sentiment with those whom he was attempting to influence, he now begged them to be content with the distance they had already climbed towards the summit of their ambitions rather than to insist on climbing higher. He failed, but his words had power outside the House, and did much to tranquillize feeling in Barcelona, whence the debates were being followed with the keenest anxiety.

Once again Sr. Azaña threw his weight into the Catalonian argument when at a later stage the Cortes considered the amended financial proposals of the Statute. Some thought the proposals over-generous; to these he replied that if any region were granted autonomy it must have, not only a sound financial status, but one capable of expansion with the region's prosperity. Others objected that the proposals were being taken altogether too quickly; to these his answer was: 'Go as slowly as you please, but the House will not rise for recess till the Statute is disposed of.' The schoolmaster-like reply was respected, if not appreciated, and—'the debate continued'.(13)

This took place at the end of August. On September 9, the Statute as a whole was approved by 314 votes to 24; the numbers of those present, in the depth of Madrid's dead season, should be contrasted with the numbers which had voted, in the preceding October, for Article 26 of the Constitution. Despite the disappointment felt at the mutilation of the Statute, the Catalonians found no difficulty in giving themselves over to jubilation for what they had achieved. On the day after the vote, Barcelona was *en fête* till the small hours of the morning. On the 11th—which happened to be the anniversary of Philip V's attack on Barcelona in 1714—the Catalonian deputies returned from Madrid and were given a public reception. Four days later, the Statute, and the decree promulgating it, were signed, most appropriately, at San Sebastián, and on the 25th it was formally delivered to the Generalitat assembled in session. It was on this last date that the full enthusiasm of the Catalonian people was outpoured to overflowing. The recipient of it was Sr. Azaña. The Republic, he declared, is establishing the new Spain on bases of equity and justice: Catalonia and the Republic must stand or fall together.

'*¡Ahora sois de la República!*' ('Now you belong to the Republic!') he cried, three times in succession.

And each time, from the dense crowd below, there came back to him, with all the force of Catalonia's gratitude and loyalty, a tumultuous '*Sí*'.

So, after centuries, Catalonia was freed from a form of union in which her individuality was crushed and her claim to be a people and a nation tacitly rejected, and given deeds of a new partnership which recognized both. It was clearly only a first step. By time and by the strain of events as yet unforeseen the partnership had to be tested. Each link in the new Statute had to prove its worth. Many problems at the complete solution of which all realized they had not yet arrived would have to be reconsidered. And there were more difficulties still. Would the Lone Star separatists be placated by this compromise of a Statute? It was feared not: and, though few, they were determined and influential. Would the Federalists remain content with a Statute which, by virtue of the very constitution of the Republic, had a unitary basis? This seemed even less likely. Sr. Macià himself, a convinced Federalist, continued to use the language of his historic declaration of April 14, 1931. 'We embrace', he declared in his address to the people on September 9, 1932, '*the other peoples of Iberia.*'(14) Nay, even the Prime Minister, on September 25, spoke similarly. 'Before long,' runs the report of his speech, 'the other peoples of Spain will have their statutes and all these peoples must take their share in assuring to Spain a new place in the world.'(15)

This is perhaps an appropriate place to speak of the aspirations of these other peoples and to give some idea of the position of Autonomists and Federalists not only in Catalonia but elsewhere.

The idea of federation, like that of regional autonomy, has its origin in the assumption that the inhabitants of Spain are not one people, but many. Every observant traveller in Spain, and every intelligent student of Spain, knows that there is truth underlying this assumption. It would be easy to find two European nations more like one another than are the Galicians and the Andalusians, the Extremadurans and the Aragonese, the Catalonians and the Castilians. Dialects quite apart, four well-differentiated languages are spoken in the Peninsula: Basque (which stands philologically alone), and Spanish, Portuguese (with its important Spanish dialect, Galician), and Catalan (with its dialect, Valencian), which are related as sister languages to French and Italian within the Romance family.

Next to the Catalonians, the Basques, with their sharply defined characteristics and their unique language, have probably the strongest claims to autonomy. Of late years Basque studies and a Basque national movement have made considerable progress, and it is significant that, three days after the Catalan State had been proclaimed in Madrid, an attempt was made to proclaim a Basque State beneath the famous 'national' oak of Guernica, a town which was once the seat of a Basque parliament. But as the move met with opposition from the military and the police, its promoters went no farther. The Basques, however, though comparatively few in number, are a determined little people and were not likely to shirk the hard work necessary to attain their ambition.

By the Basque Country is normally meant the four provinces of Guipúzcoa, Alava, Vizcaya and Navarre, though it is doubtful if the last-named, the most isolated and most rural of the four, has any desire to share in Basque autonomy; its position is not unlike that of the Balearic Islands, whose people have the closest affinities

with the Catalonians, yet seem to prefer being governed
from Madrid. Though the movement for Basque
autonomy developed largely through a revived interest
in the Basque language, its chief distinguishing feature
is its attitude to the religious question. The Basques
are passionately devoted to Catholicism; it was the
Basque deputies who withdrew from the Cortes in
protest against the anti-clerical articles of the Constitution,
and the Basque Country suffered more from Sr. Azaña's
wholesale suppressions of traditionalist newspapers than
did any other region. Consequently the first draft of
their autonomy statute, which assigned religious control
to the Central Government, was vehemently opposed by
some of the Ayuntamientos (town councils), notably by
those of Guipúzcoa, which voted for a separate Con-
cordat. This, and the lukewarmness of the Navarrans,
were obvious stumbling-blocks. At the discussion of the
first draft of the Statute at Pamplona, in June 1932, 123
Navarran delegates voted in favour of it and 109 against,
while among the remaining delegates its majority was
245 to 14. Navarre being thus, by its own act, excluded,
the town councils of the three other provinces approved
the Statute with something approaching unanimity,(16)
and, in the following November, plebiscites in Guipúzcoa,
Vizcaya and Alava confirmed this action, 87, 89 and 50
per cent of the respective electorates voting in favour.(17)
The Statute then went to the Cortes, but parliamentary
delays, coupled with the representations of the Alavan
minority, combined to keep it in Committee till the
resignation of the Government made a further postponement inevitable.

Galicia, in the extreme north-west of Spain, is a land
of agriculturists and seamen, of good servants and bad
masters, of dreamers and poets. The Galicians might
well find their niche in a Federalist Peninsula and achieve
greater prosperity than at present, but one can hardly
see them, under a unitary constitution, making any great

success of autonomy. Yet many of them, chiefly for economic reasons, ardently desire it. Every one who has travelled in these north-western provinces knows something of their isolation. Coruña and Vigo are two of Spain's chief ports, yet the communications by which they are served are appallingly inefficient. Whereas Spain as a whole has one kilometre of railroad to every 1,330 inhabitants, in Galicia the proportion is one kilometre to 3,660 inhabitants. There is no direct line from Pontevedra to Coruña nor from Pontevedra to Lugo, while the light railway from the word-famed Santiago to its natural outlet on the coast, Villagarcía, must be one of the worst in the country. These and other disabilities the Galicians have borne over-patiently. But, with the coming of the Republic, the autonomist movement, of some forty years' standing, had the courage to look Madrid in the face and prepare its draft Statute. At first, progress was slow, chiefly because of the difficulty in fixing the seat of the proposed autonomous government. Coruña, the chief port and a city with a long history of independence, had probably the best claim. Santiago challenged it on the traditional side, and Orense had long been the headquarters of the growing movement. By December 1932, the draft had been submitted to the town councils and passed by them with the necessary majority. Before the next step could be taken, the Central Government fell, and with it, for Galicia as for the Basque country, all hope of immediate progress.

No other region of Spain is likely to press for autonomy under the present Constitution, though in several there are autonomist organizations which Federalists look upon with sympathy. Each of the peoples of Iberia, say the Federalists, has a right to self-government; those who are not already demanding it will accept it when it is offered them; and the rest, whose national self-consciousness has been quenched by excessive centralization, will come in before many years have passed. Not all the promoters of the idea would use precisely that language, but it is typical both of the most distinguished and of the most moderate.

In its extremest form Federalism aims at providing for some fourteen separate States, but this is regarded by most people as merely idealistic. The more practicable scheme of a union of about four States would presumably federate Catalonia, the Basque Country, Galicia and the rest of Spain—the last and by far the largest of these divisions being bound together by the fact that the language spoken almost everywhere within its borders is Castilian. The Balearic Islands might well come in with Catalonia, though they seem to have no aspirations toward this ideal at present. The position of Valencia, which is not devoid of such aspirations, is a matter of much doubt. Very soon after the proclamation of the Generalitat, the Valencian nationalists sent a declaration of adhesion to it and issued a statement demanding the formation of an allied but independent state incorporating the three Levantine provinces of Valencia, Castellón and Alicante. But Valencian nationalism has comparatively few adherents, and the attempts which have been made to produce a Statute have only the advantage, from the agitators' point of view, of keeping the question before the public. The hope of the movement lies in its younger leaders, who realize that at present the provinces of Castellón and Alicante are indifferent, or even hostile, and that time must pass before the city and province of Valencia can convert them. Similar as Valencian is to Catalan, the positions of Catalonia and Valencia are quite different. Two Catalonians, meeting as strangers, may greet each other in Castilian, but within sixty seconds they will be talking their own language. Two Valencians, on the other hand, may talk Castilian together all day long.

Andalusia, again, in the event of the triumph of Federalism, might well, in view of its agrarian problems, demand and receive a certain degree of autonomy. It did, in fact, organize a Regional Assembly at Córdoba in February 1933 to discuss the subject, but there was so much violent disagreement and so many delegates withdrew that no progress could be reported.(18) In Andalusia itself, few take the Statute seriously. There are active autonomist minorities both in Majorca and in Aragon, though it is significant that much of the boycotting of Catalonian goods during the anti-separatist agitation of 1932 arose in the latter region.

The ideas and ideals of the Federalists, as has been hinted, are many, but the foregoing paragraphs represent the lines which would be favoured by most of them. The federal theory, it should be added, provides that regions unable, after due self-examination, to feel the quickening of national life within them, shall become territories, under the central government of 'Federal Iberia', until such time as they desire autonomy.

Those who deride the Federal idea as visionary should not forget that it is about as old as the Republican tradition in Spain. After the dethronement of Isabel II, in 1868, the Constituent Cortes which met to determine the nation's future had a Republican minority which was almost wholly Federalist. In 1873, when the first Spanish Republic was formed, the Constituent Assembly was markedly Federalist, as was the Constitution which the Assembly drew up and found itself unable to enforce. It proposed to partition Spain and her colonies into no fewer than seventeen States, both Andalusia and Castile being divided each into two parts, Navarre being separate from the other three Basque provinces, and other parts of the Peninsula, such as Extremadura, Murcia and the Balearic Islands, being isolated as self-governing entities. It seems unlikely that such a federation could ever come into being. If it did, the probabilities are that it would have a short and disturbed existence, and that the partition would result in a speedy return to complete centralization and possibly to the establishment of a totalitarian state.

There we must leave this interesting, though some-what academic question and return to our main narrative. At bottom the obstacles to Federalism are psychological. The illustration which some Spaniards give of its success-ful working—that of the United States of America—can only too easily be turned against them. The Americans have a genius for co-operation, and some of them, completely ineffective as individuals, produce fine work in the mass. The Spaniards, on the other hand, have a passion for individualism, and when they attempt to co-operate do so badly or fail altogether. Till they change their nature, as with the changing conditions of European life they may gradually do in the course of centuries, it is idle to suppose them capable of Federal government, and for that reaon, their warmest well-wishers trust that they will never be led into experi-menting with it.

III

While the Cortes were still in session—less than a month, indeed, before the Catalan Statute and the Agrarian Law were passed and the House was granted a bare three weeks' vacation—a new and alarming revolt, of the rather old-fashioned military *pronuncia-miento* type, broke out in Madrid, and another, almost simultaneously, in Seville. It will be observed that revolts, in Spain as elsewhere, never take place to time-table: they are continually predicted for Labour Day, the anniversary of the Dictatorship or the morrow of a General Election, and the days in question pass in complete tranquillity. The converse is also true. It was certainly most inconsiderate of the rebels to operate in Spain's dead season of high summer, when every one was asleep or on holiday and much too hot to take a proper interest in the proceedings.

The two outbreaks were no doubt related to each other, but were not confessedly planned with the same object. The Madrid revolt was frankly Monarchist—

the first sign of a violent resurgence of Monarchism that had yet occurred—and its rapid suppression, with its failure to evoke any marked popular response, must have been a sore blow to Alfonsist aspirations. The Seville revolt purported to strike, not at the Republic as such, but at the interpretation set upon Republican principles by the Government in power. There is no doubt that, even so early in the Government's life, a growing discontent was making itself felt among its former supporters. A short phrase charged with feeling, *No era eso*—'It wasn't *this* that we expected'—said to have been first used by the eminent philosopher Don José Ortega y Gasset, was just then the slogan of the moderates as well as of those whose sympathies inclined towards the Right. And it is possible enough that the malcontents of Seville may have desired no more than a purge of the Cortes and the Government. Nevertheless, most observers believed that, had both the revolts been successful, their leaders would at once have joined forces and attempted to carry the country.

In Madrid, the revolt broke out early in the morning of August 10. Organized by aristocrats and retired army officers, it made its first objective the capture of the cathedral-like General Post Office in the Plaza de Cibeles —the very centre of modern Madrid. To their great surprise the rebels met with stubborn resistance from the civilians whom they endeavoured to intimidate, and before they had recovered from this, they were opposed by a considerable force of police and loyal soldiers who had been rushed to the scene of battle. Street fighting followed in the Calle de Alcalá, which crosses the square at one corner of which stands the Post Office, but the result was never in doubt and in a few hours all danger to the *régime* was over.

In Seville the revolt was more serious. Its leader was no less a notability than General Sanjurjo, Director-General of the Civil Guard, known popularly as the 'Lion of the Riff', who had figured prominently in the news at the time of the village tragedies of the preceding winter and who was known to be highly disillusioned with the results of republicanism. The General had apparently planned to watch events in Madrid, and, when he judged the moment to strike his blow to have come, to journey post-haste to Seville, issue a manifesto describing his aims and protesting his loyalty to republicanism and proclaim himself Captain-General. His programme duly carried out, the movement at first seemed likely to cause a considerable amount of bloodshed. Fighting broke out all over the city, not merely between General Sanjurjo's troops and the forces of law and order, but also between extremists of the Right and Left, the latter thinking this a heaven-sent opportunity to pay off some old grudges. So they burned three clubs, a number of aristocratic mansions and the Seville offices of the Monarchist newspaper *A.B.C.*, which publishes a special daily edition for Andalusia. The *mêlée*, deplorable as were its consequences to life and property, served the good purpose of impeding the rebels' progress, and, as the Civil Guard for the most part remained loyal, reinforcements soon decided the outcome of the rebellion. There was a huge number of arrests, and General Sanjurjo, driving hard for the coast, was somewhat ignominiously captured on the high-road by a policeman. Unfortunately the flames kindled by the Sevilian rebels spread throughout Andalusia; in all the large towns of the region Socialists or Syndicalists declared strikes of protest; there was a good deal of rioting; and at Granada, where the situation was particularly tense, the beautiful church of San Nicolás, in the Albaicín, was wrecked by fire.

The prompt and determined action taken by the Government sent up its stock rapidly and Sr. Azaña very justly received a full measure of congratulations and a great accession of confidence. In the Cortes he spoke at length, and with the greatest frankness, in that phlegmatic, dispassionate tone which he can assume at will, and his hearers felt, not for the first time, that here was a man fully capable of directing the country's fortune. The Government, he assured the House, had known all about the Madrid revolt well in advance, and to crush the Sevilian outbreak had been child's play. The good impression which he made in the Cortes was intensified at the trial of the chief prisoners, which was held, a fortnight later, before a civil court, at the Palace of Justice, where the members of the then Revolutionary Committee had been tried at the end of 1930. The Public Prosecutor asked for the death sentence for General Sanjurjo and life imprisonment for his son, his aide-de-camp and the majority of their fellow-prisoners. The first of these sentences was granted, but popular opinion had no desire for executions, and within a few days the list of individuals and societies who had petitioned for a reprieve filled four columns of a daily paper. Among the petitioners, it may be noted, were the widow of García Hernández and the mother of Galán, the two officers who had been shot after the rebellion less than two years earlier. The Government made no difficulty about clemency: it unanimously counselled the President to issue a reprieve, and Sanjurjo *père* (his son had been found Not Guilty) was sentenced to a 'life' imprisonment which every one knew would soon be ended.

So far, so good; but in other respects the Government lost ground. Before the trial was held, the Cortes, after an all-night sitting, passed a bill for the confiscation of the lands, houses and other property of those to be found guilty. Article 44 of the 1931 Constitution had made such procedure perfectly legal and the strength of the Government left no doubt as to the result of the division, but both in the Cortes and in the country there were violent protests against what in the circumstances was considered an excess of severity.

Whatever may be said about this, there can hardly be two opinions as to the Government's treatment of the Press. It might be reasonable, at a time of crisis, to suspend Opposition newspapers for a day or two, but the Government's idea of the liberty of the Press, for contravening which those who now supported them had so strongly attacked Primo de Rivera, was to suspend eight Madrid newspapers, including *A.B.C.*, the *Debate* and *Informaciones*, for an indefinite period, together with a large number of periodicals in the provinces. The *Debate* and *Informaciones* were not allowed to appear till October, and, as for *A.B.C.*, its readers began to think they would never see it again. Eventually it reappeared on the last day of November, after an interval of one hundred and twelve days, during which period it had paid salaries and wages to nearly a thousand employees and had achieved a certified net loss of over two million pesetas. In the circumstances it might be forgiven a slight flourish of trumpets, and the pen of its editor had certainly lost none of its cunning during three and a half months of inaction:

'Neither in the days of Calomarde [ran its leading article], nor in those of Narváez, nor in those of Primo de Rivera—never, during all the Governments of six reigns and two republics, was there applied to a periodical so severe a governmental sanction, without any legal justification whatsoever. Granted that the Constitution is being set aside—for this prohibits the suspension of periodicals save by the firm sentence of a competent tribunal—our case cannot be justified even by the Law for the Defence of the Republic, for this empowers the Home Secretary to suspend periodicals only for a definite period, the length of which must be fixed when the sanction is decided upon and is determined by the causes or motives in virtue of which it is to be imposed. We, on the other hand, have never been informed of the reasons for the imposition of this penalty, which is without precedent in Spain.(19)

The result of such measures as these could only be, in

the Spanish phrase, *contraproducente*. It increased the discontent which had previously been felt by moderates and Conservatives; it destroyed the good effect which the Government's promptitude and prudence had created among the non-political; and it did immense harm to the reputation of the Republic abroad.

In September, an unsuccessful attempt made by the Communists to promote a revolution of their own added still more to the population of Spanish prisons, many of which even previously were full almost to overcrowding. By no means all the prisoners taken in August were tried with the same dispatch as the ringleaders, and, in Madrid's Model Prison, aristocrats in plenty found rough lodging pending deportation, with or without trial—and at their own expense!—in warships which lay in waiting for them off Cádiz. By the middle of September, the first detachment was on its way to Villa Cisneros, on the unhealthy coast of Spanish West Africa, where we shall hear of them again shortly.

The early autumn saw the most considerable purge of the Civil Service which had as yet been attempted; and to be charged with the now familiar crime, unprovable and unanswerable, of 'incompatibility with the *régime*', was an eventuality from which few could consider themselves safe. The process was in no sense initiated by the Republic but it created an uneasiness and a feeling of insecurity which were anything but desirable. The wholesale dismissals included over forty members of the Diplomatic Service, some for alleged disaffection and others for reasons not stated. In November, the long-talked-of and rather tardily staged trial of the persons chiefly responsible for the Dictatorship of 1923–30 came as something of an anti-climax, and the announcement of the sentences, which varied from six years' exile to twenty-four years' imprisonment, was heard with no great interest. The Dictatorship belonged to Spain's far-away past; the question of painful moment was what she would make of her future.

In November, the Cortes were presented with a Budget. This one would not think to be an unusual event, but it proved to be the last Budget of this history, succeeding governments finding postponement a convenient formula. Considering the way in which the deficit had been mounting up during the Dictatorship—there had been a constant increase from 417 million pesetas in 1925 to 924 million four years later—the figures were not alarming. The first year of the Republic had reduced the deficit to 576 millions and the second brought it down by 100 millions more. It was not money that was uneasy so much as men's minds.

If the greater part of Spain during this period was restive and fearful, Catalonia was quiet and content. Once the Statute of Autonomy was duly promulgated, reconstruction, despite inevitable delays, proceeded apace. Elections for the new Catalonian Parliament, held on November 20, gave, as was expected, a huge majority to the Esquerra, which in many places received more than double the votes recorded for the moderate Lliga. The Radical party, now becoming so unpopular in Catalonia that its dissolution could be but a matter of time, scored only diminutively. Returned at the head of the poll for Barcelona city, Sr. Macià, the veteran leader of the Esquerra, was elected Premier of a Cabinet of seven, which started work shortly before Christmas, ready to face the numerous problems raised by the gradual transference of the powers conceded by the Statute. The President, or Speaker, of the parliament, it may be remarked, was that interesting character of whom we shall hear more in the next chapter: En Lluis Companys, the hero of Barcelona's 'fourteenth of April' and now an ex-Mayor of the city.

IV

It might have been supposed that, after the disestablishment of the Church and the numerous other concessions and gestures made to anti-clericalism, the Government would now confine itself to matters secular. But there was still to be passed the 'Law of Confessions and Congregations', foreshadowed in Articles 26 and 27 of the Constitution, and this became a subject of controversy from its first publication, as a draft, in October 1932, until its promulgation, seven months later.

A considerable part of the Law, as eventually passed, merely confirmed guarantees already given in the Constitution and repeated regulations drawn up in the interests of religious equality. Religious bodies, for example, might worship within their own buildings, but not, except with special permission, outside them. Any notices issued by them would be subject to the same police rules as any other notices. They should be free to appoint their own officers, providing these were Spaniards, subject to the veto of the State. Their property belongs to the State, 'under whose safeguard'—ironical phrase!—they hold it. They may 'found and direct establishments for instruction in their respective doctrines and for the training of their ministers', but the State, by means of inspection, will see that none of them 'teaches doctrines which threaten the safety of the Republic'.

This is only an indication of the nature of the Law, in its early sections, and in no way an attempt at summarizing it. The latter and more important part aimed at restricting the freedom of the religious Orders—an aim achieved by means of a number of harassing regulations which intensified the opposition of Catholics without notably increasing the satisfaction of anti-clericals. The Orders were forbidden to engage in 'any kind of political activity', the penalty for disobedience being dissolution at the pleasure of the Cortes. All Orders must be recognized as associations, and submit copies of their statutes, a statement of the 'aims' of each of their 'houses or residences' and an inventory of their possessions. Each house must register the name of its Superior, who must be a Spaniard, and the names of its other members, at least two-thirds of whom must be Spaniards, together with particulars of the property which each member has brought to the Order. Each religious house must submit its books and its annual balance-sheet for inspection. Should any professed religious, or any novice, desire to leave his or her Order, the State will support his intention, and will require the Order to return him such property as he may have deposited with it, less a reasonable allowance corresponding to the time he has spent in the Order.

No Order, continues the text of the Law, may engage in commerce, in industry or (apart from what is necessary for its own subsistence) in agricultural labour. No Order may engage in teaching, save to instruct its own members; State inspection will see that the Orders neither maintain private schools of their own nor teach in schools kept by lay-folk. All teaching by members of religious Orders must come to an end by October 1, 1933, except in elementary schools, for which the period is extended to December 31.

There were two opinions, even among anti-clericals, about the wisdom of passing so drastic an educational measure, or at least of enforcing it with such celerity. The Republic had been in existence for eighteen months and there were still many thousands of children unable to go to school because there were insufficient schools for them to go to. Many educationists who placed education before anti-clericalism felt that it was impossible to provide adequately for an additional number of elementary school children estimated by the Minister of Education at 350,000, and by the Catholic Press at double that figure,(20) and that it would be better to bring in the change much more gradually. Others, however, argued that during a transitional period there might well be a reaction in favour of a Conservative government and that the Law might in that case never come into operation at all.

We may spare a moment here to look back on what the Republic had done, and proposed to do, for education in general. When Don Marcelino Domingo, an ex-schoolmaster, became the Republic's first Education Minister, he found himself confronted by problems too vast for immediate solution, even had the attack upon them not been complicated by political considerations. The universities were too numerous; having no autonomy, they were swayed by every wind of politics; their curricula were often unsuitable; their professors, generally elected by *oposición* (a species of oral examination), began at a minimum salary of 5,000 pesetas (nominally £200 yearly) and often rose little higher; the relations of undergraduates to the professors and to the university itself left much to be desired. Secondary schools were too few: many large towns had only one Government secondary school, or Instituto. In these the classes were far too large; the teachers' salaries far too small. The curriculum, which, since before the Dictatorship, had been continually tinkered with, was too wide and superficial. The teachers, to supplement their salaries, did a nefarious trade in bad little text-books which they wrote themselves and forced their pupils to buy. Elementary schools were the worst of all. Despite Primo de Rivera's efforts there were 50,000 children in Madrid alone for whom there was no seat-room in existing schools.(21) One can imagine what the situation was in the country— and what it would have been but for the labours of the religious Orders.

Though little has in fact been done in university reform Sr. Domingo envisaged far-reaching changes in all three classes of institution, and from the beginning he set out to create the *escuela única*—the single course of education leading from elementary school to university: in our own phrase, to set up the educational ladder. The first and principal thing was obviously to lay the foundations of reform by building more elementary schools, and this task he began upon with a will. Within three months, he had authorized the creation of 27,000 new schools, of which over 3,000 were already completed and 7,000 were to be finished within a year.(22) The training of teachers was more difficult, but shortened courses in pedagogy were afoot by the summer vacation of 1931 and large numbers of teachers were improvised by the following September.

The year 1932 saw further progress. Some 2,500 more schools were opened, bringing the total to nearly 10,000. The salaries of elementary school teachers had been raised to a minimum of 3,000 pesetas (nominally £120), and improvements had been effected in the scale of increments. A law had been passed obliging municipalities to contribute to the cost of new schools built in their areas. Travelling schools, or 'pedagogic missions' —to give an attractive scheme its rather repellent Spanish title—had been sent into the remotest country districts, to bring the inhabitants into new contact with music, painting, history, literature and current civilization. At the end of 1932, Don Fernando de los Ríos, who succeeded Don Marcelino Domingo as Minister for Education, summed up these and other developments. He was able to point to fine new secondary schools which had been built (or occasionally, it might be added, confiscated from the Jesuits) in Madrid and to the 70,000 boys and girls receiving secondary education, as against the 20,000 of three years earlier. In university education there was, he confessed, little to point to. The erection of the University City in Madrid was proceeding apace, but a Republican minister could hardly say much about that.(23) The miserable students' strikes continued, together with the old professorial abuses, and only in Barcelona, where the Generalitat had lost no time in asking for it, was there university autonomy. An attempt had been made, as it had also been made under the Dictatorship, to reduce the number of the universities, but, Sr. de los Ríos declared, as soon as he had suggested the suppression of two of them, the opposition was so great that he abandoned the project as hopeless.

Still, taking the situation as a whole, and not forgetting such extraneous reforms as the strengthening of the *Junta para Ampliación de Estudios*, the creation of Schools of Arabic Studies and the establishment of the rather pretentiously named 'Summer International University' at Santander, the Republic was to be congratulated on what it had accomplished. In the first year of the present century, the sum budgeted for education had been 50,000 pesetas; in the year 1932 it was nine hundred times that amount, or 45,000,000 pesetas.

When, in May 1933, the Government came to grips with the Opposition over the educative clauses of the Law of Confessions and Congregations, the Education Minister made light of the disadvantages of closing so many schools so quickly. For the complete absorption of the children in the elementary schools of the Orders, he said, it would be necessary to create 7,000 new schools, provision for 4,000 of which had already been made, while there was ample time and money for the remainder. The 17,000 secondary pupils of the Orders could also be absorbed by October and five hundred new secondary school teachers were being intensively trained during the summer.

But many besides Opposition deputies found it impossible to share Sr. de los Ríos's hopefulness. If the annual Education estimates, asked *The Times*, are to be not much more than a million pounds sterling, where are all the new buildings to come from? 'Is it proposed to confiscate the schools of the Orders? This is not clear. Nor is it clear how 7,000 new teachers are to be prepared in six months.'(24)

'A more leisurely solution would have sufficed', is this writer's conclusion, and from an educational point of view there is no doubt that a more leisurely solution would have been more effective. But, as things turned out, the change was made less violently than had been intended. For in November, only a month before the elementary instruction given by the Orders was due to cease, the Government fell, and its successor, being less advanced in character, allowed things to continue. Whether for better or for worse, since educational reforms of other kinds also slowed down considerably, is a matter on which there may well be two opinions.

V

The early days of 1933, though the fact was not at first evident, saw the hardening of the Government's unpopularity and the beginning of its downfall. In the second week of the year attention was diverted from politics by a series of Anarchist revolts—the third armed outbreak against the Republic in twelve months. These were considerably more widely spread than any others of the kind, embracing Madrid, Barcelona, Lérida, Valencia and Seville, but all of them were put down within forty-eight hours with encouraging ease. A few days previously, word had reached Spain of the escape from Villa Cisneros of twenty-nine of the August revolutionaries. For months stories had been abroad (not all from unprejudiced sources) of the indescribable hardships which they were suffering, and the news that the fugitives, now safe in Portugal, had elected to attempt a journey of nearly two thousand miles in a hundred-ton boat rather than to continue life in West Africa or to return to Spain for the trial which they were still awaiting put violent accusations of tyranny once more into the mouths of the Government's enemies.

But the event which, more surely than any other, brought about the Government's fall, and a complete, though not a permanent, change of direction in Republican policy, was the revolt at Casas Viejas. The undistinguished name of this little village, twelve miles south of Medina Sidonia, in the province of Cádiz, was at the end of the year 1932 as completely unknown to the average Spaniard as that of Castilblanco had been twelve months earlier. Yet within a few weeks the name 'Casas Viejas', instead of denoting merely a hamlet of a thousand souls, signified the most implacable enmity to a Government which (said its enemies) had from first to last been distinguished by an arbitrary rule, a severity and a tyranny which could no longer continue.

The bald facts of the affair, as they were at first reported in the Madrid papers, suggest that this was one of the village riots which have been so distressingly frequent under the Republic and are due to the violent action of subversive ideas upon the simple minds of little educated and unsophisticated peasants. The people of Casas Viejas live on the borders of an estate of 40,000 acres owned by the Duque de Medinaceli, which was about to be confiscated and distributed among the peasantry.(25) Early in the morning of January 11, a group of rebels, not all inhabitants of the village, took possession of the local Anarcho-Syndicalist centre, proclaimed a Communistic *régime*, intimidated the *alcalde* and called for the surrender of the Civil Guard.

'I will die for the Republic,' replied the sergeant, 'but I will never surrender,' and sent hurriedly for reinforcements from Medina Sidonia and Cádiz.

Meanwhile, the rebels, who, as investigations afterwards showed, had accumulated large stores of pistols, ammunition and explosives, opened fire on the Civil Guard, with such effect that, within a few minutes, three members of the small force were mortally wounded. Soon after midday, reinforcements of Civil Guards and shock troops drove the rebels to a position outside and above the village, tore down the Anarchist flag which had been hoisted and began a search of the village house by house. Only one house resisted them—that of a rebel nicknamed Seisdedos ('Six Fingers'), whose daughter Libertaria acted as his gunloader as he fired, and here the loyal troops suffered heavy losses. At last, during the night, they had to send for bombs and a machine-gun, which, even then, they hesitated to use until they received a telegram from the Home Secretary authorizing them to raze the house to the ground. Thereupon they bombed it without mercy, soaked it with petrol and set it on fire: Seisdedos, his daughter, and six other persons perished.

By seven o'clock on the next morning, when several more houses had been set on fire and over twenty people killed, the rebels surrendered. Precisely what took place in the last hours of the struggle will probably never be known. Determined as were the attempts afterwards made to obtain and sift evidence, the witnesses were so contradictory that no clear account of the affair could be gathered. What chiefly emerged was that those in command of the loyal forces had received the most drastic orders from Madrid; that the troops, being small in number, fatigued by want of sleep and exasperated by their heavy losses, had given these the most literal interpretation; and that certain of the guards and shock troops had protested vehemently at the orders which they had received, as being barbarous and inhuman. Captain Rojas, who had commanded the troops on the spot, came in for some severe criticism, and when, after sixteen months, he was brought to trial, the death of fourteen people was laid at his door and he received a heavy sentence.

At the earliest possible moment the indignation aroused by these terrible events found expression in the Cortes, whose members reassembled, after a longer recess than any they had previously enjoyed, at the beginning of February. The attitude of the Prime Minister was at first one of truculence: the Government could not be expected to quench 'the smallest revolutionary spark in the smallest Spanish village'. But the criticism which he had to face soon became too detailed and too emphatic to be met by a debating speech, especially as for some time Sr. Lerroux and his Radical followers had been growing troublesome and there was every sign that the Left coalition would shortly be rent asunder. In the end, Sr. Azaña had to agree to a two-day debate on Casas Viejas and to make the question one of confidence.

The days of the debate, ironically enough, coincided with those of Carnival. The House, for once, was crowded; passion rose to fever heat, and there were numerous *escándalos*. Members of nearly every political party censured the Government. One of the minor heroes of Jaca, Sr. Sediles, drew a parallel, amid protests from Sr. Azaña and his supporters, between Jaca and Casas Viejas. Sr. Maura, with the authority of a former Home Secretary, described the affair as an ineradicable stain on the Government's record. Sr. Martínez Barrio, who later perpetrated the famous condemnation of the Azaña *régime* as one of 'mud, blood and tears', made a personal attack on the attitude of the Prime Minister. Sr. Azaña put a bold front on the affair, but it must have been the stiffest parliamentary fight that he had as yet engaged in. On a division, he won—but only by the narrow majority of forty-three.

In Spain, and at such a time, this majority could not be considered as final. Only a week later, the more intransigent of the Government's opponents tabled a motion of censure which provided an excuse for bringing up the affair all over again. This time the Prime Minister gave an undertaking that an official investigation should be made and thereupon his majority rose by twenty.

By the middle of March the investigatory commission sent to Casas Viejas had returned. Their report gave the fullest possible account of the whole incident, and, in addition to registering the opinions which have already been reproduced, censured the new Director-General, Sr. Menéndez, who held the supreme command, for having given express orders to apply the *ley de fugas*[1] to all who gave trouble. The Government, however, it exonerated, to the extent of entering in its favour the verdict of 'Not proven'. The outcome of such a report

[1] A term applied to a proceeding of which forces of the law have in the past often been accused in Spain—shooting a person under the pretext that he was trying to escape.

131

was fairly obvious. The Director-General, following the custom so much in fashion, went to prison; an almost languid debate of some days took place in a greatly thinned Cortes; and on a new division the vote for the Government was unanimous—or, to be exact, the figures were 210 to 1.

But, notwithstanding this result, the Government's credit was mortally wounded, and every one knew it. '*Muy feo*' ('An ugly business'), murmured the man in the street. By which he meant: 'This continual severity and repression can't go on. Even at the cost of holding up Republican progress, Spain must have a change of leaders.'

At first the Government itself was unable, or unwilling, to see what was plain to every outside observer. The barometer which in 1933, as in 1931, showed the political feelings of the country was the municipal elections. As early as January the new electoral register was announced as being near completion, and municipal elections—the first since those which brought in the Republic—were fixed for April. They were, of course, to be entirely political in character, and it soon became clear that Sr. Azaña was hoping much from their results. 'The political parties which support us', he declared in February to two thousand or more of his adherents, 'will go to the country prepared, if they are beaten, to take the consequences. But if they are *not* beaten—why, then, there will be consequences for others!' (26)

Winter gave place to the early Spanish spring, and, except for the usual daily crops of strikes all over the country, accompanied from time to time by mild disturbances, Spain was quiet. Yet another of the committees on responsibilities for events of the past concluded its sittings—and for the various parts which they had played in the Jaca executions various ex-army officers received various terms of imprisonment. The prisoners arrested at Castilblanco over a year before (for the mills of the Republic grind slowly) were tried and sentenced, and the miscreants of the following August who had not escaped from Villa Cisneros were brought to the tribunals; seventeen of them, it may be said in passing, after spending six months in deportation, were acquitted as innocent. The tragic events of Casas Viejas began to recede into the past; it might appear that they too had been consigned to history.

Then, at the beginning of April, came an announcement which showed that the Government had feared to test popular opinion after all. The 'consequences' which Sr. Azaña had so boldly challenged, the votes of six million women—a factor 'unknown', perhaps, but only too accurately predictable—should wait a little longer before he faced them. There was small hope that the Left would be returned to power; let the evil day be deferred as long as possible.

So the municipal elections were indefinitely postponed and 'partial' elections were announced in their stead—to be held in some 2,500 rural districts which in 1931 had returned Monarchists and as a punishment had since that time been deprived of representation. The date fixed for this preliminary sounding of opinion was April 23, and there was fear and trembling lest the intervening days should see disorders, for did not Good Friday—an ecclesiastical holiday, though no longer an official one—coincide this year with April 14—the Day of the Republic? Flags would be flying everywhere and festivities would be in full swing—and would not this inevitably lead to clashes between Catholics and anti-clericals?

The fears were without foundation. Holy Week, as it had so often been in the past, was a week of truce, and both sides gave and took freely. On the one hand, processions and *pasos*, even in Seville, remained within their churches instead of risking disorder by parading the streets as usual. On the other hand, the more festive events arranged for the celebration of Republic Day were postponed till the Saturday and Sunday, and, though it was strange to see flags flying at full mast on Good Friday, there were few other indications of rejoicing. Popular opinion is so completely Catholic in Spain that even among anti-clericals Catholic observances have largely been taken for granted; the greater saints' days, for example, are no longer official holidays but they are quite freely observed as such and no one raises any objection. In this very year 1933, despite the permission given to Madrid theatres and cinemas to remain open on Maundy Thursday and Good Friday, only eleven out of fifty-six did in fact remain open, and five of these gave exclusively sacred performances. (27)

On the first Sunday after Easter the 'partial' elections took place and the results must have confirmed the Government's worst fears. It is true that they proved avowed Monarchism to have practically disappeared—but no one had supposed Monarchism to be at issue. The question was: 'Shall the present Government stay or go?' And by a two to one majority the answer came back: 'Go'. Of the 16,000 seats that were filled, rather over 5,000 went to Government candidates, about a hundred less to parties of the Right, and seven hundred fewer still to the Centre and Left opposition. (28)

As soon as the Cortes met, the Opposition parties called loudly upon the Government to resign, since the test which it had itself proposed had given results adverse to it. Sr. Azaña chose once again to be truculent. What were these elections after all that they should affect the Government's position? Merely a filling up of vacancies in unimportant and obscure rural constituencies—*burgos podridos* ('rotten boroughs'), in fact. He had not the slightest intention of resigning office; he had been called to power in order to build up a new Spain round the new Constitution and he would remain in power until all the laws complementary to the Constitution had been voted.

This attitude, though perhaps the only one open to him, had the unfortunate effect of bringing the coalition to a virtual end. Before making what soon became

notorious as his 'rotten boroughs' speech, he had conferred at length with the President of the Republic and it
seemed to his critics unlikely that there was any hope
of a dissolution from that quarter. So the Radicals,
who had previously been growing restive, went into open
parliamentary revolt, and the Opposition parties combined to form a frankly obstructionist block in the Cortes
in the hope of exasperating the Government into resignation. For several weeks there was chaos. The Law of
Congregations, which had been slowly passing through
the House, was held up night after night while the
obstructionists forced one political discussion after the
other. The Prime Minister made continued appeals
for concord, and various pacifist parliamentarians put
forward suggestions which might expedite public
business. But the Opposition declared that the public
welfare necessitated, first and foremost, a new Government, and remained inexorable.

Even while battle raged in the Cortes, the centre of
interest shifted for a time to the country. Social disturbances, due chiefly to the Syndicalists, were renewed
all over Spain. Barcelona was paralysed for several days
by a traffic strike; all the Syndicalist and Anarchist centres
were closed; and two companies of shock troops were
drafted into the city. Before this was brought to an end
a series of forty-eight-hour general strikes was begun
all over the country. Practically all the large cities were
affected—from Saragossa, Oviedo and Coruña in the
north to Seville in the south—and a great many smaller
towns also. In Madrid, the trouble spread to the University. Groups of youths calling themselves Fascists
organized demonstrations exactly similar to those of the
anti-Fascists in the last years of the Dictatorship. Shots
were fired; a number of people were wounded; and the
bulk of the student body struck work in protest. Through
May and June these disturbances continued with little
respite. Some thought they heralded the dissolution of
more than the Government, but the vast majority had

long believed the Republic to be safe, simply because there was no practicable alternative to take its place. 'Communism—never! The King—no!' summed up the situation. On the one hand, Catholic Spain would not tolerate a system completely out of accord with its own deep-rooted traditions. On the other hand, few could endure the thought of a Bourbon on the throne again—with all the recrimination and revenge which learning nothing and forgetting nothing imply. There was no serious fear, then, of a change in the *régime*, but there was widespread depression and a feeling that for many years Spain, struggling upwards, was condemned to unrest and conflict, and that there was no short way out of her troubles which would not again send her downwards.

VI

On May 17, 1933, after a rougher passage than any Government measure had yet met with, the Law of Religious Confessions and Congregations passed the Cortes by a majority of 278 votes to 50 and was sent to the President for his signature.

As soon as it was known that this had been done, the amiable figure of the President became the centre of interest for the first time since his election. In the intervening eighteen months he had held many consultations with his Ministers, visited various parts of the country, received deputations, made speeches, opened schools, and acted as an obliging, if not a particularly effective, figurehead. But now came a stern test impossible of evasion. Under the Constitution he was bound either to sign the Law or to take the consequences of committing a 'criminal' action,(29) which would, at the very least, lose him his high office. In the past, on a similar question, he had followed the dictates of his conscience: would he do so again?

If this was too much to expect of him, argued his fellow-Catholics, he had fifteen days' grace, at the end of which time he might send the Law back to the Cortes for re-consideration. As the majority of two-thirds which in that case would be necessary for its promulgation had already been greatly exceeded, there would be little to gain from such a course apart from a slight delay. It might, however, have a moral effect which would be of value in the future, though, on the other hand, it might equally well give provocation to the Left extremists. On the whole the choice seemed to lie between promulgation and the consequences of refusal.

As a general rule the President had approved laws submitted to him for signature within a day or two, and when, at the end of a week, the Law of Congregations remained unsigned, the situation began to assume interest. During the whole of this period protests of all kinds, coming from every part of the country, were published in the Conservative Press, and an even greater number were sent privately to the President. At the end of the week the Spanish Metropolitan Bishops issued a joint letter condemning the Law and other anti-clerical measures of the Government. Still no move: the situation began to grow tense, and even dramatic. The hopes of the Clerical party mounted.

But on June 2, the very last day of the period accorded to him by the Constitution, Sr. Alcalá Zamora capitulated. Despite a condemnatory encyclical from the Vatican, published on the following day, and of which we may safely assume him to have had advance knowledge, he chose to remain in possession of his office rather than to make a second sacrifice. The Right, which had once hoped for much from him, never entirely forgave him, and, though he was soon to offend them yet more deeply, they no longer counted on his support. History, how-ever, will find no fault with him here, for after two centuries of Bourbons Spain needed above all a president who would act constitutionally and in Sr. Alcalá Zamora she apparently had it.

A week later, on the President's initiative, the

Government had resigned, and the President attempted to find another Prime Minister capable of forming a new coalition. But the search was unavailing and within a few days Sr. Azaña was back in office with a reshuffled but otherwise almost identical Cabinet. The opportunities given to other leaders to form a Government had cleared the air, and during the three further months of office which remained to Sr. Azaña there was no more obstruction.

The principal achievement of these months was the creation of the rather grandiloquently named Tribunal of Constitutional Guarantees, which may best be described as an attempt to supply the need being increasingly felt for a Senate or other form of Second Chamber. It was to decide whether or no laws were constitutional; to settle conflicts between the State and autonomous regions; to pronounce on any alleged infringements of the Constitution by the President, the Prime Minister and others; and, among many other tasks, to protect any citizen whose constitutional rights had been overridden. The great wish of many was that this Tribunal might be impartial and non-political: of its twenty-four members, fifteen were to be elected by the various regions of Spain, and its President was to be chosen for ten years and paid an annual stipend of 100,000 pesetas (nominally £4,000)—a sum second only to that received by the President of the Republic. The first President of the Tribunal, however, was a politician—Sr. Albornoz, Socialist Minister of Justice, who vacated this office on election—and the majority of the members, when elected, were found to belong to the same category. It is indeed difficult to achieve impartiality in Spanish politics.

No tears were shed at the interment of the hated Law for the Defence of the Republic, which, at the end of July, after an inglorious career of twenty-one months, gave place to a new and rather more liberal Law of Public Order. The best-known of the provisions contained in this measure is the threefold grading of abnormal national conditions as State of Prevention, State of Alarm and State of War. With strikes still rampant all over the country, it was hoped that this gradation would make effective action easier. During the State of Prevention, for example, which can be declared by the Government and need not be referred to the Cortes until after ten days, undesirable foreigners may be detained or expelled, associations suspended, meetings cancelled and fines within wide limits imposed on individuals. The State of Alarm—unfortunately named, for again and again it caused unnecessary apprehension abroad—makes possible even more stringent action at short notice and must be renewed or revoked at the end of a month. So far as one can see in retrospect, the promulgation of the new Law made little difference to the number of strikes and riots, but it removed in part the sense of grievance felt by many under the Law for the Defence of the Republic and pacified those who believed that Spain was rapidly passing from one dictatorship to another.

By September the Opposition in the Cortes was again becoming restive. Sr. Azaña had now passed all the laws complementary to the Constitution, and still he was continuing in office. It was time, said the Radicals, that this predominantly Socialist coalition should dissolve. The country was clearly turning towards the Right: of the fifteen elected places in the Tribunal, ministerial candidates had won only five, against four gained by the Radicals and six by other groups of the Opposition, mainly of the Right. Attendances in the Cortes were thinning and Sr. Lerroux hinted plainly at a new bout of obstructionism in the near future. This time Sr. Azaña took the hint and handed in his resignation. He had been in office for almost exactly two years.

The general feeling was in favour of immediate dissolution, but in the end Sr. Lerroux consented to try his hand at forming a government predominantly Radical and Radical-Socialist. Its fate was farcical. On the very day it met the Cortes, the Socialist leader, Don Indalecio

Prieto, moved a vote of no confidence, which was so strongly supported that on the second day of the debate Sr. Lerroux began his speech with the words 'Morituri te salutant'. They proved to be a correct statement of the position. In a House from which barely a score of members was absent, over one-third abstained from voting, the Government lost by ninety-eight votes and its resignation at once followed.

This made it abundantly clear that there was no course open but to go to the country. A new Government was fashioned out of the remains of the last under the retiring Home Secretary, Sr. Martínez Barrio; the President of the Republic duly dissolved the Constituent Cortes; and the General Elections for the first ordinary Cortes of the Republic were fixed for November 19.

CHAPTER IV

TWO YEARS OF THE CENTRE-RIGHT

(*November* 1933 *to January* 1936)

I

GENERAL elections in Spain differ in many ways from those of other European countries and not least in the length of time which must elapse before the announcement of reliable figures. In the remote country districts, communications are not all they might be and the collection of ballot-papers takes, not hours, but days. Even in the large cities, where the count should be quickly over, different newspapers sometimes give different lists of the numbers of votes cast for each candidate, and, as there are numerous parties and their affiliations with Left, Right and Centre are not always easily determined, an estimate of the strength of the parties must be at best an approximate one. Further, second ballots, held a fortnight after the original polling-day, are usually necessary in some constituencies. And finally the first act of the new Cortes is the verification of election certificates, a protracted business which sometimes leads to the annulment of elections and their repetition two or three weeks later still.

All this will explain why, no doubt fortunately, the news of the great electoral landslide of November 1933 was broken to the Spanish people very gently. The first information that came through was the orderliness with which the elections were conducted and the tranquillity of the country. Then came the figures for Madrid, always a strong Socialist centre, which showed that the Left was holding its own, but also that, as no candidate had obtained the necessary percentage of the total, a second ballot would be necessary. But the next news—that of the first two hundred results in the country—gave some indication of the reaction in favour of Conservatism: nearly half these successful candidates belonged to the Right, and the Socialists numbered only twenty.

It was nearly three weeks before the Home Secretary issued the complete returns and the full extent of the landslide became evident. An electoral law passed since the last elections had increased the representation in the Cortes to 473: of these the Right parties had 207; the Centre, 167; and the Left, 99. To put it comparatively, the Right had increased its numbers by 165 and the Centre by 31, while the Left had lost 192. The composition of the three main divisions was of some interest. With the Right deputies had come back no less than 43 who described themselves as 'Traditionalists' or 'Monarchists' and 62 who belonged to the recently formed and very energetic party known as 'Popular Action'. Over 100 of the 167 Centre deputies were Radicals, and of the remainder 25 belonged to the Catalan Lliga. The Left was similarly composed—58 of the 99 were Socialists and 19 were from the Catalan Esquerra; the remaining parties, so strong in the last parliament, had all but disappeared.

At first glance, it would naturally have been thought that the Right would take office, and men began to speculate as to what degree of success they might hope to accomplish. There had been few of them in the Constituent Cortes; the old Conservatives had either left the country or retired from active politics; and the leaders of the three main groups were young and inexperienced. But a little reflection made it clear that, without the close co-operation of the Centre, the Right would be unable to count on a majority; and, while the Right and Centre combined could get their own way without fear of defeat, the Left and Centre combined—and in certain eventualities they might well combine very frequently—would be more than a match for the apparent victors in the elections.

The deciding factor in the political situation was therefore the increase of thirty-one in the representation of the Centre—not a remarkable increase in itself but a sure sign that moderate opinion was gaining ground and a sufficient guarantee that the swing of the pendulum, which it was so imperative, in the interests of peace, to bring to an end, was likely to diminish in force. The most practicable policy, therefore, seemed to be that the Centre, and not the Right, should govern, especially since the Radical leader, Sr. Lerroux, who had the largest single party in the new Cortes, was a subtle and experienced parliamentarian. When this became clear, there was much discontent among extremists, but the general feeling throughout the country was, so far as it could be assessed, one of relief. Energetic as were the reforms of the Left, its rule had been marred by actions and incidents which to the plain man savoured of tyranny. The suspensions of the Press, Casas Viejas and the Law for the Defence of the Republic would not soon be forgotten. Now, however, there would be a chance to remedy the worst excesses of the past two years and there should be little danger of passionate reprisals.

But, if the plain man hoped for so much, he was, as events showed, unduly optimistic. Instead of the clear-cut programme, the determined attempts at progress and the almost daily revolutionary strikes which adorned the calendar of the Socialist biennium, Spain was to have a period of political lethargy, with continually changing governments, hopeless confusion in the Cortes, unrest (though less than before) in the country, and one black page of strife hardly distinguishable from civil war standing between the first of the two years and the second. If the first year may be fairly described as one of pacification and attempts at reconstruction, the second was characterized by partial liquidation of the rebellion and uneasy apprehensions as to the future. If the electors of November 1933 hoped they might get something better than they had had before, the electors of February 1936 felt sure they could get nothing worse. The two years of Left rule were years of high hopes and crushing disappointments, but the two years of Centre rule were years of monotonous depression.

On December 8, almost before the results of the elections were published, the temporary Government found itself confronted with an Anarcho-Syndicalist firework display of uncomfortable dimensions. Barcelona, where a transport strike had been smouldering, sprang into revolt, and machine-guns had to be installed in the principal squares before it was ended. Simultaneously, Anarcho-Syndicalist revolts broke out in several parts of Spain. A general strike crippled Coruña; in Saragossa, Huesca, Barbastro and many other towns in the district attacks were made on the Civil Guard; churches and convents were burned at Calatayud and at Granada; and, perhaps worst of all, the Barcelona-Seville express was deliberately wrecked by revolutionaries and nineteen people perished.

The State of Alarm was proclaimed, as well it might be, and once again the loyalty of the police and the army saved the situation. Within three days, the revolts, save for a few general strikes, were over, and the man in the street turned his attention once more to politics. As many had predicted, Don Alejandro Lerroux took office with a Cabinet of thirteen members, eight of whom were Radicals, the remainder, with one single exception, belonging to the Centre also. In the Right groups there was considerable heart-searching at this, for many saw in the Confederation of Right Parties (popularly known, from the initial letters of its Spanish title, as the Ceda) the strongest party coalition in the country and hoped that its young leader, José María Gil Robles, would undo much that had been accomplished by Sr. Azaña and remain in office until it became practicable to revise the Constitution. Sr. Gil Robles, though only in his middle thirties, and completely without experience of government, had

been a tower of strength to the Catholics in opposition
and great things were hoped for from him if he succeeded
to power. His enemies called him a Fascist—but
'Fascist' on the one hand and 'Marxist' on the other are
current terms of abuse in Spanish politics and cannot
be taken seriously. Sr. Gil Robles had never given cause
to doubt his loyalty to the Republic, which he repeatedly
asseverated, accepting the Republican *régime* as legally
constituted and declaring that within its framework it was
possible to build up a constitution wholly satisfactory to
Catholics. He was what might be termed a *Debate*-
statesman: not many years previously, indeed, he had
actually been on the staff of that newspaper.

His most ardent supporters were unquestionably disappointed when their leader did no more than express
his intention of collaborating loyally with the Centre,
though as soon as the Cortes reassembled he declared
that he was ready to take office immediately if the Radicals
failed to survive. Unfortunately for himself, he talked
rather too freely about 'taking' office; his supporters
cheered him to the echo at each mention of it and no
doubt he continually saw himself as Prime Minister.
But he apparently overlooked the fact that before he
could fill this *rôle* he would need to receive an invitation;
and though, during this biennium, he was more than
once given a portfolio, he was never called upon to form
a Government. The President evidently distrusted him
as a statesman: it was freely said, too, that he disliked him
personally. Whatever the reason, Sr. Gil Robles remained
without office, a fact which greatly increased the unpopularity of Sr. Alcalá Zamora with the Right parties,
who honestly thought that their leader had not been
treated with due consideration.

Over Christmas and the New Year of 1933-4, Spain
was filled with rumours about the new Government's
policy. When the Cortes reassembled, it was seen that
it proposed to lose no time in dealing, to its own satisfaction, with the religious question. The substitution of

lay schools for religious, it was announced, would be indefinitely postponed—and already it was known that Jesuits were teaching openly in the capital. A law was quickly passed granting clergy who had been beneficed in April 1931 no less than two-thirds of their salaries for the current year. Negotiations were opened with the Holy See, and, though full relations could hardly be resumed while the Law of Congregations was still on the statute-book, an arrangement was made by which the Foreign Minister, though retaining his portfolio, went to the Vatican as 'Ambassador Extraordinary'.

These events, quite apart from rumours, showed that the Church was likely to reap benefits without number from the political reaction. Monarchism and Fascism also advanced more boldly than they had done since 1931. A new Monarchist Club in Madrid received a telegram from Alfonso XIII, in which he declared that in the Monarchist youth-groups lay his 'hope for the salvation of our beloved Spain'. Some point was given to the implications of this message by two articles in the Monarchists' newspaper A.B.C., which declared that Don Alfonso's third son, Don Juan (the first two sons having resigned their claims to the succession), was looked upon by many as the hero of the coming Restoration—'a prince who is far removed from discussions and disputes and has played no part in the quarrels of the past'. It must not be supposed, however, that either now, or in the far darker days which followed, there was a general desire for the return of the monarchy. Men were appalled at the thought of the agitation of the pendulum which would inevitably follow a restoration of the Bourbons. 'And the King?' one would query at that time of former anti-republicans pessimistic as to the country's future. 'The King?—No, never that!' would be the reply, in tones almost of horror. Whatever else might happen, it would seem, the continuance of a non-monarchic form of government was certain.

As winter passed, the probable nature of the period of

Centre rule became evident. On the whole, the country seemed quieter, for, though a small number of revolutionary strikes, notably one at Saragossa, dragged misery behind them for weeks and even months on end, the number of partial strikes grew smaller and there were comparatively few of those disconcerting lightning-strikes of twenty-four hours' duration to which Spaniards had grown quite accustomed under Sr. Azaña. When they did break out—there was a particularly effective one in Madrid that April—they were more peaceful than they had been in the past.

But it became equally clear that little of value was likely to be accomplished in parliament. For no reason, an observer would think, other than general instability, lack of a policy and the unwillingness of individuals to collaborate, one Government after another resigned. The Cabinet of the preceding December lasted only till the beginning of March. 'Giving it the benefit of every possible doubt,' remarked Sr. Gil Robles of its successor, 'I doubt if it can survive the month.' His estimate was very nearly correct: it came to an end on the twenty-fifth of April.

The March Government was notable for the inclusion, as Minister of Education, of Don Salvador de Madariaga, one of the outstanding personalities of the time and so far removed from the ordinary type of politician that to many it was a surprise that he should ever accept political office. A bold and penetrating thinker, and a writer completely at home in three languages, he had had a distinguished career, during the Dictatorship, in the League of Nations and as a Professor at Oxford, while the Republic had used him as an Ambassador, first at Washington and later at Paris. Both in Spain and abroad, speculations were rife as to the reforms which might be expected in Spanish education if a man with so keen a mind, and so vast an experience of the educational systems of other countries, were allowed to work his will on it. But alas for speculation! Sr. Madariaga, having for reasons which we can only surmise been effectively removed from Paris, spent exactly six weeks at the Ministry of Education, was dropped from the following Government and never entered another. If one day he should publish his autobiography, these events, and others lying behind them, will no doubt form an interesting chapter.

A fresh crop of strikes in March brought Spain once more into the State of Alarm: Syndicalist and Communist centres, together with a number of Socialist centres, were closed by authority. The most embarrassing of the strikes, that declared by the printers, arose from a dispute with *A.B.C.* over the employment of a single non-union workman. *A.B.C.*, no doubt remembering the months of its suspension, during which it had paid its men their full wages, declined to submit the quarrel to arbitration and for four days there were no newspapers but those run by non-union labour—notably the *Época* and the *Debate*, street-sellers of which were given armed protection by the Government. Together with the printers, came out builders, metallurgical workers, and (in Catalonia and Aragon) gas and electricity employees. Valencia, at the end of March, was in a truly deplorable condition, with no gas or electric light, no water, no theatres open and no newspapers. At Saragossa a general strike continued for nearly two months and the distress was so intense that children were sent in groups to other parts of the country—notably to Madrid and Barcelona. Nowhere, however, was there any general disturbance, and by Holy Week, which for the first time under the Republic was a fair imitation of its former splendid self, Spain had once more become tranquil.

In Catalonia, one event dwarfed all others in importance during this period—the death, on Christmas Day, 1933, of Francesc Macià, first President of the Generalitat and the protagonist in the fight for Catalonian autonomy. *L'Avi*—'Grandpa'—was the affectionate name given him by his own countrymen. He was indeed a Grand Old Man. His tall, slightly stooping figure, his quiet, determined voice and the keen eyes which flashed beneath his bushy eyebrows—all made an immediate impression on those who saw him. I remember paying him a visit only a few months before his death, and remarking that if I were able to paint a picture of him it would be entitled 'Youth in its seventy-fourth year'.

Energy, determination and fearlessness combined with an almost visionary idealism were the marks of Macià's character. Born in 1859, he had spent forty-five years of his life in his native Catalonia before becoming known as a politician at all. Then, as a Colonel in the Engineers stationed in the Catalonian outpost-city of Lérida, he attracted the attention of the leaders of the movement for Catalonian autonomy by his stern treatment of an anti-Catalanist military demonstration which had aroused great indignation in Barcelona. Once in the movement, he soon began to stand out as an advanced Catalanist. When in 1912 Canalejas agreed to sponsor that form of local government already referred to—the Mancomunitat —which duly became law, he refused to acquiesce in the compromise and stood out for complete autonomy, by revolution if necessary.

When the first weeks of Primo de Rivera's rule made it clear that the Catalonians were about to lose every one of the few privileges which had been restored to them, Macià left Barcelona and set up the headquarters of his autonomist organization, *Estat Català*, first in Paris, and later, after the unsuccessful rebellion at Prats-de-Molló, in 1926, at Brussels. With an enthusiastic staff, not inconsiderable funds, and inexhaustible personal energy, he carried on widespread propaganda in favour of the would-be State. On Primo de Rivera's fall, though over seventy, he returned to Barcelona, to pursue his never-changing aim at home. He was immediately expelled, but, in February 1931, was finally re-admitted, and unanimously acclaimed as the only possible leader of the new Esquerra Republicana party, which was about to contest the fateful elections of April 12. From that date to the day of his death, his history is that of Catalonia.

If happiness lies in the fulfilment of noble ideals, Macià died happy. Not only did he accomplish his purpose but the hands which accomplished it were clean. Few men in Spain have been more deeply loved by their intimates, and few have been more genuinely respected, even by their political opponents.

After the death of its leader the political path taken by Catalonia began for a time to diverge from that of the Republic. This, however, was not in the beginning due to the removal of Macià's influence, but to the perfectly understandable fact that Catalonian opinion had not veered towards the Right as had that of the rest of Spain. The municipal elections, postponed elsewhere, were duly held throughout Catalonia, in January, and the Esquerra won them with ease, though by a somewhat reduced majority. As, one after another, the reforms of the Left in Spain were reversed or set aside by the new Government, Left-wing opinion hardened in Catalonia, and when in March the new President of the Generalitat came to Madrid for secret consultations with the Government it was freely suggested, and not officially contradicted, that the main question under discussion was the seriousness of the results to be expected in Catalonia should the Central Government move farther towards the Right.

This new President was a man whom we have already met more than once—En Lluis Companys. In many ways he contrasted with Sr. Macià, who had been some twenty years his senior. An undistinguished-looking little lawyer, markedly *bourgeois* in manner, he had more subtlety and statecraft than his predecessor but infinitely less personality and popular appeal. As leader of the Esquerra, however, he enjoyed the confidence of his party and those who inclined towards it, which is equivalent to saying the great majority of the Catalan people. When, later, he fell, it was only to rise again with increased prestige, and even in his fall some saw the elements of triumph.

The events in Madrid which preceded the demise of the March Government showed that, despite the ostentatious attempts at resurgence made by Monarchism and Fascism, the country was still true to the principles which brought the new *régime* into being. One incident alone sufficed to indicate the national temper. A few days before the celebrations of the third anniversary of the Republic, the Cortes debated a Government Bill re-establishing the death penalty, for crimes involving murder, for a period of one year from the date of the publication of the Act if and when it should become law. The Bill was unpopular in the country, and Sr. Álvarez Valdés, the Minister of Justice, had to defend it in great detail, which he did by enumerating the crimes so continually occurring in the larger towns of Spain and declaring that there was no other way than capital punishment of putting an end to them.

Since the execution of the two officers at Jaca—an act which undoubtedly did more than anything else to exasperate the people with the Monarchy—opinion in Spain had fought shy of capital punishment and no one defending it could expect an increase of popularity. But Sr. Álvarez Valdés went farther. In full Cortes, he actually had the temerity to indulge in an outburst against the Jaca revolt and to speak otherwise than with veneration of the 'Martyrs of the Republic'. The scandal was tremendous! Protests from all over the House, and from all over the country, made only one course possible. Immediately the anniversary celebrations were ended, the Minister of Justice resigned—his portfolio (by an irony which will not be lost upon the future historian of the Second Republic) being given temporarily to Sr. Madariaga.

On the heels of this minor sensation came the dispute over the Amnesty Bill and the brief re-entry into the limelight of Sr. Alcalá Zamora. It was only to be expected that, once the Left was out of power, those who had been sentenced for offences against the Left would be pardoned; amnesties always characterize the pendulum-swing in Spain and life sentences therefore lose a great part of their terrors. The Amnesty Bill brought in by the new Government proposed to pardon political offenders for crimes committed before December 3, 1933, notable among whom, of course, were General Sanjurjo and his fellow-conspirators of the Sevilian insurrection.

The Bill went through the Cortes amid heavy weather. There were numerous incidents between Monarchists and Socialists and even scenes involving displays of physical violence. Eventually the Opposition abstained from voting and the Bill was passed at the end of April by 269 votes to 1. Hardly was the result of the division announced, however, than Madrid was afire with rumours that the President was about to refuse his signature. For days nothing happened and prophecies of new crises were heard on all sides. Eventually the President signed the Bill but at the same time published a statement setting out at length his reasons for disapproving of it. A weaker or more ineffective compromise could hardly have been imagined. True, as with the Law of Congregations, there was little hope that, by sending the Bill back to the Cortes, as the Constitution allowed, the President could have brought about its defeat. But it would at least have been a gesture in favour of the Left had he done so. Now he had incurred the enmity of both Left and Right and incidentally provoked a new change of Government, for it could hardly be supposed that after so marked a rebuff as the President had given him, Sr. Lerroux would remain in office any longer.

When he resigned, there was actually talk, after less than five months, of a new General Election, the impetus in that direction coming chiefly from the Left, who never ceased to agitate for it for nearly two years, until at length they got it. They would probably have gained very little by an election held before a new reaction had set in in their favour, and there was general relief when the crisis ended in a reshuffle. The new Prime Minister, who had previously held the portfolio of Industry and Commerce, was Don Ricardo Samper, and, except for the omission of Sr. Madariaga, the list of his colleagues contained no surprises. Nor did the Government's administration. For a little over five months Sr. Samper marked time in a more or less dignified manner, the principal diversion in the Cortes being the speeches of Sr. Calvo Sotelo. This able young ex-Finance Minister of Primo de Rivera had left Spain on the proclamation of the Republic, and, though elected to the Cortes *in absentia* at each of the General Elections, preferred to remain in exile until the Amnesty Law facilitated his return. Allowed after some discussion to take his seat in the Cortes, he lost no time in launching vigorous attacks on Republican finance and administration. During his long absence, other and less able men had supplanted him in the esteem of the Right's supporters, but, within a few weeks of his return, his trenchant parliamentary style had carried him to the front rank of his group, and during this period he was responsible for several lively sittings. Yet, notwithstanding these, the centre of popular interest shifted from the Cortes to the country, and when, after events to be described in the next chapter, Sr. Samper's Government perished, it was through something very much akin to inanition. And its demise might have taken place even earlier had it not been summer.

II

The summer of 1934 was a period of gathering troubles which came to a tragic head in October.

The least of the troubles, though one highly significant of the growing independence of regionalism, was the conflict between the Government and the Ayuntamientos of the two Basque provinces of Guipúzcoa and Vizcaya. The causes which led up to the August disputes are too complicated to detail fully. But, briefly, the Basque provinces, under what is known as the Concierto Económico, had long enjoyed the right of self-assessment and the payment of a fixed annual sum to the national Treasury in lieu of taxes. Certain new taxes appeared to the Ayuntamientos to jeopardize this privilege, and they therefore conferred together and resolved to elect representatives in each municipality, on the second Sunday in August, who would defend the Concierto. These elections the Government declared to be illegal, and, after vainly suggesting their postponement till the Cortes should re-assemble, it forbade their being held earlier. (1)

Determined to exercise what they maintained to be their rights, the majority of the Ayuntamientos duly elected their committees, under the formal protest of the Civil Governors of the provinces, and, despite (or possibly because of) the presence of police, armed guards and shock troops in great numbers, with no sign of disturbance. The elections held, a large number of the Mayors were arrested, but, except that a few ringleaders were fined or dismissed from their posts, the arrests made were merely formal, bail being accepted and the whole matter allowed to rest pending discussion in the Cortes. All this went on in the full swing of the holiday season and received the greater publicity from the fact that numerous political personalities were holiday-making in this delectable corner of the Peninsula. But, important as the incident was historically, it caused hardly a ripple on the placid surface of life in these provinces, and the alarming terms in which it was referred to abroad surprised none more than those chiefly concerned.

A much more serious embarrassment to the Government was the agrarian trouble of this summer and in particular its repercussions in Catalonia. All over rural Spain, the change of Government had been regarded with apprehension, for if the Agrarian Law was working slowly, it was at least on the statute-book, and its own promoters might be relied upon to apply it much more expeditiously than those who had abstained from voting for it, or, having voted for it, were known to be lukewarm in its favour. This gave greater significance than would otherwise have been the case to a short peasants' strike organized in June over fifteen provinces and to a grave situation which arose in Catalonia immediately afterwards.

Some weeks previously, the Generalitat had passed a new agricultural law, known as the Ley de Cultivos, which was designed to settle a long-standing conflict between *rabassaires*, or cultivators of land, and proprietors. Land is cultivated in Catalonia on the basis of contracts, which give the *rabassaires* tenure of the land for varying periods, up to a maximum of fifty years. In recent times depression had made it impossible for the cultivators to fulfil their contracts and many of them had suffered dispossession. The new law set up arbitration tribunals to decide disputes which had arisen since the establishment of the Republic. Both parties were to be represented on the tribunals, but the terms of settlement, which involved the reinstatement of dispossessed cultivators and their payment to the proprietors of only half pre-Republican rentals, seemed to the proprietors to be unjust and confiscatory, and they made vehement protests against them.

In accordance with the terms of the Statute of Autonomy, the new law was submitted to the Tribunal of Constitutional Guarantees, which on all such matters, under the Constitution, is the final court of appeal. By a small majority the law was thrown out by that body, not because it infringed the Constitution but on the grounds that the Catalonian parliament was not competent to legislate on the question.

This was exactly the kind of situation likely to occur in an initial period of autonomous rule and one which friends of peace and order had dreaded. The issues, of course, at once took on a political character of the highest importance. In Barcelona, though the Right-wing Lliga Catalana on the whole supported the Tribunal, the Esquerra, with its large majority, would not hear of compromise. The President of the Generalitat described the Tribunal's action as an attack, not only upon the autonomy of Catalonia, but upon the basic principles of the Republic. The Esquerra deputies, followed by the Basque nationalists, walked out of the Spanish Cortes. Finally, amid immense popular enthusiasm, Sr. Companys cut the Gordian knot by solemnly and publicly ratifying the law as though the Tribunal had approved it.

All this took place in early June, and for four months the deadlock continued. On the one hand, the Government upheld the Tribunal and debates in the Cortes provided no way out. On the other hand, Catalanists lost no opportunity of attacking, not merely the action of the Tribunal, but the very nature and composition of the Centre Government which had approved it. 'The Statute of Catalonia', ran a widely circulated statement, 'is being systematically undermined as a result of the advent to power of political parties with centralizing ideas.' The outspokenness of this language, however, was nothing to the violence with which Sr. Companys thought fit to abuse the Government. The situation, he declared, was 'brought about by the same mentality as was exemplified in the fallen Bourbon Monarchy' and he openly predicted a conflict in which Catalonia might 'conceivably be vanquished and lose her liberties'. Indeed, his recriminations were accompanied by scarcely veiled threats. At a meeting in Gerona on September 2, for example, he is reported thus:

'This Government, which is charged with the gui-dance of the Hispanic peoples, is no longer loyal to the Constitution. It cannot throw off the cloak of imperialism and the education which it received from the Monarchy. These men are not Liberals; they cannot understand the Federalist idea. If in Madrid they cannot create the Hispanic ideal, we will proceed to create a Catalonian nationality.' (2)

Unless the President of the Generalitat were bluffing, this language could mean only one thing—revolution. But the Cortes replied only by issuing a statement to the effect that surrender must precede any negotiations, while the Generalitat, taking no notice, proceeded to apply the law in detail. At this point, after a particularly noisy debate, in which a Socialist ex-minister created a sensation by brandishing a pistol, the Cortes passed a vote of confidence in the Government, and, leaving it to do what it pleased with Catalonia, rose for the first really long recess since the advent of the Republic.

The Prime Minister made one more gesture—a polite note to the Generalitat, 'requesting it to abstain from applying the law'—and, this naturally failing to produce any result, went off for his summer holiday.

So, for the time being, ended the conflict over the Ley de Cultivos. But meanwhile another and a still more serious danger was arising, and, though difficult at first to locate and define, this began to be spoken of with increasing apprehension. It was natural that, after the persistence with which their Radical opponents had played the game of parliamentary obstruction and their heavy rout at the polls which had followed the appeal to the country, the defeated Left should feel sore at the prospect of a period of government by the Centre or Right. But, seeing that they had made good use of their two years in office, they might have been expected to go into dignified opposition till public opinion should once more favour them. Instead of this, with less excuse than the Radicals a few months earlier—indeed, with no excuse, for the polls alone would have justified the formation of a Government, not of the Centre, but of the Right —they began in their turn to hint, first at abstentionism, then at obstruction, and finally, as the actions of the

Government grew less and less to their liking, at open revolt.

In the main, these parliamentary malcontents were Socialists, and those who upheld them began to look for leadership to two outstanding Socialist politicians, themselves rivals, Don Indalecio Prieto and Don Francisco Largo Caballero. Either, it was believed, would take risks for what they considered to be true Republican principles. ¿La libertad, para qué? the latter had asked publicly a few months earlier. 'What is the use of liberty? Is not the State by definition an absolute power? Certainly we Socialists and true Republicans are not going to be foolish enough to grant liberty if at the first opportunity it undermines the foundations of government.'

Such language suggests a Red Dictatorship, and there were undoubtedly at this time many leading Socialists to whom such a dictatorship would have been welcome. But they were not alone in deploring the new political situation. Various other of the Left-wing parties joined in the outcry; and this was supported by no less a personality than Sr. Azaña, who, on the temporary defeat of his coalition, first assumed the rôle of a disgruntled Achilles, and then, in numerous speeches since collected in the second volume of a work entitled *In Power and in Opposition*, came out into the open in the more dangerous character of a revolutionary.

He despaired, it seems, of Spain. The Esquerra Government of Catalonia, he declared, was now 'the only Republican power' in the entire country and the only 'bulwark' against the return of tyranny. He could not himself serve 'a Republic imbued with Monarchism, made to the measure of servants of the King, or rather of renegades from his service.' 'We do not want', he added, 'a Republic such as that.'(3)

Lesser men, who had been associated with him on platform and in parliament, took up his cry. 'This', for example, exclaimed a prominent deputy, Sr. Sánchez

Román, 'is a mutilated Republic. In no sense is it an authentic Republic. True Republicans are being persecuted by a Government with which they can have no solidarity.'(4) That was the attitude taken by the disappointed Left as a whole and they held it to justify passive revolt and even armed rebellion. It is hard to see how, on such principles, the democratic government for which they professed to stand would ever be possible.

By September the outlook had become still graver. In the Basque provinces of Guipúzcoa and Vizcaya, as a protest against their treatment, the whole of the Ayuntamientos resigned. All over the Basque Country demonstrations were held demanding full autonomy, and a deputation sent to the newly elected inter-municipal committee by the Catalonian Esquerra showed that the two non-Castilian-speaking regions were prepared to combine. Almost simultaneously a mass meeting of Catalonian landowners, who were opposed to the Ley de Cultivos, was held in Madrid: the Socialists, Syndicalists and Communists protested against the meeting by means of a general strike, which would have been repeated in Barcelona but for an appeal by the Generalitat against it.

In Catalonia, in the Basque Country, in Madrid and in many other parts of Spain, inflammatory speeches became more frequent and opinion was genuinely alarmed when it was announced that a consignment of over seventy cases of arms had recently been landed in Asturias. Was this in any way connected with the rumours of a Socialist rebellion, or were the arms merely Government property which had gone astray? The actions of the Prime Minister increased the general fears. First, he announced that discoveries of concealed munitions had been made on a very considerable scale, that arrests had been effected and that searches for illegally concealed arms were being made in numerous suspected quarters. Then a decree was signed establishing the State of Alarm throughout Spain. Municipal elections, eighteen months overdue, were to have been held in the autumn, but the plans for these were now cancelled. Everything seemed to be conspiring against social tranquillity and even persons usually optimistic were fearful.

Politically, things were even worse. A crisis in the Cortes was imminent. For months, in the loudest tones, Sr. Gil Robles had been publicly declaring that the time was now approaching when he would govern. On a snowy day in April, fifty thousand members of the youth-groups of Popular Action had braved the elements and flocked to a congress at El Escorial, to hear their leader indulge in oratory which, as they thought of it later, they might have considered unduly confident, if not boastful, but which at the time seemed the most natural thing in the world:

> 'Power will infallibly come to us—and I tell you this with the fullest sense of responsibility. But it will come when we will it—when it suits the interests of Spain and of our party. Then indeed we will govern and none shall prevent our determining the direction of Spanish politics in the future. . . . We will come into office soon, for the political parties are crumbling, their organizations are splitting from top to bottom, and the moment will arrive when not only the Right groups, but the great neutral masses all over Spain will turn to us as to their only hope for the future. That will be the moment when we shall say: "Now is the time!" The time to work, not for our own good but for the good of our Spain and of all Spaniards.'(5)

September came and still Gil Robles' moment had not arrived. But it would seem that it was drawing nearer. The youth-groups held another congress—this time in Asturias, at the spot venerated by all traditionalists as the cradle of the Spanish nation: Covadonga. And again the Leader made one of his confident speeches, condemning in good round periods the 'rebellion' of the Basque provinces and the encouragement given to it by

Catalonia, which, 'not content with maintaining re-
belliousness in its own territory, exploits the candour of
those whose horizons are limited by insignificant
aspirations to nationalism'. Up to the present, Popular
Action had exercised notable restraint, but things were
now in so serious a condition as to be tolerable no
longer.

'The way is clear before us. Not one moment
more! For ourselves we want nothing, but we will
no longer suffer this state of things to continue.'(6)

These words, if they meant anything, could only mean
that the Leader would rally his followers in the Cortes
to defeat the Centre Government and would then
assume office as Prime Minister. So, at least, they were
interpreted by the proletariat of Asturias, and the next
day saw Asturias in the grip of a general strike, with the
result that the delegates found it harder and more uncomfortable to travel home from the cradle of the
Spanish nation than it had been to make the excursion
thither. A fortnight later Sr. Gil Robles struck his blow,
and the world was informed that on the reassembly of
the Cortes the Ceda would withdraw its support from
the Government—and, as everybody knew, this would
drive the Radicals from office.

III

Whether it was the opposition of the Ceda that killed
Sr. Samper's Government or its own pusillanimity is a
matter of opinion. There are those who maintain that
its collapse would in any case have been brought about
by its masterly inactivity.

The scene in the Cortes on October 1 was a curious
one. After Sr. Samper had reviewed the events of the
vacation, the Leader of the Ceda rose somewhat pontifi-
cally and condemned the successive Governments of the
past eleven months as having failed to interpret the will

of the majority of the people. 'We have lent them our support,' he declared, 'but we feel that we can do so no longer. We are ready to fulfil our duty.'(7)

He sat down. The Prime Minister, hardly knowing perhaps what to do next, asked for the opinions of the party leaders. None of them obliged. There was an embarrassing silence. Then, slowly, the one 'Agrarian' member of the Government, Sr. Cid, rose from his seat, not to speak, but to walk out of the Chamber. It was an acknowledgment of defeat—a signal that the Government would resign without a struggle. The sitting was adjourned, and, a few minutes later, the announcement was made that the inevitable had happened.

Three days later, after the usual crop of rumours and the almost hourly reports of new Presidential consultations, the composition of the next Government was made public. To the single-minded followers of Sr. Gil Robles it came as a bombshell. Their Leader had not 'taken', 'assumed' or 'stepped into' office, as he had so confidently forecast. He was not the head of the new Government. He was not even a member of the new Government. He had (so they said in public), with his well-known modesty and complete freedom from self-seeking, remained in the background: he would, for the time being, fill the *rôle* of unseen power behind the *banco azul*. But what they thought, and said in private, was that the unspeakable President of the Republic had inexplicably passed him over and so added one more crime to those of which they had already found him guilty.

The new Prime Minister, commissioned to 'form a Government (to use the fine Presidential phrase) within the limits of Republican cordiality', was none other than the ubiquitous Don Alejandro Lerroux. His team still showed a small majority for his own party. Eight of the fifteen ministers (including Sr. Samper, who took the portfolio of Foreign Affairs) were Radicals; two were Agrarians; one was an Independent; one a Liberal Democrat; and three were members of the Ceda.

To help counterbalance the inclusion of the Cedistas—which constituted, of course, the novel feature of this large Cabinet—two ministers without portfolio were appointed. But if the list brought disillusionment to the Right, it caused a dismay and an exasperation among the Left such as must have amazed the 'great neutral masses' by its vehemence. After all, said the latter, there were 207 deputies of the Right in the Cortes against 99 of the Left and it was surely reasonable enough that the majority group should be given some small place in the Government. The Left would have been the first to complain if they themselves, as the majority group, had been excluded from office. Why, then, being democrats in principle, and having been rejected by the electors, should they breathe fire and slaughter, and claim that what they had been unable to win by fair means must be taken by means which the man in the street calls foul? If one could judge by what one heard, reaction was already beginning to set in against Centre government and a few months of Centre-Right would probably set the pendulum swinging in their favour again. They had but to wait patiently and they would infallibly come back with a larger majority than ever.

But considerations of this kind had no effect upon politicians who were determined to have their own way, and have it quickly. Their first blow fell upon the unlucky but well-meaning President, who, having incensed the Right, found that he had now made implacable enemies of the Left also. Don Miguel Maura, the Republic's first Home Secretary, drew up and circulated a document denouncing him as a traitor. Sr. Albornoz protested by resigning his presidency of the Tribunal of Guarantees. Quite a number of Sr. Alcalá Zamora's former colleagues censured him vigorously and publicly, going so far even as to announce that they would have nothing more to do with him.

The remaining blows fell upon Spain. On the morning of October 5, a nearly complete general strike was declared throughout the country. It reached its height in Asturias, where martial law had to be proclaimed and the police and Civil Guard were reinforced by the Army. From Coruña to Valencia, from San Sebastián to Málaga, it was effective in all the great cities. In Madrid, a few trains, trams and omnibuses were run by the military, but there were no other communications of any kind, no letters, and, except for the non-union *Debate* and *A.B.C.*, no newspapers. Censorship was imposed upon news telegrams, and citizens were strongly advised not to go out between 8 p.m. and sunrise—a self-denying ordinance, indeed, for Spaniards. For the moment, however, there was no violence, and few would have thought that within twenty-four hours two of the most populous districts of Spain would be in the grip of the most violent revolution.

Upon Barcelona, where the general strike had been accompanied by complete tranquillity, revolution came without warning. On the evening of October 5, Sr. Companys had broadcast an appeal for calm, declaring that the Generalitat would defend 'the freedom of Catalonia and the democratic essence of the Republic'. What this meant became clear on October 6, when, after a day of growing rumour, the President of the Generalitat appeared on the balcony of the Palace, as his predecessor had done three and a half years earlier, proclaimed the Catalan State as part of the 'Federal Spanish Republic' and invited the 'anti-Fascist' leaders in Spain to establish the Provisional Government of a new *régime* in Barcelona. (8)

'Catalonians!' he cried to the crowds that thronged the Square of St. James below him:

'Catalonians!
'The monarchizing and Fascist forces which for some time have been attempting to betray the Republic have attained their object and have captured power. . . .
'Recent events have given all citizens the clear

impression that the Republic, as to its fundamental democratic principles, is in the gravest peril.

'All the authentically Republican forces in Spain, and the advanced social sectors, without distinction or exception, have risen in arms against this audacious move of the Fascists.

'Catalonia—liberal, democratic and republican as she is—cannot stand aside from this protest, triumphant throughout the land, nor can she keep silence or fail to proclaim her solidarity with those who, like herself, are fighting in the Hispanic countries, even to death, for liberty and right. Catalonia raises high her banner and summons all to fulfil their duty and to render absolute obedience to the Government of the Generalitat, which severs all relations with these adulterated institutions from this moment.

'In this solemn hour, in the name of people and parliament, the Government over which I preside assumes all the functions of power in Catalonia, proclaims the Catalan State of the Federal Spanish Republic, and, re-establishing and strengthening its relations with those who direct this general protest against Fascism, invites them to establish the Provisional Government of the Republic in Catalonia. . . .

'Catalonians! The hour is grave and glorious. The spirit of President Macià, restorer of the Generalitat, is with us. Each man to his place and Catalonia and the Republic be in the hearts of all.

'Long live the Republic and long live Liberty!' (9)

What did these words, which it is no mere form to describe as sincere and eloquent, tell the listening crowds below the Palace? Certainly they depicted a state of affairs very different from that actually obtaining. One would have supposed, on hearing them, that a new Primo de Rivera had proclaimed a Fascist dictatorship in Spain, that the whole country had risen in arms against him and that everywhere the enemy was being repulsed by

Republicans loyal to the 1931 Constitution. What had actually happened was that in a reconstructed Republican Government had been included three members of the group most strongly represented in the Cortes constitutionally returned at the last General Election. The Ceda was in fact neither a Monarchist nor a monarchizing organization; still less was it Fascist. In no sense had the 'protest' been 'triumphant throughout the land', unless the maintenance of a twenty-four-hour strike could be described as triumph, in which case the 'authentic Republicans' of the Socialist biennium had been triumphed over pretty frequently. All this, though it became clear enough within a day or so, might not have occurred to an uncritical crowd strongly influenced and deeply moved by an oratorical appeal to their patriotism. But even they must have seen that, since the 1931 Constitution expressly discards Federalism, those guilty of disloyalty to the Constitution were those who not only advocated the Federalist idea in their speeches but endeavoured to enforce their advocacy by inciting others to take up arms for it.

So much needs to be said here, but it is also right to say with equal emphasis that the aim of the Barcelona rebellion was not, as has frequently been alleged, any form of separatism. Precisely what moved Sr. Companys to this insensate act of rebellion we may never know: at the time, some of his own friends asserted that extremists had threatened to shoot him if he resisted this course, to which they impelled him. However that may be, there is no reasonable doubt that he believed himself to be saving the Republican principle in Spain. Certainly he never had the idea of creating an independent Republic in Catalonia. The poet and Councillor for Education in the Generalitat, Sr. Gassol, who followed him in addressing the people, made this perfectly clear. 'This movement,' he called it, 'in defence of the Republic of the 14th of April'—not, it will be observed, 'the Republic of the 6th of October'.

The speeches made, there followed action. In 1931, there had been some hours of hesitation on the part of the Army and men had waited anxiously to hear whether it would support the new *régime* or force civil war. This time, said the revolutionaries, there must be no delay about capturing the Army; and, as the high commands were now held by Catalonians, they probably anticipated little opposition. Sr. Companys sent for General Batet, who, in proclaiming martial law, had expressed the hope 'as a Catalonian, a Spaniard and a man' that there would be no fighting, and called on him to transfer his allegiance to the new Federal *régime*.

It was now nearly nine o'clock in the evening and the City Council was about to meet to pass a resolution of adherence to Sr. Companys. General Batet demanded time to think the matter over. He went away and returned at half-past ten, with the simple, but pregnant, decision: 'I am for Spain.'

Already his troops were in possession of the great central Plaça de Catalunya. Sr. Companys, called upon to surrender, refused, and, before midnight, fighting had begun. Except in so far as was necessary for defence or the restoration of order, the attack was limited to the Generalitat Palace, which had been fortified with machine-guns and rifles and was bombarded by trench mortars and aeroplanes. There could be only one end to a combat with rebels who had so little support from the people. Soon after 6 a.m. on October 7, Sr. Companys and the remainder of the Councillors (except Sr. Dencás, who with a companion had contrived to escape—it is said by a sewer) surrendered unconditionally to General Batet, and, with the Mayor of Barcelona, were taken to a Government boat which was at anchor in the harbour, and imprisoned there.

So, in twelve hours, ended Sr. Companys' ill-fated attempt to lead a revolution. It is true that for forty-eight hours various attempts were made by the rebels to rally, that both sniping and machine-gun fire were heard intermittently in Barcelona and that the *rabassaires* made sporadic trouble in the country. But in its essentials the revolt collapsed upon Sr. Companys' surrender and there was no serious apprehension as to its recrudescence.

One important fact remains to be chronicled: Sr. Azaña found himself, at the time, in Barcelona. Was this the effect of chance or of design? Most people thought at the time, and many believe still, that he had been designated by the rebels as President of the Federal Republic, and the fact that he was arrested and held for trial increased that suspicion, though some afterwards discredited it. But there is no doubt that his presidency would have given such a Republic its best chance of success, especially in Catalonia, where he has always been a hero. To the Catalonians of the sixth of October, he was not the promoter of the hated Law for the Defence of the Republic, the enemy of the religious Orders, the chief agent in the deportations to Africa or the sinister figure behind the slaughters of Casas Viejas. He was a 'pure Republican' and friend of Catalonia. He had been a signatory to the Pact of San Sebastián in 1930. In 1931 he had helped to smooth the path between Barcelona and Madrid. In 1932, as Prime Minister of Spain, he had championed the Statute of Autonomy through its four months' struggle in the Cortes. Can it be wondered that, when he was so heavily defeated at the polls, the Catalonians, always a chivalrous people, should have remained faithful to him? When in power, he had dominated the Cortes, and they had looked at him with admiration; now, impotent in Madrid, he was even more necessary to them, and (as I can testify from personal knowledge) those who in 1931 had spoken with misgivings of the possibilities of a Red dictatorship were in the spring of 1934 contemplating an Azaña dictatorship with complacency, if not with eagerness.

The rebellion in Asturias—or, more exactly, the short

period of civil war—was more stubborn and disastrous than the rebellion in Barcelona, and is harder to describe, since the Press censorship was strict and the accounts of the fighting that appeared are diverse and sometimes contradictory. Of no event that had yet occurred during the life of the Republic were related stories more terrible, and more incredible, on both sides, of cold-blooded torture and murder, mutilation, wanton destruction, rape and arson, horrible enough to make one believe that, if they were true, Spain had returned to barbarism. That any large proportion of the total number was true seems unlikely: one had them, never from eye-witnesses, but always from those who had themselves had them from eye-witnesses. But that they were all false, or even all exaggerated, is equally improbable, and this for several reasons. In the first place, some of them were confirmed, in writing, by several independent witnesses, or by individuals who, though admittedly partisans, would hardly be disbelieved on matters of pure fact. Secondly, a large number of cases of alleged cruelty on the part of the Civil Guard and other forces of the law were set out in two documents presented to the Prime Minister, each by a prominent Left-wing politician (Sr. Gordón Ordás and Sr. Álvarez del Vayo), with names, dates and signatures of attesting witnesses. Thirdly, the outrages reported on both sides from Asturias are, though on a much larger scale, strikingly similar to those related in connexion with Castilblanco and Casas Viejas, all of which were proved, by independent investigation, beyond the possibility of doubt. There is, of course, not a shadow of justification either for atrocities committed by the rebels or for brutality on the part of those who suppressed them, and one cannot but regret the partisan uses to which both have been put. Still more, however, must one regret that they could ever have happened.

Although the details of the Asturian rebellion may be difficult to isolate, its main course is fairly clear. On the very day of the general strike shooting and explosions began without warning in Oviedo, and the massing of rebels in the hills and mines of Asturias determined the Government to concentrate the strongest possible reinforcements. But they were not in time to prevent a determined onslaught on Oviedo. Here the loyal troops were hampered by the one element which was lacking to the revolution in Barcelona—popular support. Again and again, as for example when they marched to the rescue of the headquarters of the Civil Governor, which was attacked by the rebels, they found themselves fired on by snipers from private houses, so that all they could do was to retire to barracks, whence parties went out to take up strategic positions in the city. By October 7 it was calculated that the rebels numbered about six thousand—all fully armed and provided with tanks, machine-guns, armoured cars and large quantities of dynamite.

For the next three days Oviedo was the scene of continual fighting. As soon as the troops were forced from hotels, shops or banks, the rebels attempted to set these on fire, and in addition they attacked or burned numerous other buildings—notably the Asturian Bank, the Instituto (or Government High School), the University and the Cathedral. The almost complete destruction of the University and the wrecking of the famous Cámara Santa in the Cathedral were two of the most disastrous acts of violence that the Republic had yet witnessed.

During these days of battle in Oviedo, General López Ochoa, who was in command of the loyal troops in Asturias, was fighting a fierce engagement, with less than four hundred men, near the little town of Avilés, some fifteen miles to the north-west. As soon as the rebels were routed here, he hastened to reinforce his men in Oviedo, but the destruction of bridges and the blocking of the road with trees greatly delayed his progress. He found his regiment very short of provisions, and totally without water. The arrival of reinforcements, however, raised its morale and by the 13th the city was taken.

The loss and havoc wrought by the week's fighting can be imagined. Months later, the Government published official figures, which showed a total of 1,335 killed, of whom 1,051 were civilians, 100 officers and men of the Civil Guard, 98 soldiers and 86 police and excise officers. The wounded numbered 2,951, rather more than two-thirds of whom were civilians. The buildings destroyed or damaged by fire totalled 730. The arms and ammunition captured included 89,000 rifles, 33,000 pistols and 350,000 cartridges.

The testimony of observers makes even more painful reading. 'Oviedo', wrote a correspondent to *A.B.C.*, 'gives the impression of a ruined city in the Great War'; and the *Sol*, always moderate in its statements, describes the scene in a passage of which a few lines may be quoted:

> In the whole city can be seen traces of the fury which has engulfed it. The Calle de Uria, Oviedo's principal street, an aristocratic thoroughfare both architecturally and from the size and quality of its shops, presents the depressing perspective of an interminable row of houses totally destroyed. . . . Cafés, offices, shops—nothing is left of any of them. . . . The principal streets, in which were situated the Audiencia, the Instituto, the Gobierno Civil, the University, the Hotel Covadonga: all are destroyed. . . . Some streets will have to be rebuilt in their entirety. . . . From the Plaza de la Escandalera and the Campo de San Francisco alone the Red Cross recovered 475 dead bodies. . . . There has been war in Spain and the city devastated by it has been Oviedo.(10)

The complete liquidation of the Asturian rebellion was estimated to last not months but years. As far as the destruction of property was concerned, subscription lists were opened and grants made with all possible dispatch. But it is easier to destroy than to build; the cost of rebuilding the University alone was given as over a million pesetas, and the ruined city became an object of European compassion. The questions of responsibilities and penalties were even graver, for not only were different views taken at the time by those in authority, but after the 1936 elections other policies than those of the Centre-Right prevailed, and much that they had done was then undone, with consequences even more disastrous than any which unhappy Spain had yet suffered.

The net result of the rebellion, which was commonly described as having been organized by the Socialist party and as having cost it something like a million pounds sterling, was to defeat the very purpose for which it had been planned. On the one hand, the leaders of the Left, notably Sr. Azaña and Sr. Largo Caballero, found themselves in prison, many municipal councillors belonging to the Left, and even entire councils, were dismissed from office, the Madrid Ateneo was closed, and the Left newspapers in Barcelona (not, however, in Madrid, which remained perfectly quiet) were suspended. On the other hand, not only did the Government remain exactly as it had been constituted, but the stock of all the Right parties went up by leaps and bounds. Both the Fascist party, under Primo de Rivera's son, the young Marqués de Estella, and the Monarchist party, known as Renovación Española, offered their services unconditionally to the Government for the prevention or suppression of any further outbreaks.

For weeks, Ministers went to and from Oviedo and Barcelona to investigate conditions there, while the rounding-up of arms proceeded throughout the remotest districts of rural Asturias. At Barcelona, as minor arrests were made, the prison-ship in the harbour became more and more populous, and the bloated haul soon included suspected municipal officials, men of letters, university professors and even the Rector of Barcelona University.

The transference of powers to autonomous Catalonia, which had been proceeding very slowly, was of course brought to an end; its local administration was again centralized under Madrid; and peace-loving Catalonians, who had been intensely loyal to the Republic through thick and thin, found to their mortification that the rashness of the leaders whom they had trusted was for the time being costing them their liberties.

For two months the whole of Spain remained under martial law, and, even at the end of that period, the State of Alarm was substituted for it very gradually, in a province or two at a time. In actual fact, the restrictions of martial law were considerably relaxed and tourists might often have traversed the entire country without realizing the abnormality of its condition. The measures taken were precautionary: it would never have done to have risked another outbreak like that of October. But, as a matter of fact, the winter months of 1934-5 were about the most peaceful in the history of the Republic. The forces of unrest were exhausted; strikes came almost to an end; and the Government began to talk once more of holding its long-postponed municipal elections.

But if there was a minimum of revolutionary violence, there were frequent and fierce conflicts of opinion, the first of which raged around the future of Catalonia. After the rebellion, the Central Government very naturally took control of the essential services of the region, such as policing, taxation and the administration of justice. The opponents of Catalonian autonomy, who had fought so determinedly against the Statute two years earlier, were now strongly represented in the Cortes and had every intention of pressing home their advantage. The Monarchists demanded that the Statute should be annulled entirely: such rebellions, they said, as had just been witnessed would occur again and again till the Catalonian extremists achieved complete separation. The defenders of the Statute, who included the Radicals, listened with respect and approval to a notable speech by Sr. Cambó, the leader of the Conservative Lliga Catalana, who under the Monarchy had been a protagonist in the cause of autonomy, had lost credit and been obliged to leave Spain at the advent of the Republic, but had returned recently to political life and with the eclipse of the Esquerra now took his natural position in the Cortes. He argued, with perfect justice, that it was not Catalonia as a whole, but the Esquerra, that had brought the Statute to grief, and that the Lliga could be trusted to administer it loyally. There had been nothing but enmity, he said, between the Esquerra and the Lliga. 'For three years they have humiliated and insulted us. When the papers of Sr. Dencás were examined by the police, a list was found among them of twenty-eight people who were to be shot if the rebellion was successful. I was one of them.'

This presentation of the case made a great impression, and in a few days' time the Ceda deputies, resisting the attempts of the Monarchists to capture their votes for the annulment of the Statute, came to an agreement with the Radicals along lines which eventually prevailed. The Statute was not to be revised but would remain in suspense until the Cortes should determine to begin its gradual restoration. A Governor-General would be appointed to assume the functions of the President of the Generalitat during the transitional period, and, after this was over, the Government would still have the right to appoint a delegate to represent it. The compromise was unfortunately not acceptable to the Lliga, but, considering the shock which Sr. Companys' attempted *coup* had given to public opinion, it was probably as favourable a solution to the problem as they could have expected.

Towards the end of the year there were a number of resignations from the Government, and the Christmas recess saw its reconstitution, with much the same party representation as before. The changes, however, did nothing to dispose of rumours that the Cedistas and the Agrarians were clamouring for more portfolios and that members of the Government were sharply divided on the question of the death-penalties awarded by the military tribunals to the ringleaders of the Asturian rebellion.

The charges against Sr. Azaña had fallen to the ground, and, though he was to be re-arrested later, he had been set at liberty. But several well-known people were among those condemned by the tribunals, and rumour, stimulated by discontent, was busily disseminating stories about the way they had been treated in captivity. One of them, D. Teodomiro Menéndez, a Socialist deputy, had made an unsuccessful attempt to commit suicide while in prison, a fact out of which the Socialist party made excellent capital. The crux of the situation, however, lay in the number of death-sentences which had been awarded by the military tribunals and the attitude to be adopted by the Government. At first, there were only two or three such condemnations, but the number had slowly mounted until at the end of March, excluding eight which had been commuted two months earlier and two which had been carried out, the total stood at twenty.

What would the Government decide upon—reprieve or execution? Obviously, since opinion was as sharply divided in the country as in the Cortes, whichever decision it took would be wrong in the eyes of a large section of the community, and the question resolved itself chiefly into one of expediency. The 'martyrs' of 1930 must have appeared in the dreams of Cabinet ministers as spectres warning them against repeating the errors of the Monarchy. Yet, on the other hand, might not revolution be expected to break out with impunity if its proved ringleaders were let off with sentences certain to be reversed as soon as the Left again came into power?

A decision had sooner or later to be taken and its result was the fall of the Government. The Radicals favoured commutation of the sentences; the Cedista, Agrarian, and Liberal Democrat ministers voted for execution. As no agreement could be reached, the majority decision, for commutation, was announced, and the minority ministers immediately handed in their resignations.

The reconstruction or resignation of a Government in Spain is always termed a 'crisis', but the situation which now arose was a crisis in fact as well as in name. The Right still pressed for increased representation: Sr. Gil Robles, in fact, demanded a minimum of six portfolios for his party alone. But, from the point of view of the Radicals, there was vastly more reason for resisting these demands than before. The President of the Republic talked amiably about forming a 'Government of concentration and concord', but nobody could be found who was capable of such a feat, and, after nearly a week's uncertainty, the strangest solution was reached —Sr. Lerroux formed a minority Cabinet of thirteen members of his own party, of whom no less than eight were without seats in the Cortes.

Clearly such a Government had little hope of survival, and all the parties began to talk about a new General Election. Fortunately, perhaps, public attention was diverted from politics by the anniversary celebrations of April 14, which were marked by the decoration of the two generals who had quelled the October risings and by the raising of martial law in the parts of Spain where it was still in force. For days after the celebrations were over, the Press had nothing to report but conferences between party leaders. Then, exactly one month after its formation, came the long-expected news of the minority Government's resignation. It had certainly been a farcical experiment, and Sr. Samper must have felt that his own inglorious performance in the Cortes had been surpassed by his former leader. For this Government had died almost at birth: not only had it not waited to be defeated, as it must have been, on its very first division; it had not even stayed in office long enough to meet the Cortes at all.

IV

The supporters of the Ceda, which since the October risings had been growing enormously in numbers and prestige, now believed that they had their opportunity. The 'great neutral masses', they argued, were certainly in their favour, keenly resenting the bloodshed and destruction caused by the extremist rebels, and recognizing in the Ceda the surest guarantor of future peace. The Radical leader, they considered, had made himself a laughing-stock with his thirty-day Government which had run down like a worn-out clock that no one thinks worth winding up again. The President of the Republic could hardly fail to call upon Sr. Gil Robles now: the only alternative would be an immediate general election.

So the slogan went round: 'Gil Robles or Elections!', which meant, said the Cedistas, 'Gil Robles or Chaos!' But again the unexpected happened, for the crisis was resolved in twenty-four hours, and the solution was neither Gil Robles nor a general election, but yet another Centre-Right coalition under the imperturbable 'Don Ale.'

The only crumb of consolation which the Cedistas could gather from their disappointment was that their leader was in the new Cabinet as Minister of War and four of his followers were with him. The carefully mixed team, indeed, included only three Radicals, and the remaining ingredients, besides the five Cedistas, were two Agrarians, two Independents and a Liberal Democrat. The Prime Minister, with unconscious humour, described it as a non-party Government bent only upon constructive policy. The country learned, however, with some uneasiness, that the chief item in the constructive policy, apart from the presentation of a Budget, which had been postponed for so long that nobody quite believed in it, was the reform of the 1931 Constitution. Even many who disliked that Constitution were concerned to find that it was to be added to the already numerous subjects of controversy which events and a rapid succession of Governments had bandied about like a tennis-ball. Any attempt to make vital amendments to it, they argued, will certainly last so long, and cause so many crises, that, before it can be completed, political reaction will once more have set in and the Left will be returning to power, undoing all that has been done, and perhaps trying its own hand at emendations of precisely the contrary kind to those now proposed. The prospect was certainly not an inviting one.

Other matters, however, claimed the attention of Cabinet and country before these could become practical politics. The first was Catalonia. A decree signed in April had restored to her a strictly limited autonomy, together with many of the public services taken from her, the chief service still entirely dependent upon the Central Government being public order. A month later, the new councillors of the re-formed Generalitat— a coalition of Lliga, Ceda and Radicals—took office. Now came the trial, before the Tribunal of Guarantees, of Sr. Companys and his six fellow-conspirators, each of whom, by a majority vote of 14 to 7, was condemned to thirty years' imprisonment, the death penalty not being even considered. Sr. Companys made an excellent and convincing speech in his own defence, denying that any pact whatever had existed between Catalonians, Basques and Galicians, or that Sr. Azaña had been thought of for the presidency of the Federal Republic, and taking upon himself, in the most chivalrous manner possible, the fullest responsibility.

Two minority reports considerably mitigated the effect of the judgment, especially one signed by five dissentients who argued that, since all that the accused had desired was the substitution of federal for unitary

government, they could hardly be said to have con-
spired against the *régime* at all. But, plausible as it was,
the argument did not save them; by the end of June
they were immured in convict prisons—three at Puerto
de Santa María, near Cádiz, and the remainder at Cartagena.

On the heels of the trial of the Catalonian conspirators
came the second trial of Sr. Azaña, who, as long ago as
February, had been accused, together with his former
colleague, Sr. Casares Quiroga, in a document emanating
from the Right, of encouraging Portuguese revolutionaries, and in various ways conspiring against the Republic.
The next month, the Cortes held a two-day debate on
the charges, which, in a House of hardly more than half
its full strength, resulted in an adverse vote of 194 to 49.
Sr. Azaña himself rebutted the accusations in a speech
of nearly four hours, referring with deep feeling to the
campaign which had been going on against him—'seven
months,' as he called it with pardonable exaggeration,
'of a campaign of personal persecution unprecedented
in history'.(11) A committee appointed by the Cortes
to consider the charges further reported them after
three months' interval, by nine votes to five, as proven,
but the Cortes, to which they were then sent back for
ratification by an absolute majority, gave them only
189 votes against 68 and they therefore fell to the ground.
This single-session debate, full of personalities and
of incidents described by the Press as 'noisy and picturesque', marked the lowest point reached by Sr.
Azaña's credit and popularity. From this day onward,
by one of those extraordinary barometrical reactions so
difficult to forecast or explain, they rose continuously,
until, without a shadow of doubt, they were higher
than those of any public man had been in Spain since
the advent of the Republic.

Two subjects, Constitution reform and public economy,
occupied public interest until the end of July, when the
Cortes rose for a two months' vacation. The first has

a good deal of interest, for though events impeded its materialization, it gives some indication of what the Centre-Right would have done had it remained longer in power. The 1931 Constitution had been drawn up by a House strongly under the influence of anti-traditionalist feeling and what the Cabinet neatly described as 'speculative fervour'. As, therefore, it provides for its own revision, after four years from its promulgation (i.e. after December 8, 1935), by no more than an absolute majority of the Cortes, there was little doubt that revision would be attempted. As long previously as January 1935, President Alcalá Zamora, whose legal mind did its best to maintain an attitude of objectivity, had made an elaborate report to his Ministers upon the working of the Constitution during the three years of his experience of it. Seeing that at least three-quarters of the deputies in the Cortes must have been in favour of revision, there seemed little doubt that the President's report had this in view and that revision would duly take place during the following winter.

At midsummer the Cabinet published a document summarizing its own proposals. These included the modification of the articles on regional autonomy; the suppression of the Socialistic article authorizing expropriations of private property, 'which has proved a menace and a cause of instability . . . without bringing any compensating benefit'; the re-definition of the functions of the State as instructor and inspector of instruction; and the restoration of the Senate, the unicameral system being generally allowed to have been unsuccessful. Deputies in the parliaments of autonomous regions would be prevented from sitting in the Cortes of the Republic. The Tribunal of Constitutional Guarantees was marked down for reform; it had been felt to be too political in character, and its members, even its Presidents, had been chosen according to their party affiliations, rather than for their legal capabilities and personal prestige. Important changes were proposed affecting the powers of the President, amnesties for political offences and the dissolution of the Cortes. Some modification of the articles on the religious question was foreshadowed, without, however, any suggestion of a departure being made from the original conception of the lay State. The article on marriage and divorce was described as altogether too radical and as having exercised an unsatisfactory influence on family life. These extracts from the Government's proposals will make it clear that, had the political situation not changed, Spain would have been in for a period of long and possibly stormy discussion and much would have depended upon the character of the new Constituent Cortes.

The second subject which the Government gave the country to think about during the summer was its energetic programme of public economy. For years the presentation of a Budget had been a subject of frequent discussion in the Cortes but nothing had been done beyond talking about it. Successive Finance Ministers, one of whom, Sr. Marraco, was a prominent banker, had urged the immediate presentation of a Budget, but they were overborne by the inactivity of their colleagues or by the pleas of ex-Finance Ministers that such a course would be impossible.

But the Government now in office included a new Finance Minister, Sr. Chapaprieta, a man labelled 'Independent', who determined that efforts should be made to effect immediate economies, that a Budget should be presented in October 1935 and that, though this must of necessity show a large deficit, the Budget for 1936–7 should be balanced. There had been no Budget presented at all since 1932, the nearest approach to such a thing being the statement of the Finance Minister that the approximate deficit for 1934–5 was in the neighbourhood of 750 million pesetas—normally thirty millions and at the current exchange about twenty millions sterling.

Before the Cortes rose for the summer vacation Sr. Chapaprieta introduced a 'Law of Restrictions', which was passed almost immediately and came into force in October. It was certainly a drastic law, aimed chiefly, like most Spanish economy measures, at the Civil Service, with its duplications of office, its multiplications of salary and its bad old system of *gratificaciones*, all of which die hard. 'There are Government offices', declared Sr. Chapaprieta in the Cortes, 'where employees draw their salaries for not attending in the mornings and draw *gratificaciones* for attending in the afternoons. On the other hand, there are ill-paid officials who work both morning and afternoon continuously.' When the seventeen decrees entailed by the new law were published, it seemed possible that these abuses might at last be remedied. An enormous number of posts in Government offices were abolished; large cuts were made in diplomatic and consular salaries and in all types of fee and allowance; and every class of Civil Servant, it was announced, would in future be required to attend at his office for purposes of work, as well as for the drawing of his salary.

But there was, of course, another side to these economies. Many of them would do harm to education, which had already suffered severely through the closing of schools kept by the religious Orders, and the substitution, in many places, of State schools, with teachers insufficiently trained, owing to the rapidity with which new posts were created, and often paid starvation wages. A debate in the Cortes in July revealed the miserable nature of the remuneration still thought sufficient for teachers. A university professor in Spain, said Sr. Sánchez Albornoz, a Rector of Madrid University who soon afterwards went, as another of the Republic's 'intellectual' Ambassadors, to Lisbon, often earned no more than would be given in France to a cook or a porter. His statement was not disputed that there were 43,000 elementary teachers in the country earning between

£80 and £90 a year; and, when the Minister of Education contended that there were now 51,000 schools in Spain as against 21,000 under the Monarchy, he replied that it is not sufficient to create new schools and appoint teachers: one must also keep the teachers alive.

All these considerations showed that economy would bulk largely in the Government's programme during the autumn. But with the autumn came a new series of crises which effectively prevented the transaction of any business and eventually brought the Centre-Right coalition to an end altogether. During the summer the country had been quiet and deputies had either anticipated their summer vacation or had remained in Madrid, placidly voting with the Government and asking no questions. Apart from a bout of obstructionism by the Left, recalling that of the Radicals two years earlier, everything was calm. When suddenly, at the end of September, the two Agrarian ministers resigned from the Government over the re-transference of services to Catalonia, and Sr. Lerroux, unable to find substitutes for them, had no choice but to hand in his resignation also.

Here, of course, was a chance for further economies— this time in the salaries of Cabinet Ministers. As economy was to be the order of the day, the new-broom Finance Minister took the reins of office, and the Cabinet which he formed consisted of only nine Ministers—himself, three Radicals, three Cedistas (including Sr. Gil Robles), the leader of the Agrarian party and a representative of the Catalan Lliga. With a programme of economy and Constitution reform here and now, a Budget as soon as possible, and elections some time in the future, the new Government went bravely forward. But it was doomed to meet with reverses, to be reconstructed within five weeks and to fall altogether in eleven. First, a petty gambling scandal involved the resignation from the Foreign Office of Sr. Lerroux and this brought with it consequential changes. And finally the Prime

Minister quarelled with the Cedistas, and the Cabinet broke up in disorder. He went out of office with a fine flourish of trumpets, claiming in a letter to the President of the Republic that in seven months he had saved the country two hundred million pesetas and that he had only failed for want of the co-operation of his colleagues. No doubt he was right—co-operation has never been Spain's strongest point and financial reforms make many enemies. No more, needless to say, was heard of the Budget, or of the Law of Restrictions. As for those long-postponed municipal elections—they seemed farther off than ever.

The political situation was now about as complicated as it had been for many a long year. This was the sixth Cabinet crisis within twelve months and (according to *A.B.C*, which would be unlikely to have overlooked any) the twenty-sixth since the establishment of the Republic. It lasted for a full week. Almost every one who was conceivably capable of forming a Government declined the honour. The Radical leader was under a cloud; the Agrarian leader preferred to remain in the background; the outgoing Prime Minister refused to play at Cabinet-making any longer. As to Sr. Gil Robles, he had long ceased talking of 'assuming' office, and the great neutral masses must by this time have decided that he was unlikely to be head of a Government until the Republic had changed its President. There seemed no hope of any further progress: it was now mid-December and the country had been marking time since early autumn. A general election appeared to be the only remedy, and perhaps, as Spain was quiet, this would be as good a time as any other.

So the President decided upon a figurehead as his new Prime Minister, and a magnificent figurehead he chose. Don Manuel Portela Valladares, once Civil Governor of Barcelona, and quite recently, under the transitory *régime*, Governor-General of Catalonia, was a fine, upstanding man with an intellectual brow and a great shock of white hair—just the man to look well in the numerous photographs that would be published in the papers during the period of the election. Round him he gathered nine ministers—Sr. Chapaprieta (rather ironically) still in charge of Finance; the Agrarian leader at the Foreign Office; a General in the War Office; an Admiral to look after the Navy; and an assortment of Radicals and Independents—no Cedistas—to look after everything else. The team was not so deep as a well, nor so wide as a church door, but 'twould serve. . . .

Demoralizing as all these changes were for the unfortunate country, the situation was really becoming more than a little Gilbertian. Portfolios were changing hands so frequently that one could hardly keep pace with their movements. Here, for example, was the case of the new War Minister, General Molero. Peacefully engaged in commanding the Seventh Division at Valladolid, he was summoned post-haste to take a portfolio by Don Miguel Maura, one of the President's numerous choices for Prime Minister. Arriving at the earliest moment, he discovered that Sr. Maura had failed to form a Cabinet and that his successor had another nominee for the War Office. Whereupon, instead of becoming Minister for War, he found himself arrested for leaving his command without permission and imprisoned in a convenient fortress. But no sooner was he there than Sr. Portela, having succeeded in forming a Government where others had failed, decided that the General would be as useful a figurehead as he could discover. Back, therefore, came the General from prison to succeed to the War Office.

Then, to crown all, after a fortnight in office, the Government resigned, and a fresh supply of figureheads had to be provided by the same leader. 'Yesterday,' wrote *A.B.C.* on December 31, 1935, with justifiable sarcasm, 'came the seventh and last political crisis of the year—we say the last, as we presume that there will hardly be a fresh one before nightfall.' In the fifty-seven months of the Republic's life, it calculated, there had been twenty-eight governments—an average of just over two months' tenure for each. It was worse than the state of things that had existed under the Monarchy before the coming of the Dictatorship! And there were not wanting those who carried the conclusion further.

Nothing need be said about the new set of figureheads, for the interest of the story now suddenly and dramatically changes, and, almost for the last time in his career, the limelight plays on the benevolent features of President Alcalá Zamora. Would the President sign the decree approved by the late Cabinet dissolving the Cortes? If so, this would be the last time he could do so before the end of 1937, when his term of office would normally cease, for he had already dissolved the Cortes once and the Constitution gave him only two opportunities. If he should refuse to sign it, what hope of political peace or social progress could there be for Spain, muddling along as she was with minority governments and the most unstable of coalitions? An election of course, might well reproduce the same position as Spain had already had to tolerate for two long years, but on the other hand, it might bring back Right or Left with a clear mandate.

Evidently Sr. Alcalá Zamora needed time for thought, for though, on the next day (January 1, 1936), he signed a decree, it was merely one suspending the meetings of the Cortes for a month instead of dissolving it. Six days later, his mind was made up, and in a decree with a lengthy preamble in which he animadverted on the reasons for his decision, he dissolved the Cortes and appointed February 16 for the General Election. At the same time, presumably as a mark of confidence in the people, which in the event they fully justified, he raised the States of Alarm and Prevention in districts where these were still in force, as well as the heavy weight of the censorship which for so many months had lain upon the long-suffering Press.

During the six weeks of election campaigning, opinion was probably as uncertain as it had ever been of what was likely to happen. In ordinary circumstances, one would have expected the poor record of the Centre-Right and the lapse of as long a space as two years to have sent the pendulum swinging towards the Left again. But the indignation aroused among the non-party section of the electorate by the rebellion in Asturias had gone deep, and many felt, at the same time, that, though the Centre had indeed had its chance, the Right had hardly had a fair deal from the President. On the whole, men inclined most to the belief that the Right would come back again, but with so small a majority that it would once more be unable to govern except with the support of the Centre. Yet there was no firm foundation either for this view or for any other. Though over thirty seats in the Cortes had become vacant during the past two years, no by-elections had been held to fill them, and by-elections are always a useful political pointer. Municipal elections, again, are in Spain always fought on a political platform, and there had been none of these for nearly five years, with the exception of the 'rotten borough' elections of 1933, which had preceded the last General Election. The only index to popular feeling was popular demonstration, and this, on the whole, suggested that the Left was gaining.

The most significant fact under this head was the now rapidly growing prestige of Sr. Azaña. Since the events of October 1934, he had refused to respond to the President's repeated summonses to consultations, issued to all party leaders, and this consistent attitude of aloofness, while not without its drawbacks, had the advantage of giving him complete independence. With the people, his credit had been mysteriously rising, for no discernible reason, since he had defended himself so vigorously in the Cortes on the day of his impeachment. In October 1935, he had electrified the capital with a rousing speech, delivered, with all his old energy,

before what was freely described as one of the largest
political meetings ever held in the country. To his
followers of the Republican Left (*Izquierda Republicana*)
he was Spain's greatest leader, and many members of
other Left groups realized that they had in him the one
hope of a return to power, if they could but combine.

And combine under him they did—Republican Left,
Republican Union, Socialists, Syndicalists, Anarchists,
Marxists and Communists—forming, for the purpose
of the election campaign, a united phalanx, a 'Popular
Front', as they called it: *Frente Popular*. How long it
would remain united, like a similarly named coalition
in France, nobody knew: so completely different were
the ideals of its component groups that there was little
ground for optimism. But, unless all the fruits of the
Republic's first two years were to be lost, win these
elections the Left must, at whatever sacrifice. 'We
co-operated to establish that other Republic, not this
one', Sr. Largo Caballero had said in December when
he was being tried, after fourteen months' detention,
for military rebellion, of which charge he was in the
end acquitted.(12) Well, they would co-operate once
more to bring 'that other Republic' back again—to
give the workers of Spain progress and increasing prosperity after two years of apathy and reaction. It must
have been a moment of great hopefulness and inspiration
when, after so long a period of depression, they made
that decision.

The joint election manifesto of the 'Popular Front'
parties was given great publicity. The Right, whose
prize poster depicted a bloated Gil Robles staring glassily
into futurity, had united under the banner of Law and
Order, calling the whole of their opponents Anarchists
and Marxists with about as much justification as there
was for the name of Fascists with which they were
vilified themselves. But their opponents' election
address was much the more inviting of the two. It
promised, first and foremost, immediate amnesty for

all political prisoners who in their tens of thousands were languishing in confinement or squandering their energies in exile. It promised, next, immediate re-instatement to hundreds of thousands more who had been dismissed, for political reasons, from employment. There would be indemnities for 'families of those victimized by the revolutionary forces or by illegal repressive acts of the authorities and the forces of the law'. The Constitution should not be tampered with as the Right had proposed; it should be retained with only such slight and reasonable modifications as ex-perience (i.e., the experience of the Left) might be found to have suggested, and above all it should be strictly enforced, and not (as in some respects it had been) allowed to fall into desuetude. All the reforms so rudely interrupted in 1933 should go forward again—educational, financial, agrarian.

If such an address as this were read uncritically, it would surely have been difficult for any progressively minded elector to resist it. Those who did so, and voted for the Centre and Right, would no doubt be actuated by memories of the Socialist biennium and the conviction that the leopard had not changed his spots but had merely shifted his lair and varied his method of approach.

So the sixteenth of February drew near, with few signs of excitement apart from student ebullitions in the universities, and with every indication that yet another general election was being taken with the greatest possible seriousness and that the votes to be cast would be given with the fullest sense of responsibility.

CHAPTER V

CHAOS

I

AT half-past ten on the morning of polling-day, the wealthy Majorcan banker and deputy, Don Juan March, crossed the frontier, with his entire family, into the healthier land of France. Unlike most of his fellow-traditionalists, he anticipated a triumph for the Left, during whose earlier reign he had been in prison for a year and a half without the formality of a trial, making a dramatic escape and a successful dash from Alcalá de Henares to Gibraltar only a fortnight before the 1933 elections. This time he was taking no risks, and, though he was subsequently elected at the head of the poll for his constituency, he probably congratulated himself on his foresight. Before many weeks had passed, he was being followed by flocks of like-minded supporters of the Right, while extremists of opposite political views were returning in great numbers from either forced or self-imposed exile.

These facts would suggest that the Popular Front had won a spectacular victory and the actual figures might perhaps hardly seem to justify the general exodus. The instability of the affiliation of a fair number of individual deputies makes it impossible to group the returned members otherwise than approximately. But no one, in February 1936, would have taken strong objection to the supposition that 256 of the new deputies would normally vote with the Left, 52 with the Centre, and 165 with the Right.[1]

The increase of 157 in the size of the Left groups was of course remarkable, and more than justified the

---

[1] The official figures given by the Home Office before the second ballots were: Left, 240; Centre, 46; Right, 176. Those given in the text are the figures most commonly circulated in the Press after the second ballots.

subsequent jubilation. But it will be seen at once that the victory had been gained much more at the expense of the Centre, which lost 115, than of the Right, which lost only 42. It was government by the Centre, rather than by the Right, that was discredited; and it must not be forgotten that, while 87 of the Left deputies were Socialists and 81 belonged to Sr. Azaña's party of the Republican Left, the largest party in the Cortes was still that of the Ceda, which numbered nearly 100 members. Further, the solidarity of the Right parties was much greater than that of the Left, whose coalition was liable at any time to be irremediably cleft asunder.

Academically minded observers, therefore, like the disappointed supporters of the Right and a considerable proportion of the 'great neutral masses', thought it unlikely that the Left would regain the ascendancy which it had enjoyed in the Constituent Cortes. Then, Sr. Azaña, who, it was already taken for granted, would be the new Prime Minister, had nearly forty more followers than now, and practically no opponents. To-day, should the Centre for any reason combine with the Right, as it well might, the Left would have difficulty in getting a majority, even if its own uncertain union were to hold together. There seemed, therefore, every reason to look forward to another period of crises and changing governments, and, while abroad the sensational papers rang with reports of 'Wild scenes in Madrid', 'Red Riots in Spain', Madrid itself, ruminating peacefully one morning over its coffee and rolls, observed that Bagaría's inimitable cartoon in the *Sol* was headed 'Tranquillity', and represented two old gentlemen yawning at each other and indulging in the following political commentary:

'Well, nothing much seems to be happening. . . .'
'No, and there's going to be another Government. . . .'
'Yes, that's just what I said. . . . Nothing happening. . . .'

Things were to happen, as it proved, quite soon enough, but this profound indifference was the temper of work-a-day Spain in the few days immediately following the elections. The country had gone to the polls once more in exemplary order, which persisted until it became perfectly clear that the Popular Front had gained its majority. Then the supporters of the Popular Front began to grow violently impatient. They wanted those amnesties that had been promised them for their friends and relatives, and they wanted them at once. Dispossessed officials clamoured for immediate reinstatement; penalized families demanded their financial compensation; Catalonia insisted upon the return of its exiled councillors. Few disturbances occurred, but pro-amnesty demonstrations were held in Madrid, and political rhythm in the country became alarmingly rapid. The Government saw that for a few days at least it must be something more than a figurehead, or there would be open revolt.

So the State of Alarm was proclaimed, for a week, throughout the country; the Governor-General was recalled post-haste from Catalonia; the more important officials who had been deprived of their posts were reinstated and the nominees of an earlier Government who had supplanted them were deprived of employment. Having effected these concessions, Sr. Portela Valladares promptly resigned.

All this happened within a week after the elections and long before the publication of its complete results. Many critics of the figurehead Government reproached it bitterly for running away. But the fact was that the reaction in the country had been greater than the election figures indicated and the sooner a strong man was in the saddle the better. So the President lost no time in commissioning Sr. Azaña to form a Government, and in a few hours' time a complete list of Ministers was in his possession. It contained the former number of thirteen members, excluded the Socialists, put the Army

in the hands of a General and gave the remaining portfolios to Republican Left and Republican Union in the
proportion of three to one. Not until midnight was
the list made public, but when the new Prime Minister
appeared on the balcony of the Home Office to address
the crowds which had gathered in the Puerta del Sol,
it seemed as if all Madrid were present. In a few telling
words he repeated the promises of the election manifesto
and told them that amnesties and reinstatements should
be carried into effect without delay.

On the next morning the Cabinet decided to reinstate
the former Ayuntamientos and to appoint new Civil
Governors throughout Spain, and also to reinstate the
Rector and Council of the once-again-to-be-autonomous
University of Barcelona. On the day following, the
President signed the Amnesty Decree, leaving it to be
approved by the Cortes when opportunity offered.
But already even this energetic action had been out-
stripped by popular sentiment. General strikes and
noisy, though harmless demonstrations had opened
prison doors with remarkable celerity: in Oviedo alone
several hundred prisoners had been set free and many
thousands in other parts of the country. Sr. Companys
and his six fellow-councillors were converging by
different routes upon the capital, making speeches and
receiving tributes of admiration all the way, and, in a
broadcast speech to Catalonians, their former President,
soon to resume his office, described his rebellion as
having 'confirmed and strengthened Catalonia in the
glorious work of the Republic.' (1)

By the beginning of March, a new decree had empowered the Catalonian parliament to re-elect its government, and the ex-Councillors had made a triumphal
progress from Madrid to Barcelona. A special session
of parliament was at once called and Sr. Companys was
again elected President. 'The title', said the Speaker
to him, 'is yours more than ever. You enjoyed our
confidence before your imprisonment, you enjoyed it

during your imprisonment and now that you are free you enjoy it still.' So, whatever might have been said under the former Government, the October Revolution was completely whitewashed, and, even while the Barcelona parliament was glorying in it, the Tribunal of Guarantees in Madrid was declaring (by a majority of sixteen votes to seven) that the annulment of Catalonian autonomy had been illegal.

The first act of the Catalonian parliament, as one would have expected, was to re-enforce the Agrarian Law which it had defied the Tribunal of Guarantees by promulgating eighteen months earlier and against which, owing to the changed circumstances, the Tribunal was now unable, or unwilling, to do battle. Barcelona was contented, other parts of Spain, however, were less quiet. The best that can be said about the riots that took place during the months following the General Election is that they seem nearly all to have been spontaneous, unorganized acts of hooliganism, due to the return of exiled extremists and to the ebullition of feeling at the return to power of the Left after a period of eclipse.

It was unfortunate that the first targets of popular violence should have been churches, for the inactivity of the forces of law and order in suppressing the outbreaks was interpreted, at least by implication, as pointing to a new period of official anti-clerical policy. As a matter of fact, it seems to have been due rather to a desire not to excite mob feeling and to the hope that, if left alone, it would in the course of a few weeks die a normal death. Churches and convents, however, formed the most natural and conspicuous targets for incendiarism, and cases of arson were reported all over the country—notably in Madrid, where the offices of *La Nación* and the churches of San Luis and San Ignacio were burned down; at Logroño, in the north, where two churches and four convents were set on fire; and at Elche, in the extreme south-east, which lost three churches, including Santa María, the scene of the famous medieval play given annually on the festival of the Assumption.

A rigid Press censorship prevented many of these facts from becoming known, while it magnified others beyond belief, and created, especially in Madrid, a higher degree of panic than had been known since the coming of the Republic. The State of Alarm was prolonged month after month; many people left the country, taking with them as much money as they could smuggle through the Customs; many more remained in their houses after nightfall and observed the most elaborate precautions when leaving them. And it must be admitted that they had cause, for to widespread incendiarism was added an epidemic of murders by gunmen, for at least some of which there was an uncomfortably and rapidly growing suspicion that Fascism was mainly responsible. The victims of these murders had included Don José María Maura, a Bilbao insurance official, brother of three famous political figures and son of one of Spain's greatest prime ministers; Don Alfredo Martínez, an Oviedo doctor, leader of the Liberal Democrat party in Asturias and a member of the last Government; and En Miquel Badià, one of the two ringleaders in the October rebellion who upon its failure had made his way into France, whence he had just returned. Among those who escaped was the Socialist professor, Sr. Jiménez de Asúa, a vice-president of the Cortes, shot at in the open street as he was leaving his house for the University. During a military review held in Madrid to celebrate the fifth anniversary of the Republic, shots and explosions were the signal for a general stampede, and street fighting resulted in the death of a Civil Guardsman. At the funeral there was further rioting and three Fascists were killed. All the time, Fascists in great number, from the young Marqués de Estella downwards, were being put into gaol, till it seemed that there would soon be none left outside.

The nerve-ridden state of Madrid in April 1936 exceeded anything that Spaniards with long experience could remember. Indiscipline and lawlessness, which had made themselves felt during the first month of the Republic's life, seemed at last to have reached a climax. The smallest street incidents made one feel that this state of affairs could not go on much longer. Other cities of Spain, however, even in the south, were, though apprehensive, quite reasonably tranquil, and there was little sign of the approach of organized revolt.

The Government, none the less, took precautions. One of its first acts had been to appoint April 12 for the holding of those oft-postponed municipal elections which had not now taken place for five years. It was an unlucky date, said the superstitious, for on April 12, 1931, municipal elections had brought about the fall of the Monarchy: what if those of April 12, 1936 should bring about the fall of the Republic? They need not have troubled: a week or two before the elections should have been held they were postponed yet once again. This was no time to risk such fresh disorders as might follow a new and decisive party victory. Besides, as we shall see, the Government had other urgent business due for transaction.

One last form of disturbance took place in the agricultural districts of central and southern Spain—the forcible seizure of land by impatient peasants. For over two years the Agrarian Law of 1932 had been held up by the Centre-Right Governments and an unusually rainy winter in the south of Spain had increased unemployment and caused intense distress. When the return to office of the Left enabled the Institute of Agrarian Reform to start work in earnest, it became clear that the rate of progress would have to be expedited. Labourers who, four years earlier, had, as they themselves believed, been promised their small holdings then and there, had waited patiently, but fruitlessly, for the promises to materialize. Now they were told that their friends had come back to power and all would be well—but two months had passed, there was still no news of a distribution, and it would soon be too late for this year's sowing. So, although in these two months 70,000 men had been given their holdings, and at the end of March a decree was published authorizing the Institute to proceed more rapidly still, thousands of *yunteros* (as labourers are termed who have their own *yuntas* or yokes of mules or donkeys) determined to take the law into their own hands. It must not be supposed that the proceeding, which was organized by the Socialist Agriculturist Federations, was normally accompanied by either disorder or violence. An eye-witness thus describes a typical scene in a rural district of the province of Badajoz.

At 5.0 a.m. on March 25, organized groups of labourers armed with ropes, spades and other implements mustered secretly and trooped out from 150 of the 163 villages of the province; they proceeded— many of them on their donkeys, of course—to the neighbouring big estates and calmly marked out the strips which they proposed to occupy for cultivation under the new land settlement system. Then, after a lusty cry of ¡*Viva la República!* they marched back to their villages, held a demonstration meeting in front of the local Government Building, and then sent a commission to get formal approval for their land-taking: their case being that they had been promised the land in the Government election programme, but that all kinds of bureaucratic obstacles were being put in their way.(2)

In most cases the *fait accompli* seems to have been accepted and regularized with all due speed, but in some places the peasants were driven off the land they had taken, and this caused a great deal of confusion, though not as a rule any serious disorder. But as a sign of the prevailing chaos, due chiefly to the dilatoriness of two largely wasted years, the incidents were disturbing in the extreme; and the more one read and thought of them, the more perplexed did one feel about the immediate future.

II

Anxious as it was to give general satisfaction, the Government had no sooner met the duly constituted Cortes than it provided the country with the greatest political sensation that it had enjoyed since the fall of King Alfonso. By doing so it created a situation which might have seemed insoluble had not the solution been evolved well in advance, and it brought about a dramatic change in the administration of the *régime* of which great things were being expected at the very moment when pent-up passions broke loose and involved Spain in disaster.

The sensation was nothing less than the deposition by the Cortes of the President of the Republic. To say that to all but a very few it came as a surprise is to understate the effect which it produced upon the country. The unfortunate 'Botas' had contrived to give mortal offence to both the chief political groups and to become anything but popular. Unseemly jokes, indeed, about the need for a national bootblack (*limpiabotas*) were current, and it was freely rumoured that on the advent to power of Sr. Azaña he would tender his resignation. But the more general opinion was that he would remain in possession of his office in the National Palace, and of his more than kingly salary, till his term came to an end in December 1937, and that he would then bury himself in decent obscurity and retire from politics. If such were his intention, however, it was certainly not the intention of those who now held power.

The technical ground on which it was decided to depose the President was his recent action in dissolving the Cortes. It will be remembered that the Constitution provides for such dissolution by a President twice during his six years of office, but it also lays down that, after a second dissolution, the first act of the new Cortes shall be to examine its necessity: 'an unfavourable vote by an absolute majority of the Cortes', runs the article, 'shall automatically involve the deposition of the President.'(3) The Government, therefore, had the way clear before it, for its coalition was unlikely, at so early a stage, to come to pieces, and, unless this happened, the President could only be saved by the votes, or the abstention, of the whole of the Centre and Right and by the abstention of a considerable group in the Left.

The protagonist in the debate (or, as some might have said if it had gone in the President's favour, the monkey's paw) was the Socialist, Don Indalecio Prieto; Sr. Azaña, possibly from motives that did credit to his delicacy of feeling, remained in the background. From beginning to end the discussion ran on party lines. The argument which the President had himself used at the time of the dissolution—that the dissolution of the Constituent Cortes 'did not count'—was disposed of by the Socialist orator without further ado, after which he accomplished the preternatural feat of delving into the President's mind and bringing up what he conceived to have been the motives of his action. The Cortes had been dissolved, he declared, with no sincere intention of obtaining the country's verdict upon the political situation, but 'with the illogical desire to trample upon the sovereign will of the people and to bring parliament into conformity with the President's own opinions, instead of these opinions being, as the Constitution provides, subordinated to the opinion of the country'. The intention was frustrated, continued Sr. Prieto, with tinsel eloquence, by the 'noble reaction of the Spanish people', who for so long, 'in the depths of their hearts, had concealed their grief' at a *régime* of repression which they had at last brought to an end.

The debate lasted for five hours, but from the beginning its result was certain. The Right were naturally critical of the Socialist leader's arguments, but after the President's treatment of Sr. Gil Robles they had no more use for him than had the Popular Front, and they therefore decided upon abstention. Only Sr. Portela Valladares and those of his former colleagues who were present defended the unlucky successor of King Alfonso, offering to take full responsibility for the dissolution if the Left would accept them as a propitiatory sacrifice. But all they could do was to register five solitary votes in the President's favour, and, as the annulment of a few election results had brought the effective strength of the House down to 417, the number of votes recorded for the motion—238—was more than sufficient to secure its passing.

It was at 10 p.m. on April 7 that the result of the vote was announced and no time was lost in making it effective. A Committee of the House was appointed to inform Sr. Alcalá Zamora of his deposition, the sitting of the Cortes to be resumed upon their return. As so often happens in Spanish politics, the proceedings, conceived with all proper dignity, were enlivened with a touch of unintended humour. The committee, preceded by the usual gang of journalists, drove in two cars to the deposed President's house, and asked for an interview. But, instead of seeing them, the President sent a message by one of his sons to say that he was 'resting', and that, so far as he knew, no clause of the Constitution made it obligatory for him to receive them. The Committee insisted, but the President was firm, and the best they could do was to drive to his office in the National Palace and make their report to his principal secretary. This done, they returned to the Chamber of Deputies, where, at 12.20 a.m., the session was resumed.

A quarter of an hour sufficed for the remaining business. Since the Constitution provides that, during any such interregnum as this, the Speaker of the Cortes shall occupy the President's place, the senior Vice-President and Chairman of the Committee just appointed formally invited the recently elected Speaker, Sr. Martínez Barrio, to hold the presidency until after the new election. The Speaker assented, mounted the platform, and, then and there, with the deputies standing, gave the 'promise' of fidelity to the Republic and the Constitution. (4)

Its work well done, the House prepared to disperse.

'Long live the Republic!' cried a member, enthusiastically, as the deputies rose.

His voice was lost in a chorus of *Vivas*.

'Long live the Popular Front!' shouted a Communist, with slightly less conviction.

But only one voice greeted this sally, the voice of a deputy who had been tried, imprisoned and all but condemned to death after the October Revolution. And in that voice, there was no lack of conviction, as it cried: 'Long live Asturias!'

One may speculate on the number of deputies who awoke on the following morning with slight misgivings as to the effect which their act of the night before might have upon the stability of the Republic. Possibly more than one of them remembered how the First Republic of 1873–4 had had four presidents in eleven months and wondered if the first step towards a similar *débâcle* had now been taken. But, whatever their thoughts might have been, their speech was all of Sr. Alcalá Zamora's successor.

The constitutional procedure laid down for the election of a President is, as we have seen, a rather clumsy one. It depends neither directly upon the people nor upon the Cortes, but upon an Electoral College composed of all the deputies of the Cortes and an equal number of *ad hoc* members, or *compromisarios*. (5) As no names for the presidency were to be publicly put forward until after the College had been constituted, nearly a month elapsed before such names were canvassed in the Press. The election of the President was not to be until May 10, and it was about the end of April that vague speculation began to give place to insistent rumour.

For a month the names of numerous political leaders had been bandied about as those of likely candidates for the Presidency. It was notable that no such names of really great non-political Spaniards were spoken of as had been the case four and a half years earlier: party candidatures were by now inescapable. As the Right had retired from the field and taken no serious part even in the elections of *compromisarios*, it was pretty clear that the new President would belong to the Left, and really when one glanced down the list of persons suggested there seemed no reason why any of them should be elected (or rejected) rather than any of the others. As time went on, however, one name, which had first been mentioned only to be dismissed as *hors concours*, became more generally favoured. It was the name of the Prime Minister, Don Manuel Azaña.

To the very last there were those—not, of course, behind the scenes, but closely in touch with Spanish politics—who declared that for Sr. Azaña to allow his name to go forward was unthinkable. True, to have a strong man in the Presidential office was highly desirable, but to have him as Prime Minister, with Madrid a bundle of nerves and Spain seething with unrest, was far more so. They could not believe that Sr. Azaña would leave the Popular Front, which he alone, if any one, could hold together, to the mercy of individual passion and inevitable political disunion. But as, each day, certain newspapers advocated the election of Sr. Azaña more and more strongly, one began to suspect that their fervid commentaries were inspired. One has no information, and perhaps never will have, as to precisely when the idea of becoming President first occurred to Sr. Azaña, but there is no doubt that his election was arranged with great dramatic effect. By the beginning of May he was accepted as the sole candidate of the Popular Front; by the day of the election he was the only serious candidate at all.

On a warm Sunday morning the presidential election was held in the Crystal Palace of the Retiro Gardens, in the heart of the modern city. Voting, appropriately enough, was by political parties, and, once the votes were recorded, the greater part of the time was spent by the electors in the shade of the trees or at the open-air bar which had been erected in the vicinity of the Palace. Except for a fight between two Socialist deputies, all was peace.

The election had begun at eleven o'clock in the morning, but it was nearly two—the Madrid luncheon hour—when the electors were recalled to hear the result, which they had awaited with no particular eagerness.

The number of electors, it seemed, was 911. Of these, 874 had voted. One hundred and fifteen papers (for the most part, those of the Right) had been returned blank. Don Alejandro Lerroux, the Radical leader, had received one vote. Don Francisco Largo Caballero, the Socialist leader, had received one vote. Don José Antonio Primo de Rivera, the Fascist leader, had received one vote. . . .

(It would take some time, at this rate, an outsider might have thought, to complete the 874.)

Don Ramón González Peña—the deputy who had shouted *¡Viva Asturias!*—had received two votes.

(The number was rising!)

And Don Manuel Azaña Díaz had received 754 votes! So Don Manuel Azaña Díaz was elected.

'*¡Viva la República!*' cried the electors, as the presiding officer left to greet the new President, who was reported, in due course, to have received the news of his election 'with emotion'.

The Socialists and Communists raised their fists, and their voices, and sang the *Internationale*.

The Catalonians, not to be outdone, sang their own national hymn, *Els Segadors*.

The Basques made answer with the *Guernikako arbola*.

The Monarchists sang nothing, which for the sake of the public peace was perhaps just as well, and the rest of the Republicans sang nothing, because they had nothing to sing, Republican talent not having yet produced a new national anthem. But a few of the musically inclined were heard to hum the Hymn of Riego, which honours a Spanish patriot shot exactly a century before the coming of the Dictatorship, by the orders of Alfonso XIII's great-grandfather.

On the next day, Don Manuel Azaña Díaz duly promised fidelity to Constitution and Republic. 'At last,' he had said to his own party some days before with the same momentary expansiveness as he had shown when he first became Prime Minister, 'Spain will have a President who is a true Republican. I shall be incapable of corruption, insensible to bribery, and impervious to threats. To defend the Republic, if need be, I will shed the last drop of my blood.' (6)

After his election, the new President announced his intention, not merely of maintaining an office in the National Palace, as his predecessor had done, but of taking up his permanent residence there.

It was an announcement worth making. Somehow to know that Sr. Azaña was in the Palace gave Spaniards a badly needed feeling of confidence.

III

The Presidential crisis over and the Government having for the second time formally resigned and been confirmed in office, the next thing was for the Cortes to get down to business. After a two-days' interim ministry Sr. Casares Quiroga, a member of the new President's late party, took office—the fourth Prime Minister within three months—and his Cabinet was one of similar composition to that of Sr. Azaña.

A perusal of the Spanish Press for May and June 1936 will convey the impression of great parliamentary activity—and in fact the Government worked hard at its preparations for giving effect once more to the Agrarian Law and the Law of Confessions and Congregations. But in the light of after events the interest of these months lies outside the Cortes rather than within it —in the intense and increasing social unrest and in the alarming rapidity of the growth of militant Fascism.

To give any adequate idea of the barrage of revolutionary strikes that was maintained by the extremists during this period is impossible: even to enumerate them all would require many pages. In a parliamentary debate held exactly four calendar months after the General Election, Sir Gil Robles declared that there had been 113 general strikes and 218 partial strikes during that period. The figures were not challenged, and may therefore presumably be taken as correct. But if the statistics were extended to take in the calendar month following they would be more impressive still. Never, as during this month, had there been such social unrest in the Republic's entire history. Day after day, pages of the newspapers were filled with reports of old strikes settled, new strikes declared, demonstrations, shootings, casualties, violent scenes at funerals, riot, arson, destruction. There were also numerous reports of arrests in connexion with these disturbances; what one hardly ever saw was that any particular crime had been brought home to anybody. Unhappy Spain was rapidly moving towards a condition of complete chaos.

Naturally, the Right-wing parties in the Cortes, numerically so strong, lost no opportunity of reproaching, and even taunting, the Government for its powerlessness. The protagonists in the attack were the disappointed leader of the Ceda, Sr. Gil Robles, and Primo de Rivera's former Finance Minister, Sr. Calvo Sotelo. The Government was as impotent within the House as without. The Prime Minister could not deny that in four months

170 churches, 69 clubs and the offices of 10 newspapers had been set on fire, and that attempts had been made to burn 284 other buildings, including 251 churches. He could only contend that it was really the result of the repression practised when his opponents were in office; that, while there was certainly not 'absolute quiet' in the country (ironical phrase!), his critic's descriptions were 'purely fantastic'; and that, for so long as the Army continued loyal to the Republic, 'nothing would happen' —*no pasaría nada*. So the old tag of the Dictatorship did duty once again in a new setting. But the Opposition's main contention was unanswerable and its demand was quite reasonable, as the Home Secretary would no doubt have been the first to admit had he been able to satisfy it. The contention and the demand were merely these:

> 'A country can perfectly well live under a Monarchy or under a Republic, under parliamentary rule, Soviet rule or the rule of a dictatorship. But a country cannot live in a state of anarchy, and Spain is in a state of anarchy to-day.
>
> 'This situation in which Spain is living cannot go on. We ask you to put an end to it.'(7)

Being unable to control the extremists on its own flank, the Government endeavoured to oblige its opponents by rounding up the extremists on theirs. Towards the middle of June 1936 began that month of intense activity and violence on the Fascist side and of intense repression on the side of the Left which proved to be the prelude to disaster. Spanish Fascism was, of course, a very different proposition in 1936 from anything that it had been during previous Governments. Then it was an almost academic party—just one group among many which could be counted on to support the Right in the Cortes. It had no very effective parliamentary leader, for Sr. Gil Robles was an anti-Fascist, and even Sr. Calvo Sotelo, though he would presumably have held office in a Fascist state, was not a member of the Fascist party but only of the Monarchist party which styled itself 'Spanish Renovation'. Had the Right been successful in the February elections, Fascism would no doubt have continued to develop within it, but it would have developed slowly, with formative rather than militant aims, hoping that by patient methods it might gradually attract to itself leaders of other parties, who, though freely described as Fascists by their opponents, were in fact very far from being so.

But, when the Popular Front came into power in February 1936, there set in a reactionary movement not at all unlike the movement in the opposite direction which had begun after the victory of the Centre two years earlier. The majority of the Right-wing groups were content to abide the consequences of the electorate's decision and to go into opposition until their turn came at last for power. But the Fascists were not. In the first place, they were no doubt elated by the success of Fascist Italy's campaign in Abyssinia and heartened by the results of the self-assertive actions of Nazi Germany. Next, they had already seen what two years of Left rule had been like, and the next period, they thought, would be far worse, since Syndicalism, Anarchism and Communism were all much stronger. Further, they probably thought, if at this moment of disillusion and incipient psychological reaction they began a determined offensive, they would enlist many new and useful supporters— notably the leaders of the Army, who were finding themselves, according to the usual formula of Spanish pendulum-rule, in danger of being tried, degraded, imprisoned and expelled for the parts they had played in suppressing the risings of October 1934, the promoters of those risings now being in power.

Such reasonings as these, no doubt, were in the minds of the parliamentary Fascist Party and the so-called Military Union, if, as seems likely (for the history of this period is still imperfectly known), they prepared deliberately to follow the example set by the extremists of the opposite camp two years earlier. The Government, without the least doubt, recognized the danger and answered their unspoken challenge with words of asperity. 'There is one thing,' announced the Prime Minister to the Cortes in the middle of May,

> 'There is one thing which I wish to make clear with regard to the Government's attitude to Fascism. . . . The purpose of the Fascist groups is to attack the fundamental principles of the democratic Republic. Here the Government cannot maintain an attitude of neutrality. In its relations with Fascism, the Government is a belligerent.'(8)

So the field was set, and, with Fascism directly menacing it on the one hand and Left extremism clamouring for power by means of illegal strikes on the other, the Government went helplessly on with its self-allotted tasks, though it could have had small hope of accomplishing them. In normal times, for example, one would have expected a Left-wing Government to proceed steadily with the problem of regional autonomy. But it was with a sense of the complete unreality of the event that one read, at the beginning of July, of Galicia's plebiscite for her Autonomy Statute, which had just been approved by seventy-five per cent of the voters: all this seemed so far away when the two chief political groups in Madrid were each at the other's throat, when the whole country was torn with anxiety and when the very existence of the Republican *régime* was threatened—as far away as ex-President Alcalá Zamora, who, freed against his will from the cares of office, had conceived the excellent idea of leaving Spain for a three-months' holiday abroad, just (as it chanced) at the moment when Spain was heading for chaos. Not the least to be envied of the leaders of the Second Republic has been Sr. Alcalá Zamora!

Meanwhile, the most disturbing feature of each day's

news became, no longer strikes and riots, but political assassinations. The complete impunity with which these were committed, despite the efforts, or at least the existence, of detectives, police, Civil Guards and Shock Troops, was agonizing. The only thing the authorities seemed able to do was to arrest Fascists, by the score, or even by the hundred, on suspicion. By the beginning of July there must have been thousands of them in prison. And yet the murders went on. On July 4, a crowd was emerging from a Socialist meeting at the Casa del Pueblo. From passing cars, gunmen fired at it pointblank—and disappeared: seven Socialists were killed, and a dozen wounded. Eight days later, Don José Castillo, a lieutenant in the Shock Troops, was leaving his home in a small Madrid street between two main thoroughfares. Four men stepped across to him and fired: in a moment he was dead.

Presumably these crimes, like the majority of those already enumerated, were the work of men with Fascist or traditionalist sympathies. How much was known about their authors by those who determined to avenge them it is impossible to say. But it is said that, standing by the body of Sr. Castillo, who had shot a prominent Fascist in the April riots and had since received several letters threatening his life, one of his companions swore to execute immediate vengeance. If that companion was responsible for the crime of July 13 he certainly acted with remarkable speed.

At three o'clock on the morning of that day, the militant Monarchist deputy, Sr. Calvo Sotelo, was awakened by a loud knocking on the outer door of the house in which he lived in the Calle de Velázquez. Going out, he found a police van in the charge of an officer holding a warrant for his arrest. Such arrests being common enough (his late chief's eldest son, for example, had been for some time in prison) he first satisfied himself of the officer's *bona fides* and then went away with him. He was never seen again by his friends alive.

Early in the afternoon, the police headquarters received an inquiry from the East Cemetery, in the mortuary of which some police had deposited a body in the small hours of the morning, saying that they had found it in the streets. They had promised to send in a formal report in a few hours' time. The report had never arrived. The body was at once examined. It was that of Don José Calvo Sotelo.[1]

Of all the political murders of this troubled *régime*, this was perhaps, if only for the methodical way in which it was planned and executed, the most revolting. It was also, from the point of view of the traditionalists, the most disastrous. Though only forty-three, the victim had frequently been spoken of as a future Dictator; with his long political experience, he might well have become a Spanish Salazar and, in more senses than one, have saved his country's fortunes. The Left, of course, would not have shared this view, but Left and Right alike were shaken at the audacity of the crime, while the man in the street, dumbfounded with horror, saw it as the climax beyond which crime could not farther go. 'This', he said, perhaps not knowing exactly what he meant, 'must be the end.'

IV

The end came only a few days later, in the shape of a military revolt, which caught fire over all the country and in the course of a short week-end developed into civil war. (9)

How closely the outbreak of the revolt was connected with the murder of Calvo Sotelo is a question to which we may never have a conclusive answer. Taking place, as it did, at the end of the same week, it was at first assumed to be a direct consequence. But it soon became

[1] He had been shot in the breast and through the right eye. The story, current in the English Press, that his eyes had been gouged out with a dagger, finds no confirmation either in the Spanish Press reports or in the evidence of the medical expert (cf. *Sol*, July 14 and 15, 1936).

clear that this was no mere impulsive outbreak provoked by current events but another revolution of the *pronunciamiento* type, like the rising under General Sanjurjo almost exactly four years earlier: a revolution carefully planned and skilfully organized by able military leaders on a nation-wide scale. The date on which the initial blow was struck may well have been advanced with a view to capturing the sympathy of those who had been appalled by so cold-blooded a murder, but it seems more probable that the coincidence of the two events was fortuitous and the timing of the various outbreaks followed a pre-arranged plan.

Some weeks earlier, Sr. Casares Quiroga had spoken lightly in the Cortes of a projected Fascist revolt, the details of which, he claimed, were perfectly well known to his Government. If this was the revolt to which he had referred he was either grievously mistaken or greatly to blame. But once again it seems likely that there was no connexion between the projected and the actual rising and that the form taken by the latter was as complete a surprise to the Government as to the world at large.

The trouble began in Spanish Morocco, where on July 17 a number of regiments rose in mutiny against the Republic. Their leader, General Francisco Franco, a brother of the intrepid airman of Cuatro Vientos fame, had for some time been stationed in the Canary Islands and flew over from Las Palmas to Morocco on the day before the revolt. Although, with the backing of the Foreign Legion, the rebels took possession of both Ceuta and Melilla, no great anxiety was felt in the Peninsula: more disturbing events than these had been happening at home. At noon on the next day, the Government issued a note condemning the Moroccan revolt with rather suggestive vigour, and adding, with an emphasis which distinctly seemed to protest too much, that 'nobody, absolutely nobody' in the Peninsula had 'taken part in this absurd scheme'.

But, even as this note was being written, the 'absurd

scheme' was rapidly turning into something more formidable. By the evening of July 18, news reached Madrid from one large town after another that garrisons were revolting and distinguished generals were leading insurrections. On the following morning, it was clear that the revolt had spread to almost every part of Spain. General Franco had landed his first detachment of troops on the mainland and was in firm command at Algeciras and Cádiz. Seville, which was to become the southern metropolis of the rebels, had been taken without resistance. In Saragossa the entire garrison had come out in support of the insurrection, as also in Pamplona, the capital of traditionalist Navarre.

These mutinies, it was clear, were ably and gallantly commanded. Officers of the highest rank, who five years earlier had been unwilling to risk anything to save the Monarchy, were now risking all to further whatever ends they had in view. Some of them, indeed, such as General Queipo de Llano, who was commanding the insurgents in Andalusia, had actually participated in pro-Republican activities before the Republic's birth. In the north, the commanders were a veteran officer, General Cabanellas, and General Mola, who had once been Director-General of Police. In Majorca, General Goded had pronounced for the insurrection, and, leaving Palma in rebel hands, had flown over to take part in a more important task at Barcelona. During its early stages, however, he had to surrender, and in due course was court-martialled and shot. This was a serious setback to the rebels, and almost at the outset of their campaign they suffered another loss more serious still. The intrepid but ill-starred General Sanjurjo, flying from Lisbon to some unknown destination in Spain, met with an aeroplane accident near the Spanish frontier and was burned to death.

Could so many independent revolts be checked before the armies became mobile, joined their forces and involved the entire country? That was the one question asked on that fateful Saturday and Sunday, July 18 and 19, and on the answer to it everything depended. The Socialists believed they could secure peace and order by applying once more their long familiar panacea: wherever the rebels proclaimed martial law, announced the General Union of Workers, their adherents would declare a general strike. But somehow this failed entirely: even in Seville, where Left-wing extremism had for so long been dominant, the workers failed to get their way. By Sunday afternoon, the proletariat of the large cities of Spain were preparing on a large scale for armed resistance. Bearing in mind past events, we cannot doubt that most of them were already well supplied with weapons. Those who were not soon acquired them, and, in cities where the rebels had not obtained a hold, the workers made themselves responsible for public order. 'At midnight on Saturday,' wrote an observer in Madrid, 'armed Marxists began to appear. On Sunday morning every street was being patrolled and all passers-by were rigorously though politely searched. The police had almost disappeared.'(10)

Meanwhile, what of the Government and what of the Republic's strong man—its President, Don Manuel Azaña? Had Sr. Azaña, weeks earlier, taken power into his own hands, as so many had prophesied that he would, it is possible that he might have cemented the insecure allegiance of the Army to his Government and to the Republican *régime* before a rival group of leaders sprang into being and claimed its loyalty. But from the beginning he chose to be strictly constitutional; and, though abroad men wondered what had happened to Spain's indomitable leader, in Spain the course that he took earned for him the respect, at least, of every democrat. He remained at his post, appealing to the nation as he was entitled to do at a time of national emergency, and, for the rest, fulfilling the *rôle* marked out for him by the Constitution.

His first duty was to preside at a series of lightning

changes of Government which in rapidity exceeded anything that even this kaleidoscopic Republic had known. There were three ministries in twenty-four hours. By the Saturday night it was clear that the 'absurd scheme' ridiculed by the Casares Quiroga Government had developed into a situation of the gravest danger, and a Prime Minister who had cried 'Nothing happening here!' down to the very moment of a nation-wide insurrection, and had then, in an official note, made light of the insurrection, could hardly be expected to remain in power. Sr. Casares Quiroga therefore resigned office—at three o'clock on the Sunday morning.

The President took the opposite course to that which most observers would have predicted: instead of attempting to meet the common danger with a Popular Front Coalition Government, plentifully sprinkled with extremists, he sent for the moderately minded Speaker of the Cortes, Sr. Martínez Barrio, and entrusted him with the formation of a Cabinet, which proved to be of so mild a character that it even included Sr. Sánchez Román, who had revolted against the Popular Front manifesto in the preceding February.(11)

At this the leaders of the extremist groups protested vehemently. It was primarily extremism, they said, and not merely the 'pure Republicanism' of the incorruptible and indomitable Sr. Azaña, that was taking arms to save the Republic. The militia now being formed was largely Communist. The bonfires soon to be lit would be sponsored by Anarchists. The new Government, whatever its composition, would probably be of the smallest practical importance. 'The Government do not exist', declared the Marxist leader, Andrés Nin, a day or two afterwards in Barcelona. 'We are collaborating with them, but they can do no more than sanction whatever is done by the masses.'(12) Still, said the extremists, if only a figurehead, the Government should still represent the not yet sundered Popular Front.

The strong man had no alternative but to surrender.

It was a humiliating situation. The rebel leaders had earned the condemnation of all good Republicans by pronouncing against a constitutionally elected Government, but here were the very supporters of the Constitution interfering with the prerogative which it gave him. So, after the second Cabinet had held office for only a few hours, it made way for a third, which was substantially the first, with a former Minister of Marine, Don José Giralt, at the helm, and a loyalist General, Sr. Pozas, in the Home Office. (13)

Fighting in the streets of Madrid, between the workers and the Military Union, had already begun—first spasmodically; then, in some of the main streets, more steadily. Where victorious, the extremists took their usual toll: by the Sunday night churches and convents were once more blazing. On the Monday, the regiments in the Montaña barracks, behind the Northern Railway station, mutinied, but, after heavy bombardment, surrendered in a few hours. It was a short but bloody engagement. Some of the officers, it is said, committed suicide; other officers were forced to yield by their own men; the leaders of the rising, General Fanjul and Colonel Quintana, were taken prisoners and shot, and the total number of soldiers killed was estimated to be as large as two hundred. (14)

Bad as was all this, worse still was happening elsewhere. Barcelona was the scene of a battle which lasted for three days, and in which, no sooner had the Government troops put down the rebels, than there began wholesale burnings, mutilations and cold-blooded murders, to say nothing of violent dissensions among the victors. Seville was still firmly held by the rebels, and Don Fernando Primo de Rivera, a son of the late Dictator, was fighting for Córdoba. Despite the marked loyalty of the Navy, troops were crossing steadily from Morocco to Andalusia, in preparation for a great march northwards. Galicia was now said to be rebel, together with Gijón in Asturias, while heavy fighting was foreshadowed in Oviedo. Near the western frontier the rebels were fighting for the road into France; soon Irún was to be fiercely bombarded. Elsewhere General Mola's army was on the move: a march on Burgos had begun. Already in imagination one could see the northern and southern armies closing on Madrid. . . .

It was civil war! That was the terrible realization which during the short week-end was gradually dawning, and then, at its close, suddenly burst upon the Spanish people. In a day or two General Franco had publicly announced that the object of the insurgents was to put down Bolshevism and that the victorious entry of the anti-Government forces into Madrid would be followed by the establishment of a military Directory. From Burgos, the temporary capital of the new *régime*, if such it was to be, General Mola proclaimed the establishment of this Directory, addressed messages to foreign powers and announced the dismissal of all Ambassadors and Consuls of the Second Republic.

As the war went on, the papers began to speak glibly of the northern and the southern fronts, of the battles being fought in the Guadarrama mountains, of the forthcoming siege of Badajoz, of the possibility of an action before Madrid. Then the ripples of the stone flung into the Spanish pool quickly widened. Russian workers contributed large sums to the funds of the Spanish Government; Italian planes were flown to the rebels in Morocco; members of the Popular Front in France urged intervention in the interest of their Spanish comrades; the French Government approached the British Government over a non-intervention pact; Germany demanded satisfaction for the shooting of four Germans. . . . So, in a way which few could have foreseen, Spain at last came into the international news: and the country which for centuries had maintained a not too splendid isolation became the centre of interest in Europe.

With the growth of a number of apparently scattered mutinies into a revolution and the transformation of the revolution into the bloodiest and most ferocious of civil wars this history of Spain's Second Republic comes to a tragic close. Any discussion of the civil war and its consequences belongs clearly to another volume, for which the historian will find material in only too great abundance. But the Second Republic, in every real sense, is dead. Even if in name it continued it could never again become what it was intended to be at its foundation. Its fate was sealed from the moment the Martínez Barrio Cabinet was deposed from office. From that moment men talked, not of the future of the Republican *régime*, but of the nature of the *régime* that was to succeed it. What manner of government would Spain, who had suffered so much, have to suffer now?

There was little doubt in any one's mind that the immediate effect of the war, whichever side won, would be to agitate the pendulum more violently than ever. The peace, when it came, could not but be succeeded by a period of repressive rule—a dictatorship, no doubt— in which such partisans of the losing side as were left alive would have the choice of transferring their allegiance, of conforming indefinitely to opinions which they could never conscientiously hold or of leaving the country. This, no doubt, together with the effect of the freeing of passions for so long repressed, explains the terrible bitterness and sometimes almost bestial savagery which was remarked on both sides. Neither side could even contemplate the possiblity of the other side winning. Victory simply *must* be its own.

V

In reflecting upon the war, and upon the tragedy of the Republic of 1931, one must at all costs resist the temptation to assign responsibilities. To reflect in that retaliatory spirit which was the bane of the Republic would tempt one to an excessive simplification of issues which have throughout been closely interdependent on each other and thus extremely involved.

It is a strange and a terrible paradox, for example, that the nation should have been plunged into bloodshed by the deliberate act of men fighting for the ideals of the party which had so recently gone to the country with the slogan of 'Law and Order', and that it should in fact be for this law and order—as they conceived it—that they fought. The politicians of the Right, no doubt, would say that the war was begun by an Army revolt in which they had no part, and of which many of them, if not all, were ignorant. However that may be, it soon resolved itself into a conflict, and a conflict to the death, between Left and Right. Men had to be on the one side or on the other: there was no longer any Centre.

Abroad, we have tended to think of the war as of one between Fascists and Communists, between the raised hand and the clenched fist, between Mussolini and Moscow. But in reality, though Fascism inspired the rebels and their followers, and it was largely the Communists who were responsible for rallying the forces of the Government, the opposing parties were by no means of such simple composition. On the one side were Generals of the Army dissatisfied with Republican rule and rebellious at having been struck by the latest swing-back of the pendulum. With them they carried the Foreign Legion in Morocco and large sections of the rank and file of the Army, not necessarily because these were Fascists, or even knew what Fascism was, but partly because their officers were distinguished soldiers in high positions and with fine army records, and their officers had told them that it was their duty to resist Bolshevism, and partly because many of them, like their leaders, were genuinely opposed to a Government which had trampled underfoot so much that they and their fathers had held dear. On the other side was the Popular Front Government, followed by all who supported any one of the groups which made up so precarious a combination: the chief of these were Republican Union, Republican Left, Socialists, Syndicalists, Unified Marxists, Communists and Anarchists. This side was also supported by a great many law-abiding and democratically minded people, who had been on the side of the Centre-Right in October 1934 but held that, whatever their political opinions might be, it was their clear duty to take the side of a Government constitutionally elected and therefore representing as nearly as possible the will of the people. Thus there were partisans of the Centre-Right who supported the Government, just as there were former allies of the Left who hoped, privately if not publicly, for the victory of the rebels, because, for all their dislike of military rule, they disliked it less than continued chaos or the rule of Anarchism or Communism. And here, it may be recalled how Sr. Largo Caballero, advanced Socialist as he was, had declared his implacable opposition to Communism, and that Sr. Azaña, only a few days before his election to the Presidency, had replied to a Conservative member, who had taunted him with Communistic sympathies: 'I have as much to lose from the possible advent of Communism as the honourable member has.' As a matter of fact, he very soon had a good deal more.

These will be sufficient indications of the very mixed nature of the forces on either side, inexactly labelled as Fascists *versus* Communists, chiefly because in this modern world every one has to be labelled as something. The rebels were fighting for one form or another of the *ancien régime*: for the Church, for the nobility, perhaps for the King. Some, no doubt, for a return to 1923 and a Fascist State in a Europe now riddled with Fascism. Others, undoubtedly, for a return to 1931 and a fresh start along the road to reform, but for slow and moderate progress, not for a continuance of the pace at which Spain had rushed downhill to her own destruction. The loyal troops were fighting for rather more diverse aims: some merely for the inalienable right of the people to a government of its choice; some for the reforms on which the Left had already embarked—for 'that other Republic' to which Sr. Largo Caballero had referred at his trial; some for the proletarian revolution, which at last, after five years of Republic, had been thoughtfully precipitated by capitalists and the Army; some for the destruction of hated institutions, for the destruction of anything, for destruction alone.

It is easy, and natural, to condemn the military leaders for rising against a lawfully constituted Government, but it must be remembered that less than two years had passed since a large section of the Left had done the same. They in their turn might have declared that General Sanjurjo's insurgents of 1932 had set them an example, and General Sanjurjo might have argued in his own favour from the influence exerted upon public opinion by the Republican rising at Jaca in 1930, even although this rising failed in its immediate objective. In the same way, precedents can be found for the brutality of which both sides in the conflict were undoubtedly guilty, as also for the earlier repression and the futile reprisals which stain the history of the Republic. Nor will it suffice to refer everything back to the Dictatorship of Primo de Rivera, for an examination of the condition of Spanish politics before its advent will convince one that there was ample cause for exasperation then as later.

A truly objective view of the Spanish arena will reveal patriotism and idealism on one side and on the other, and on both sides there are leaders whom we can admire for their ability and sympathize with for their defeat. No less deserving of condolence than Primo de Rivera and his royal master are the men who brought in the Second Republic. Moments there may have been in their short careers when the robe of their importance fell from them and left them standing all unconsciously in the garb of comedy, but it would be an intensification of the present tragedy if the Spanish state were to be permanently deprived of their usefulness. Some of them, at least, their sternest opponents will remember with honour and even with affection. They were men of high ideals, of amazing industry, of undoubted probity and of notable ability in administration. They failed in their main task for two reasons. First, like most of their race, they suffered from so intense an individualism that they were unable to maintain a coalition, such as that of April 1931, which represented fairly accurately the different views of Spanish progressives, and, had it remained united, would unquestionably have made numerous converts. Secondly, they were unable or unwilling to stop the pendulum, and the pendulum is the curse of Spain.

These views were powerfully expressed by one of the ablest of Republicans, Don Salvador de Madariaga, in a remarkable *Idearium for the Constitution of the Third Republic* which he published when the Second Republic was four years old. 'Those few of us,' he writes, 'who in 1931 dreamed that Spain had at last won her redemption and was about to take seriously in hand the fashioning of her new Constitution before setting herself to labour in earnest,

> 'have seen how the ambition of a few, the negligence of all, divisions in the ranks of the Centre and the intransigence of the extremists have dealt Spain a terrible blow both in her economy, her *morale* and her prestige abroad. We know that they will end by causing her ruin, unless we Spaniards can be inspired by passions of a generosity sufficient to raise us above our ambitions and prejudices, our impatiences and evil habits, and to fill us with a sense of our responsibility.'(15)

He was right. They could not or would not see—these idealists of the Left—that, by encouraging reaction instead of striving to check it, they were merely inviting extremists to use them as stepping-stones to their own desires. The extremists could afford to tolerate the Republic till the time was ripe for their long-desired revolution, after which they would be able to throw aside the Republic's founders as men who had served their purpose and for whom they had no further use.

Some of these founders would doubtless reply in all good faith that in the early days of the Republic severity was necessary for its consolidation and that malcontents with deeply implanted grievances against the old order would never have tolerated slow and gradual reforms. To discuss this reply would take us more deeply into the realm of hypothesis than it would here be practicable to enter. It must suffice to say that there are degrees of severity, as those who thought that Primo de Rivera had touched the maximum soon found, and that a great leader, had he arisen, could have kindled enthusiasm for reform based upon a ten or a twenty years' plan—the only road it would seem, to Spain's ultimate salvation.

The fundamental weakness of the Second Republic has been the lack of a great leader. It has produced no man powerful enough to rule yet capable of ruling with moderation and prudence, of rising above the recriminative aims of party politics and of persuading others to accept him and to believe that he holds the key to his country's prosperity. Such a man must of necessity arise before Spain can be saved. Government by the Left parties produced little but reaction. Government by the Right, had it been tried, would probably have produced no less. Centre government failed to do more than mark time and liquidate the results of reaction. But at some time, whether in the near or distant future, a Centre Government must come again, and this time it must come, not to compromise, but to rule.

The immediate outlook is almost indescribably dark. The hopefulness and buoyancy of five short years ago have given place to something like despair. 'Have proclaimed the Republic'; telegraphed the apocryphal *alcalde* of 1931 to the Home Office, 'what shall I do with the priest?' We laughed, for this was comedy—the priest was in little danger. 'Have slaughtered officers,' telegraphs the crew of a warship in 1936, 'what shall we do with the bodies?' We laugh no longer, for this is tragedy. Slaughter and counter-slaughter seem the only prospects. The rhythm of reaction has gathered speed till rhythm itself is lost in the whirl and clash of warfare. Men are at each other's throats. Civilization has given place to chaos. And there is one 'martyr of the Republic' above all others—Spain.

Yet I believe in Spain, as firmly as ever I have believed in her in the past, and I believe that the millions of her citizens who still place country above party will in due time, in a re-united and prosperous land, have their reward. There may be various opinions about kings, presidents, statesmen, demagogues and party politicians, but nobody who knows Spain, and to whom she is a second home, can have the smallest doubt as to the intrinsic greatness of her people. If Nature has endowed her with riches, history has crowned her again and again with enduring laurels. High above tyrannical rulers, capricious favourites and vacillating governments she has risen, and high she will yet rise above even the fiercest party strife. For she still retains those essential virtues without which, in the old warlike Europe, she could never have enjoyed her splendid past; and those same virtues, in the new Europe, now struggling, like herself, in the throes of rebirth, will give her a still more splendid future.

APPENDIX

SOME BOOKS ON CONTEMPORARY SPAIN

OUTSTANDING works in Section III are marked with an asterisk (*); books published in Spain which are written in Catalan, with a dagger (†).

Students might also consult the first three and last chapters of *Spain, a Companion to Spanish Studies*, London, 1929; F. Sánchez: *Bibliographical List relative to the Dictatorship of Primo de Rivera*, North Carolina, 1931.

The order of books within each section is alphabetical.

I. HISTORIES OF SPAIN WRITTEN IN ENGLISH

Altamira, R.: *A History of Spanish Civilization.* Trans. P. Volkov. London, 1930.

Atkinson, W. C.: *Spain, a Brief History.* London, 1934.

Bertrand, Louis, and Petrie, Sir Charles: *The History of Spain, 711–1931.* London, 1934.

Chapman, C. E.: *A History of Spain.* New York, 1925.

Hume, Martin: *Modern Spain, 1788–1898.* London, 1899.

Moran, Catherine: *Spain, its Story Briefly Told.* London, 1931.

Petrie, Sir Charles: *Spain* (Modern States Series). London, 1934.

Sedgwick, H. D.: *Spain, a Short History.* London, 1925.

II. BOOKS IN ENGLISH OR FRENCH ON CONTEMPORARY SPAIN

Alcalá-Galiano, Álvaro (Marqués de Castel-Bravo): *The Fall of a Throne.* Trans. Mrs. Steuart Erskine. London, 1933. [An anecdotal history of the last days of the Monarchy, written from a highly Monarchist standpoint and translated from the second book named in Section III.]

'Anonymous': *The Spanish Republic: A Survey of Two Years of Progress.* London, 1933. [Anti-Republican. Interesting documentation.]

Benoist, Charles: *Cánovas del Castillo: La Restauration rénovatrice.* Paris, 1930.

Brandt, Joseph A.: *Toward the New Spain.* Chicago, 1933. [A history of political development in Spain from 1812 to 1933, by an American author. Sources for the latter part of the narrative are often indicated in footnotes. Contains a good bibliography, chiefly on the period before the reign of Alfonso XIII, which should be consulted by students of the period.]

Chapman-Huston, (Major) D., and Princess Pilar of Bavaria: *Don Alfonso XIII: A Study of Monarchy*. London, 1931.

Dwelshauvers, G.: *La Catalogne et le problème catalan*. Paris, 1926.

Erskine, Mrs. Steuart: *Twenty-nine Years: the Reign of King Alfonso of Spain*. London, 1931.

Greaves, H. R. G.: *The Spanish Constitution*. London, 1933. [Day-to-day Pamphlets, No. 15, 48 pp.]

Ludwig Ferdinand of Bavaria, Princess: *Through Four Revolutions, 1862–1933*. London, 1933.

Madariaga, S. de: *Spain*. London, 1930. ['An examination of the history of Spain, tracing her development to the present day.']

Manning, Leah: *What I saw in Spain*. London, 1935. [Deals with the Asturian rebellion of October 1934. Written from the standpoint of the Left. Appendices on alleged atrocities.]

Mirkine-Guetzévitch, B., and Reale, E.: *L'Espagne*. Paris, 1933. (Bibliothèque d'histoire et de politique.) [Contains French text of Constitution of 1931 and Agrarian Law of 1932.]

Sencourt, Robert: *Spain's Uncertain Crown*. London, 1932. ['The story of the Spanish Sovereigns, 1808–1931.' Attractively written, the later chapters from the Conservative standpoint.]

Tharaud, Jérôme et Jean: *Rendez-vous espagnols*. Paris, 1925.

Trend, J. B.: *The Origins of Modern Spain*. Cambridge, 1934. ['A collection of essays—intimate personal sketches of the reformers and educators of the generation of 1868' (Preface). Written from the standpoint of the Left.]

Young, Sir George: *The New Spain*. London, 1933. [Deals appreciatively with the early achievements of the Republic.]

III. BOOKS IN SPANISH OR CATALAN ON CONTEMPORARY SPAIN

Albornoz, Álvaro de: *Al Servicio de la República*. Madrid, 1936.

*Alcalá-Galiano, Álvaro: *La Caída de un trono, 1931.* Madrid, 1933.

Álvarez, Basilio: *Dos Años de agitación política.* Alcalá de Henares, 1933. 2 vols.

Álvarez y Blanco Gendín, S.: *Regionalismo. Estudio general. El Problema en Asturias,* etc. Oviedo, 1932.

Araquistáin, Luis: *Entre la guerra y la revolución: España en 1917.* Madrid, 1917.

Araquistáin, Luis: *El Ocaso de un régimen.* Madrid, 1930.

Arrabal, Juan. *José María Gil Robles: Su vida, su actuación, sus ideas.* Madrid, 1933.

Asamblea Nacional: Biografía y retratos de los 400 asambleístas y numerosos datos de menor interés. Madrid, 1927.

*Azaña, Manuel: *En el poder y en la oposición (1932–1934).* Madrid, 1934. 2 vols. [Political speeches.]

*Azaña, Manuel: *Una Política, 1930–1932.* Madrid, 1932. [Political speeches.]

*Bermejo, I. A.: *Historia de la interinidad y guerra civil de España desde 1868.* Madrid, 1876–7. 3 vols. [Also later editions.]

Blanco, Carlos: *La Dictadura y los procesos militares.* Madrid, 1931.

Blasco Ibáñez, V.: *Lo que será la República española.* Paris, 1925.

Blasco Ibáñez, V.: *Una nación secuestrada. El terror militarista en España.* Paris, 1925.

*Calvo Sotelo, J.: *Mis Servicios al Estado. Seis años de gestión. Apuntes para la historia.* Madrid, 1931.

Camba, Julio: *Haciendo de República.* Madrid, 1934. [Sketches by a well-known humorist.]

Cambó, Francisco: *Por la Concordia.* Madrid, 1930. [A translation of Francesc Cambó's Catalan work *Per la concòrdia.*]

Canals, Salvador: *España, la Constitución y la Monarquía.* Madrid, n.d.

Casares, F.: *La C.E.D.A. va a gobernar. Notas y glosas de un año de vida pública nacional.* Madrid, 1934.

Castrillo y Santos, J.: *La Orientación de la República.* Madrid, 1933.

Castro, Cristóbal de: *Al servicio de los campesinos: Hombres sin tierra, tierra sin hombres.* Madrid, 1931 (2nd edition).

Castro y Hernández, M. de: *Nacionalismo, Humanismo y Civilización.* Madrid, 1922.

*Ciges Aparicio, M.: *España bajo la dinastía de los Borbones: 1701-1931.* Madrid, 1932.

Claridades, Capitán (Vicente Clavel): *Fermín Galán y su nueva creación.* Barcelona, 1931.

Constitución política de la República Española. Madrid, 1931.

Cordero Pérez, M.: *Los Socialistas y la Revolución. Temas de actualidad.* Madrid, 1932.

Cortés Cavanillas, J.: *La Caída de Alfonso XIII.* Madrid, 1932.

Domingo, Marcelino: *¿A dónde va España?* Madrid, 1930.

†Estelrich, Joan: *De la Dictadura a la República.* Barcelona, 1931.

*Fernández Almagro, M.: *Historia del reinado de Alfonso XIII.* Barcelona, 1933.

Franco, Comandante: *Madrid bajo las bombas.* Madrid, 1931.

García Gallego, J.: *¿Por dónde se sale? El momento actual de España.* Madrid, 1931.

*Giménez Caballero, E.: *Genio de España.* Madrid, 1932.

Giménez Caballero, E.: *Manuel Azaña. Profecías españolas.* Madrid, 1932.

González Araco, M.: *Castelar: su vida y su muerte.* Madrid, 1900.

González López, E.: *El Espíritu universitario.* Madrid, 1931.

González Ruiz, N.: *Azaña. Sus ideas religiosas, sus ideas políticas, el hombre.* Madrid, 1932.

Heredia, M. de: *Semblanzas. Figuras de la revolución española.* Madrid, 1933.

Hernández Mir, F.: *La Dictadura ante la Historia.* Madrid, 1930.

Jiménez de Asúa, L.: *Notas de un confinado.* Madrid, n.d.

Jiménez de Asúa, L.: *Política, figuras, paisajes.* Madrid, n.d.

*Jiménez de Asúa, L.: *Proceso histórico de la Constitución de la República Española.* Madrid, 1932.

*Juderías, J.: *La Leyenda negra.* Barcelona, n.d.

*Lerroux, Alejandro: *Al Servicio de la República.* Madrid, 1930.

Lerroux, Alejandro: *Trayectoria política de Alejandro Lerroux.* Madrid, 1934. [Selections from his speeches and writings.]

Llopsis y Pérez, A.: *Historia política y parlamentaria de D. Nicolás Salmerón y Alonso.* Madrid, 1915.

Llorens, E. L.: *La Autonomía en la integración política.* Madrid, 1932.

*López Ochoa, E. (General): *De la Dictadura a la República.* Madrid, 1930.

*Madariaga, S. de: *Anarquía o Jerarquía. Ideario para la Constitución de la Tercera República Española.* Madrid, 1935.

*Maeztu, Ramiro de: *Defensa de la Hispanidad.* Madrid, 1934.

Marco Miranda, V.: *Las Conspiraciones contra la Dictadura.* Madrid, 1930.

Marsá, Graco: *La sublevación de Jaca: relato de un rebelde.* Madrid, 1931.

Martínez de la Riva, R.: *Las jornadas triunfales de un golpe de estado.* Barcelona, 1923.

*Maura Gamazo, Gabriel: *Bosquejo histórico de la Dictadura.* Madrid, 1930. 2 vols.

Maura Gamazo, Gabriel: *Dolor de España.* Madrid, 1932.

Maurín, J.: *La Revolución Española. De la monarquía absoluta a la revolución socialista.* Madrid, 1932.

Maurín, J.: *Los Hombres de la Dictadura.* Madrid, 1930.

Medina y Togores, J. de: *Un Año de Cortes Constituyentes. Impresiones parlamentarias,* etc. Madrid, 1932.

Mola, Emilio (General): *Memorias de mi paso por la Dirección General de Seguridad.* Madrid, 1932. 2 vols.

*Mori, Arturo: *Crónica de las Cortes Constituyentes de la Segunda República Española.* Madrid, 1932, ff. In progress.

†Nicolau d'Olwer, Ll.: *La lliçó de la Dictadura.* Barcelona, 1931.

Ors, J.: *España y Cataluña.* Madrid, 1930.

Ortega y Gasset, E.: *La Verdad sobre la Dictadura.* Madrid, 1931.

*Ortega y Gasset, J.: *Rectificación de la República.* Madrid, 1931.

Orts González, J.: *El Destino de los pueblos ibéricos.* Madrid, 1932.

*Pérez de Ayala, Ramón: *Política y toros.* Madrid, 1925 (2nd edition).

Pérez Serrano, N.: *La Constitución Española.* Madrid, 1932.

Pi y Margall, F.: *La Federación.* Madrid, 1880.

Pi y Margall, F.: *Las Nacionalidades.* Madrid, 1882.

Pi y Margall, F.: *Lecciones de Federalismo. Recopiladas por J. Pi y Arsuaga.* Barcelona, 1931.

Posada, Adolfo: *La Reforma Constitucional.* Madrid, 1931.

*Primo de Rivera, Miguel: (1) 'Génesis de la Dictadura'; (2) 'Constitución y labor del Directorio'; (3) 'La Dictadura civil'; (4) 'Fin de la Dictadura española'. [Four articles written for *La Nación* of Buenos Aires, reprinted in the *Debate* of Madrid, March 21, 22, 23, and 25, 1930, and included in this list of books on account of their unusual historical interest.]

Primo de Rivera, Miguel: *Epistolario del Dictador*. Ed. J. M. and L. de Armiñán Odriozola. Madrid, 1930.

Recaséns Siches, L.: *El Poder Constituyente. Su teoría aplicada al momento español*. Madrid, 1931.

Reparaz, Gonzalo de: *Alfonso XIII y sus cómplices*. Madrid, 1931.

Reparaz, Gonzalo de: *Páginas turbias de historia de España que ahora se ponen en claro*. Madrid, n.d. (1929).

Rivera y Pastor, F.: *Nueva práctica y estilo de la República*. Madrid, 1935.

*Rodríguez-Solís, E.: *Historia del partido republicano español*. Madrid, 1892–3. 2 vols.

*Romanones, Conde de: *Las últimas horas de una monarquía. La República en España*. Madrid, 1931.

Romanones, Conde de: *Las Responsabilidades políticas del antiguo régimen de 1875 a 1923*. Madrid, n.d.

†Rubió Tudurí, M., and Mart, N.: *Estat espanyol, Societat Anónima*. Barcelona, 1930.

Salazar Alonso, R.: *La Justicia bajo la Dictadura*. Madrid, 1930.

Salmerón, Nicolás: *Discursos parlamentarios*. Madrid, 1881.

Sánchez Guerra, R.: *Dictadura, Indiferencia, República*. Madrid, 1931.

Sánchez Guerra, R.: *Proceso de un cambio de régimen*. Madrid, 1932.

Sandoval, A. de: *El Hombre que necesita España. Ensayo político-social*. Madrid, 1934.

Tusquets, J.: *Orígenes de la Revolución española*. Barcelona, 1932.

Vila, E.: *Un Año de República en Sevilla*. Seville, 1932.

Villanueva, F.: *La Dictadura militar*. Madrid, 1930.

Yáñez, T. R.: *La Soberanía popular y su fuerza emancipadora. Ante la situación de España*. Madrid, 1931.

NOTES

THE chief reference is to the *Bulletin of Spanish Studies*, to which, since 1929, I have contributed a diary of events in Spain entitled 'Spain Week by Week'. Under each chapter heading below, references are given to the pages in this diary which correspond approximately to each section of the chapter, so that readers who so wish may study events in the strict chronological order, which here, of necessity, has sometimes been departed from, and may find quotations in their original Spanish form.

CHAPTER I

THE COMING OF THE REPUBLIC

(I) *B.S.S.*, Vol. VII, pp. 50–5,140–1; II: Vol. VII, pp. 137–45, 172–6; Vol. VIII, pp. 33–7, 124–7; III: Vol. VIII, pp. 128–31; IV: Vol. VIII, pp. 131–3; V: Vol. VIII, pp. 133–5; VI: Vol. VIII, pp. 122–3, 133–4; VII: Vol. VIII, pp. 132, 135–6.

(1) See the first of two articles by S. de Madariaga (reprinted in *Spain*, pp. 429–33) on 'The New Spain', in *The Times* of July 23, 1929. This, if allowances be made for the respect accorded to the man in power, gives an excellent picture of Primo de Rivera's character.

(2) For the Dictator's own account of this, see his article reproduced in the *Debate*, March 21, 1930.

(3) These achievements are summarized, though not exhaustively, by Primo de Rivera in an article, 'La Dictadura Civil', reproduced in the *Debate*, March 23, 1930.

(4) See *The Times Educational Supplement*, August 9, 1930. The University City was built on King Alfonso's initiative, though it was supported by Primo de Rivera and has been considerably developed under the Republic.

(5) On this question see Sir George Young: *The New Spain*, p. 99.

(6) Joseph McCabe: *Spain in Revolt*, London, 1931, p. 227.

(7) See Primo de Rivera: 'Constitución y labor del Directorio', in *El Debate*, March 22, 1930.

(8) Fernández Almagro (*op. cit.*, p. 497) puts it politely ('Firmaron en listas colocadas al efecto en sitios públicos, cuantos quisieron, o fueron llevados o fingidos, en número de 6,697,164'), but stranger things have been written about this notorious plebiscite than there

is space to record. Cf. 'The Dictatorship in Spain' in *The Times*, October 4, 1926.

(9) *Op. cit.*, pp. 497, 504–5. See an interesting leading article, 'The Spanish National Assembly', in *The Times* of September 14, 1927, and Primo de Rivera's own views in his article reproduced in the *Debate*, March 25, 1930.

(10) *The Times, art. cit.*

(11) *Debate*, March 7, 1929.

(12) *The Times, art. cit.*

(13) Fernández Almagro, *op. cit.*, pp. 498–9.

(14) Cf. leading article in *The Times*, June 30, 1926.

(15) 'The Spanish Crisis and its Sequel', *Nation*, April 6, 1929. Cf. 'The Spanish University Question', *Nation*, May 4, 1929.

(16) Actually, the Royal Decree re-opening the universities was signed on May 20. On the whole question, see Asim: 'The Spanish University Crisis', in *B.S.S.*, 1929, Vol. VI, pp. 92–101. This article gives the text of Sr. Menéndez Pidal's letter and the Dictator's reply. For a critical commentary on the correspondence, see also the *Debate* of April 3, 1929.

(17) 'Fin de la Dictadura española.' In *Debate*, March 25, 1930.

(18) Note reproduced in the Spanish Press of January 26, 1930.

(19) *Ibid.*

(20) The whole story is succinctly related in *A.B.C.* for December 27, 1930.

(21) For a description of the meeting, an outline of the Pact and references to the rather scattered sources, see Fernández Almagro, *op. cit.*, pp. 557–8.

(22) *Sol*, November 15, 1930.

(23) There are various accounts of this rebellion. I follow chiefly Fernández Almagro, *op. cit.*, pp. 562 ff.

(24) On this question, see the testimony of General Mola (*cit.* Fernández Almagro, *op. cit.*, p. 567).

(25) Reproduced fully, *op. cit.*, p. 568, n.

(26) *Op. cit.*, p. 572, n.

(27) *Op. cit.*, p. 576. Cf. *A.B.C.*, February 17, 1931.

(28) Cf. the leading article of *A.B.C.*, February 19, 1931.

(29) *Daily Telegraph*, February 20, 1931.

(30) *Sol*, March 13, 1931.

(31) Roberto Castrovido in *El Pueblo* of Valencia, March 26, 1931.

(32) Cf. *B.S.S.* 1931, Vol. VIII, p. 126.

(33) *Sol*, March 25, 1931.

(34) *B.S.S.*, 1931, Vol. VIII, p. 129.

(35) The full official figures of these elections were never published, and it is possible that the Republicans actually polled more votes than the Monarchists throughout the country, though they

certainly won fewer seats. The *Times* correspondent in Madrid (cf. *The Times*, July 29, 1932) applied, several months after the Revolution, to the Home Secretary for permission to examine the results, but it was refused him.

(36) *Sol*, April 14, 1931.

(37) Reproduced in translation in *The Times* of July 29, 1932. 'If the Republican Committee itself', added *The Times* correspondent, 'had been called upon to circularize the military commanders it could hardly have drawn up instructions better calculated to serve the purpose of paving the way for a peaceful Monarchist surrender.'

(38) Such are the Conde de Romanones' book *Las últimas horas de una monarquía*, Gabriel Maura's *Dolor de España*, and Alcalá Galiano's *La caída de un trono*. Other sources are enumerated in the list of books given above.

(39) E.g. Bertrand and Petrie, *op. cit.*, p. 523. For the views of a non-apologist critic, see S. de Madariaga, *Spain*, pp. 428, 436. ('A devout Catholic, he made the sacrifice of his oath on the Gospels; a king, he broke his royal word.')

(40) *A.B.C.*, February 18, 1931.

(41) Madariaga, *op. cit.*, p. 187. Cf. the King's alleged commentary on this judgment in Fernández Almagro, *op. cit.*, p. 579.

(42) G. Maura, *cit.* Fernández Almagro, *op. cit.*, p. 591, n.

(43) Fernández Almagro, *op. cit.*, p. 595.

(44) Alcalá Galiano, *op. cit.* (English edition), p. 205; Fernández Almagro, *op. cit.*, p. 597.

(45) Fernández Almagro, *op. cit.*, p. 599, n.

(46) *Op. cit.*, p. 592.

(47) *Op. cit.*, p. 600.

(48) Cf. Manuel Bueno: 'Los Iconoclastas', in *A.B.C.*, April 30, 1931.

(49) *B.S.S.*, 1931, Vol. VIII, p. 133.

(50) *Ibid.*

(51) For the original, see *B.S.S.*, 1931, Vol. VIII, p. 135. There are various other translations.

CHAPTER II

THE REPUBLICAN CONSTITUTION

I: *B.S.S.*, Vol. VIII, pp. 138–43; II: Vol. VIII, pp. 193–5, Vol. IX, pp. 2–3; III: Vol. IX, pp. 65–89; IV: Vol. IX, pp. 3–18; V: Vol. IX, pp. 18–24, 89–94.

(1) Cf. 'Homenaje de la República: Galán y Hernández', *Sol*, April 16, 1931.

(2) W. Horsfall Carter in *Contemporary Review*, April 1931, ('Spain and her Immaculate Republic.')

(3) Niceto Alcalá Zamora: 'La Sorpresa y la preparación de la República Española', *Sol*, May 3, 1931.

(4) *Ibid.*

(5) *A.B.C.*, May 5, 1931.

(6) *Ibid.*

(7) The quotations are from an encyclical of Leo XIII.

(8) *Sol*, May 7, 1931.

(9) Statement of Don Fernando de los Ríos, *Sol*, May 8, 1931. Cf. *B.S.S.*, 1931, Vol. VIII, p. 140.

(10) *A.B.C.*, May 8, 1931.

(11) The lengthy statement will be found in *Informaciones* for May 11, 1931, and in other Madrid daily papers for May 12. The same papers may be consulted for details of the disturbances.

(12) *Sol*, May 13, 1931.

(13) The full Spanish text of the Constitution will be found in *B.S.S.*, 1932, Vol. IX, pp. 65–89.

(14) Arts. 1–3.

(15) Art. 7.

(16) Art. 6.

(17) Art. 11.

(18) Art. 13.

(19) Art. 25.

(20) Arts. 33, 34.

(21) Art. 36.

(22) Art. 42.

(23) Art. 26.

(24) Art. 27.

(25) Art 26.

(26) Arts. 44, 45.

(27) Art. 43.

(28) *Ibid.*

(29) Art. 48.

(30) *Ibid.*

(31) Arts. 51–3.

(32) Art. 67.

(33) Art. 68.

(34) Art. 71.

(35) Art. 72.

(36) Arts. 75, 76.

(37) Art. 81.

(38) Art. 82.

(39) Art. 83.

(40) Art. 85.

(41) Cf. *B.S.S.*, 1932, Vol. IX, p. 11.
(42) *Sol*, October 14, 1931.
(43) *Ibid.*
(44) *Ibid.*
(45) *Sol*, October 15, 1931.
(46) Cf. *B.S.S.*, 1932, Vol. IX, p. 148.
(47) Cf. *Sol*, October 21, 1931.
(48) *Sol*, November 7, 1931.
(49) *The Times*, November 27, 1931.
(50) *Ibid.* The translation which follows is not that of *The Times*, but my own.

CHAPTER III

Two Years of the Left

I: *B.S.S.*, Vol. IX, pp. 94–101, 145–9, 193, 197; Vol. X, p. 32; II: Vol. VIII, pp. 196–7; Vol. IX, pp. 199–208; Vol. X, pp. 16–28; III: Vol. X, pp. 29–34, 62–5, *passim*. IV: Vol. X, pp. 34, 62–7; V: Vol. X, pp. 68, 117–27; Vol. XI, pp. 151–2; VI: Vol. X, pp. 180–7; Vol. XI, pp. 23–30.

(1) *Sol*, January 17, 1932.
(2) Official *communiqué, cit. Sol*, January 2, 1932.
(3) This detail was reported by General Sanjurjo, then Director-General of the Civil Guard (*Sol*, January 3, 1932). Further particulars are given by General Sanjurjo in the *Sol* of January 5.
(4) *The Times*, July 27, 1931.
(5) *Publicitat*, January 26, 1932.
(6) G. Marañón: 'Un año de República. España en franquía.' *Sol*, April 14, 1932.
(7) *The Times*, March 22, 1932.
(8) For a readable account of agrarian conditions in Spain during the last years of the Monarchy, see S. de Madariaga: *Spain*, pp. 191–203.
(9) Numerous references under this section will be found in an article in *B.S.S.*, 1932, Vol. IX, pp. 199–208, 1933, Vol. X, pp. 16–28, at the conclusion of which the full Spanish text of the Statute is given.
(10) Statute of Autonomy, Art. 2.
(11) For the original Catalan text of this clause, and for other particulars of the Draft Statute, see *B.S.S.*, 1931, Vol. VIII, pp. 196–7.
(12) Statute of Autonomy, Art. 7.
(13) Cf. *B.S.S.* 1933, Vol. X, p. 17.
(14) *Op. cit.*, p. 19.

(15) *Ibid.*
(16) *B.S.S.* 1933, Vol. X, p. 187.
(17) *B.S.S.* 1934, Vol. XI, p. 30.
(18) *B.S.S.*, 1933, Vol. X, pp. 69–70.
(19) *A.B.C.*, November 30, 1932.
(20) *The Times*, June 6, 1933; *B.S.S.* 1933, Vol. X, p. 179.
(21) *The Times Educational Supplement*, June 6, 1931.
(22) *Sol*, July 28, 1931.
(23) Cf. *B.S.S.*, 1933, Vol. X, p. 69.
(24) *The Times*, July 6, 1933.
(25) *The Times*, January 14, 1933. The account which follows is quoted from the report of the Parliamentary Committee printed in full in the *Sol*, and other Madrid papers of March 12, 1933.
(26) Cf. *B.S.S.*, 1933, Vol. X, p. 118 and Manuel Azaña: *En el poder y en la oposición*, Vol. I, p. 368.
(27) Cf. *B.S.S.*, 1933, Vol. X, p. 123.
(28) The remaining seats went to independents. For the figures, see *B.S.S.*, 1933, Vol. X, p. 124.
(29) Art. 85 (*B.S.S.*, Vol. IX, p. 82).

CHAPTER IV

Two Years of the Centre-Right

I: *B.S.S.*, Vol. XI, pp. 30–1, 85–92, 141–9; II: Vol. XI, pp. 209–16; Vol. XII, pp. 5–8; III: Vol. XII, pp. 9–21, 89–96, 127–31; IV: Vol. XII, pp. 132–7; Vol. XIII, pp. 21–7, 79–87.

(1) A summary account of the question at issue, written by a Basque, will be found in 'Desde Bilbao' (*B.S.S.*, 1934, Vol. XI, pp. 225–8).
(2) 'Catalonia and the Sixth of October' (*Contemporary Review*, December 1934, pp. 671–6).
(3) Cf. *B.S.S.*, 1934, Vol. XI, p. 211.
(4) *Op. cit.*, p. 214.
(5) *Sol*, April 24, 1934.
(6) *Sol*, September 11, 1934.
(7) *Sol*, October 2, 1934.
(8) Cf. reference in note 2, above.
(9) For the full Catalan text of the speeches of Sr. Companys and Sr. Gassol, see *B.S.S.*, 1935, Vol. XII, pp. 11–12.
(10) *Sol*, October 23, 1934.
(11) Cf. *B.S.S.*, 1935, Vol. XII, p. 128.
(12) Cf. *B.S.S.*, 1936, Vol. XIII, p. 79.

NOTES

CHAPTER V

CHAOS

I: *B.S.S.*, Vol. XIII, pp. 87–92, 132–5; II: Vol. XIII, pp. 135–42; III: Vol. XIII, pp. 142–3, 172 ff.; IV: Vol. XIII, pp. 172 ff.

(1) Cf. *B.S.S.*, 1936, Vol. XIII, p. 92.

(2) W. Horsfall Carter: 'Spain To-day', in *The Listener*, 1936, Vol. XV, pp. 797–9, 826. The whole article is extremely inform-ative.

(3) Art. 81.

(4) Cf. *Sol*, April, 8 1936.

(5) Cf. p. 66 above.

(6) Cf. *B.S.S.*, 1936, Vol. XIII, p. 141 ('Seré un Presidente incorruptible, insobornable e inacobardable').

(7) *Sol*, June 17, 1936.

(8) Cf. *B.S.S.*, 1936, Vol. XIII, pp. 143.

(9) Very few Spanish newspapers being available at the time when this section was written, the chief sources have been *The Times* and private letters received from Spain.

(10) *The Times*, August 5, 1936.

(11) *Ibid.*

(12) *The Times*, August 3, 1936.

(13) *The Times*, August 5, 1936. Confirmed by private corres-pondence.

(14) *Ibid.*

(15) *Anarquía o jerarquía*, p. 10.

It should be added that the narrative in this chapter was brought down to August 10, 1936.

INDEX

INDEX

Foreign Legion, 218
franchise, extension of, 60. *See also*
women's suffrage
Franco, (General) Francisco, 211, 212,
216
Franco, (Commandant) Ramón, 16,
211
Frente Popular, 188, 200, 201, 202,
206, 207, 214
victory of, 190–2
impatience of its supporters, 192
Governments of, 204, 214, 215
Fuenteovejuna, 89

Galán (Fermín) and García Hernández
(Ángel), 14, 15, 20, 32, 48, 77,
119, 151, 175
Galicia, 13, 112, 215
and autonomy, 112, 113, 114, 208
Gassol, Ventura, 166
General Union of Workers, 21, 34,
213. *See also* Socialism.
Generalitat, adoption of the title by
the Catalonian Government at
the request of the Provisional
Government in Madrid, 41, 104
Gerona, 156
Gibraltar, 190
Gijón, 215
Gil Robles, José María, 144–5, 160,
183, 184, 200, 205, 206
demands six portfolios for the
Ceda, 176
becomes Minister for War, 177
leads Right parties in 1936 elec-
tions, 188
Giner de los Ríos, Francisco, 21
Giralt, José, 215
Goded, General, 212
Goma, Mgr., becomes Primate of
Spain, 59
González Peña, Ramón, 203
Good Friday, 1933, 133–4
Gordón Ordás, atrocities described
by Sr., 169
Government by the Left, 48–140,
192–217
by the Centre, 141–61
by the Centre-Right, 161–92
Gran Vía (Madrid), 62
Granada, 13, 57, 98, 144
Jesuit college at, 94
Church of San Nicolás burned, 118
gratificaciones, 182
Guadalajara, 59
Guadarrama mountains, 216

Guadiana, river, 87
guardias de asalto. *See* Shock Troops.
Guernica, 111
Guernikako arbola, 204
Guinea, Spanish rebels exiled to, 95
Guipúzcoa, 30, 111, 112, 154, 159

Haya and Rodríguez' aviation feat, 86
Holy Week in 1931, 23
in 1932, 96–7
in 1933, 133–4
in 1934, 148
hotels, improved under Primo de
Rivera, 4
Huesca, 15, 26, 144

Iberian Federation of Anarchists, 89,
188, 214, 219
Iglesias, Pablo, 49
Ignatius of Loyola, St., 95
Informaciones, 120
Institución Libre de Enseñanza, 80
Institute of Agrarian Reform, 100–1,
196–7
Institutos. *See* Education
intellectuals and Primo de Rivera, 2
and the Republic, 16–17, 48–9
Irún, 59
Isabel the Catholic, Grand Collar of, 84
Isabel II, 37, 115
Italian help to rebels in Civil War, 216
Italy and Abyssinia, 207
Izquierda Republicana, 188, 191, 193,
218. *See also* Azaña

Jaca, rebellion of, 14–15, 37, 48, 131,
132, 151, 220
court-martial of prisoners, 20–1
Játiva, 102
Jesuits, their property burned in
Madrid, 56
in Málaga, 57
attacked in the Constituent Cortes,
72
attacked in a dramatized version of
A.M.D.G., 76–7
expelled from Spain, 85, 92–5
their schools confiscated, 95, 126
known to be teaching in Madrid,
1934, 146
Jesus, Society of. *See* Jesuits
Jiménez Asúa, Luis, 195
Juan, Don (son of Alfonso XIII), 45,
146
Junta para Ampliación de Estudios, 6,
127

243